PRAISE FOR *ON EDWARD SAID*

"This book moves elegantly between anecdotes in Edward Said's life and a profound analysis of the intellectual contribution of one of the most influential thinkers of our times. Hamid Dabashi guides us skillfully between Said's universalist, humane, and moral position and his total commitment for the liberation of Palestine. With the help of this book we revisit, in a very accessible language and a straightforward style, Said's intellectual prominence and impact on cultural studies. We are also introduced once more to the extent of his commitment to the struggle for justice in Palestine. Whether you are a devoted 'Saidian' or a newcomer to his world, this book is essential reading." —ILAN PAPPÉ

"In this beautifully written book of profound reflections and vivid recollections, Hamid Dabashi conveys from the perspective of a fellow traveller precisely how and why Edward Said stands as one of the most important intellectuals of his times. The book carries the torch of Said in its literary sensibilities, in its ethical inflection of the political, and in a shared understanding of how the particularity of the Palestinian struggle is universal in its import. Inspired by Said, Dabashi's critical and creative memoir becomes a true source of inspiration in its own right." —CAROLINE ROONEY

"Reading Dabashi is like going for an extended coffee with a very smart friend." —VIJAY PRASHAD

"Said's influence . . . was far from being confined to the worlds of academic and scholarly discourse. An intellectual superstar." —MALISE RUTHVEN, obituary, the *Guardian*

"Hamid Dabashi's respect and affection for Edward W. Said and his intellectual legacy are manifest throughout this book. As a former colleague and friend of Said's, Dabashi's engagement is not only personal, but also emphatically political and intellectual." —JOSEPH MASSAD

"Hamid Dabashi has written a deeply moving text that pays tribute and engages with one of the most important thinkers of our time, Edward Said. The book is composed of essays, documents, and shorter poli̇t̶ ̶l pieces which skillfully highlight the impact of Said's work on pres̶c̶ ̶sues. The original presentation shows Said's influence o̶v̶ Dabashi himself but on so many others who s̶ th what it means to challenge Eurocentr̶ ̶is is a book that is a must-read not only ̶ ̶ who reads him for the sake of a life comm̶ ̶ CORNELL

"A lyrical homage to his friend and colleague, the great Palestinian theorist, humanist, and agitator Edward Said. Dabashi follows in Said's footsteps, reliving his own march through Mideast war zones, and jousts with Islamophobes with lively turns of phrase and a soul laid bare." —TIMOTHY BRENNAN

"If you want to know more about Edward Said, the person, the intellectual, the friend, the political public figure, this a book to read. And it is more than that. Palestinian American Edward Said is revived in the memories of Iranian American Hamid Dabashi. At a time when hate is propelled by the state to extreme heights, what transpire from these pages are care, respect, and decolonial love between a Palestinian American and Iranian American connected through colonial wounds inflicted upon migrants from the Middle East. Through the chapters, you will find also the dignified anger with which Said and Dabashi responded to the intolerance and hate toward free thinkers in the public sphere. The account of personal and professional ethics that Dabashi learned from Said is not only a distinctive feature of the book but it is of extreme relevance when free thinking at the university has been mutating into corporate thinking." —WALTER D. MIGNOLO

"By turns skeptical and erudite, passionate and poetic, Hamid Dabashi's book is animated by his love for Edward Said and his work. It will raise many hackles, but in its provocations it challenges one to rethink many of the standard clichés and prejudices of our time. Some pages are threaded with melancholy, others with anger, as in his white-hot assessment of the films of Michael Haneke and the books of his academic opponents. Above all, *On Edward Said* is powered by Dabashi's commitment to the ideal that 'Palestine belongs to the Palestinians—whether Jews, Christians, or Muslims.' There is not a page in this book that does not challenge its reader. Whether one disagrees with it or not, this is a work that will leave its mark on all who read it." —DAVID FREEDBERG

"This remarkable collection of essays and interviews represents a long and diverse journey with a constant companion: the living memory of Edward Said. In lucid and passionate prose, Dabashi reminds us how much we need to return to Said's thought and work, especially in 'the darker moments of our despair,' when we can, if we concentrate, find him 'waiting for . . . us to awake, to arrive.' This is how death, for Dabashi, becomes a form of suspension rather than a terminal loss." —MICHAEL WOOD

ON EDWARD SAID

REMEMBRANCE OF THINGS PAST

Hamid Dabashi

Haymarket Books
Chicago, Illinois

Published in 2020 by
Haymarket Books
P.O. Box 180165
Chicago, IL 60618
773-583-7884
www.haymarketbooks.org
info@haymarketbooks.org

ISBN: 978-1-64259-273-3

Distributed to the trade in the US through Consortium Book Sales and
Distribution (www.cbsd.com) and internationally through Ingram Publisher
Services International (www.ingramcontent.com).

This book was published with the generous support of Lannan Foundation
and Wallace Action Fund.

Special discounts are available for bulk purchases by organizations and
institutions. Please call 773-583-7884 or email info@haymarketbooks.org for
more information.

Printed in Canada by union labor.

Library of Congress Cataloging-in-Publication data is available.

1 2 3 4 5 6 7 8 9 10

Contents

For Abdelwahab El-Affendi . . . the Quiet Revolutionary

INTRODUCTION

The memory of a few people
  Brightens me
  Gives me strength
  Sends me on my way—
  And the cold and old
Furnace of my home
  Is warmed
  By the warmth of their noble breath—

  The memory of a few people
  Is the sustenance of my soul —
  Anytime I'm saddened
  I turned to them—
  Their memory gives me courage —
  Brightens me —

  —Nima Yushij (1897–1960)

This volume is something of an intellectual autobiography of my prolonged and fruitful relationship with the late Edward W. Said (1935–2003)—at once personal, collegial, and intellectual and all of that in a spirit of political comradery. I decided to put together in a single volume the essays, articles, and chapters that I wrote and published on various occasions beginning with my obituary for Edward Said when he passed away on September 25, 2003, at the age of sixty-seven, and concluding with the short essay I wrote when his arch nemesis Bernard Lewis (1916–2018) passed away on May 19, 2018, at the age of 101. Needless to say, I had a deeply personal and affectionate relationship with Said, while Bernard Lewis gave me the creeps any time I thought of him and his deeply racist and treacherous thoughts and actions on Arabs and Muslims. Yet my affection for Said has never prevented my critical encounter with his monumental work, and my distaste for Bernard Lewis does not mean I ever harbored any ill will toward him. I am happy he lived a long and satisfying life. I just wish he had been less of an evil man. There is just a poetic justice between these two moments, when a towering intellectual with enduring significance in my thinking passed away, and when a man who stood for everything I detest rushed to meet his Creator.

The pieces I have gathered here and ordered chronologically range from the very personal, written soon after Said's passing and on certain anniversaries of our loss, to the very scholarly and critical. They are not everything I have written that relate to Said and his ideas. That would be an impossible task. My *Persophilia*, for example, I have always considered a fusion of my response to his *Orientalism* and *Culture and Imperialism* combined. My *Europe and Its Shadows* traverses furthest from him backward and forward into the analytic foregrounding of his *Orientalism*. My *Brown Skin, White Masks* takes some serious exceptions to his work on *Representations of the Intellectual*—at once conforming to his insights and yet going off on a tangent from what he could sense but not see.[1] The point of this volume is not to give a full itinerary of my indebtedness to him but rather to map out a particular trajectory of personal and professional conversations that in many significant ways have defined my own intellectual journey in the United States.

I have taught at Columbia University in New York for over thirty years now. When Said died in September 2003, Columbia suddenly changed for me. I have many dear and close friends and colleagues at Columbia, and I have continued to teach there and live in New York after Said's passing, but I have been just doing my job; the passion, the moral thrust of being at Columbia with Said, a sense of belonging that comes with a common purpose, are all gone. Meeting him was a landmark in my intellectual trajectory. While Said was alive, Philip Rieff and George Makdisi, the two towering intellectual forces with whom I studied, were far more important in my thinking than he was. But after his passing, when he was physically no longer here, I was more aware of his looking over my shoulder when I wrote, and the weight of his thinking began to increase on me. To be sure, by then I was a fully grown-up and mature thinker of my own thoughts. But even when I was seriously parting ways with him, I thought him looking at me and wondering.

Said was always a catalyst in my thinking—not because we thought alike but precisely because we thought differently. The very cast of our critical thinking is quite different. But something about the power of his prose, the urgency of his insights, and the provocative twists of his thinking enabled others to think their own thoughts more pointedly. As I have always said, he liberated our tongues to speak our minds. Said's own legacy is alive and well in many of his own closest and most gifted students. I was not his student. I entered his horizons as a younger colleague, and he left our midst as a senior colleague under whose shadow we all felt part of a larger project. In Mahmoud Mamdani's apartment on Columbia's campus, we once gathered with Said and a few other colleagues to map out a letter to ask Columbia to divest from companies that sold military equipment to Israel. We were able to collect a few dozen signatures from colleagues mostly in the social sciences and humanities departments. We were of course soundly defeated at the Senate, where our political adversaries had mobilized many more signatures than us (mostly from the medical and business schools). But the list of signatories to that letter we had prepared became a list of professors not to miss, as Columbia students put it, for undergraduate education on our campus. This was long before Boycott, Divestment and Sanctions had become a progressive political banner. We were a very small group. Our political adversaries were enormously more powerful, all the way to the office of our president. We were not powerful. We had reason, sanity, and the joy of truth on our side.

I was not among Said's closest friends. Our more senior colleagues like Michael Rosenthal and Jonathan Cole were far closer to him. He was my senior by many significant years. But even younger scholars like Joseph Massad were much closer to him, being both Arab and Palestinian. I am neither an Arab nor a Palestinian, but there was a connection between us that was and remained rooted in Palestine but extended into our common intellectual concerns. He had an uncanny ability to make almost all his friends feel very special to him. I was drawn to him because of Palestine. I was not drawn to Palestine because of him. And he knew that. My commitment and connection to Palestine predated my coming to the United States and eventually meeting Said by decades. Those who are familiar with his work and mine know they are very different in many significant ways. But in some enduring ways close proximity to him enabled my voice in ways that I could never anticipate. If he was, as he once said, "the last New York Jewish intellectual," he enabled me to be the first New York Muslim intellectual. That trajectory and that genealogy are the reasons I have decided to collect my scattered work on and about Said into a single volume.

Before I came to the United States and eventually joined Columbia in New York, the towering public intellectual of my generation of Iranians was Jalal Al-e-Ahmad (1923–69). We read him, admired him, and debated and disagreed with him, but in all such occasions he was and he remained a force to reckon with. Al-e-Ahmad has not fared well in the aftermath of the Iranian Revolution of 1977–79. Many Iranian critical thinkers hold him responsible for the terror of the Islamic Republic. This is neither fair nor accurate. He died long before the Islamic Republic came into being. He was the measure of our time and timbre.

Said's stature and the importance of his ideas have, on the other hand, only increased after his passing. Although only tangentially related to him, I became a Columbian, a New Yorker in significant parts because of Said, the same way that I became an American because of my children, who are all born and raised in the United States. This collection is a footprint of my memories, a passageway from an Iranian to an American intellectual journey, at once a political and scholarly reminiscence about Said, as over the last thirty years I have had reason and occasion to read and think about his ideas. I decided to put these pieces together as a record of my recollections, of how I have read and responded to Said, as an act of remembrance of things past. The future of our critical thinking depends on our recollections of this past. How we respond to the most pressing crisis of our day depends on how we keep a record of our own location next to towering figures who have bracketed our intellectual life, in my case extending from Al-e-Ahmad in Tehran to Edward Said in New York.

EDWARD SAID: THE PALESTINIAN

I write this introduction to a collection of my reflections on Said at a time that demands and exacts a slightly different sort of engagement and commitments than either Jalal Al-e-Ahmad or Edward Said offer. If either of them were to come back to life today, they would not recognize the worlds closest to their minds and hearts when they passed away. Said in particular would not believe what depth of terror and racism Donald Trump has unleashed in a country he called home for much of his adult life. He would not recognize his beloved Arab world, either in the euphoria of the Arab Spring that he would have loved to see, or in the savagery of the Islamic State of Iraq and Syria, the butchery of the Saudis, the murderous mayhem in Yemen, the barefaced massacre of Palestinians in Gaza, or other atrocities elsewhere in his ancestral homeland. He would have not recognized the post–Brexit United Kingdom and the unleashing of xenophobic neofascism in the rest of Europe. The worlds beyond these three worlds would not be any more recognizable to him. The rise of Jair Bolsonaro in Brazil, the brazen racist Hindu fundamentalism of Narendra Modi in India, the genocide of Muslims in Myanmar under the watchful eyes of the Nobel Laureate Aung San Suu Kyi, the emergence of Muslim concentration camps in China, ad nauseam. From Al-e-Ahmad and Said and scores of other towering critical thinkers from around the world, we would learn much, but are still left to our own devices as to what to think, what to say, what to do.

The world demands and will exact fresher visions of what needs to be done. Neither the legacies of European humanism and Enlightenment modernity, nor the promises of American democracy in the aftermath of the Civil Rights Movement; the revolutionary aspirations of Asia, Africa, and Latin America; or the vacuous promises of liberal democracies have left us a shred of hope that the visions of a "democratic criticism" or "secular humanism" Said gave us as his parting gift will actually deliver us to any promised land. We are all the grateful beneficiaries of his enduring ideas of contrapuntal thinking, of secular humanism, of his magisterial critique of Orientalism as the modus operandi of knowledge and power, of his monumental works on culture and imperialism. But if he were alive today, he would be part of a whole different genealogy of struggles.

All of these groundbreaking ideas and theories, today the very conceptual alphabets of our critical thinking, fade in comparison to one lasting unfinished project Said left behind when he closed his piercing eyes for the very last time: his uncompromising voice speaking bold truth to pernicious power as a stateless Palestinian. Without Palestine as the towering cause of his moral and intellectual commitment, his noble soul would have never achieved the global reach it did during his lifetime. More than any other aspect of Said's moral and intellectual commitments, it is his enduring presence as a Palestinian that should command our undivided attention. The measure of our truth, the timbre of our courage, the reach of our intellectual commitment anywhere else in the world are all determined by how absolutely and unconditionally committed to Palestine we will remain.

Said's eminent contemporaries like Jean-Paul Sartre or Michel Foucault or Noam Chomsky have cared a little bit about everything.

Said, on the contrary, cared for Palestine as if it was the very first and the very last reason for justice on planet Earth. Everything else he cared for and articulated came out and flowered theoretically from that singular cause of his moral outrage. This is the same way it was for Frantz Fanon and Algeria, Malcolm X and African Americans, Che Guevara and Cuba. They were all rooted in one ground and nourished by caring for the world. A decade and a half after Said's passing, Palestine remains an open wound and an open-ended metaphor. It is an uncompromising commitment to the openness of that wound and the open-endedness of that metaphor that every single word Said ever wrote, any single idea he mapped out, any powerful theory he made proverbial, any deconstructive gesture he ever taught us categorically point. Palestine is today the most enduring fact and metaphor of truth speaking to lies, justice revolting against tyranny. No other site of struggle anywhere else in the world is clearer cut or more precise than in Palestine—millions of defenseless adults and children revolt against a barefaced European colonial savagery. People around the globe need not have known, seen, heard, or counted Said among their personal friends to be able to place themselves at the heart of the Palestinian cause and from the depth of the indefatigable struggles of Palestinians learn the enduring rectitude of any moral voice that may reach out and teach them not just how to resist but how to triumph.

Prologue

FOR THE LAST TIME

CIVILIZATION

In September 2001 I published this essay (in International Sociology 16, no. 3), almost a year after I had originally presented an earlier version of the essay at the American Sociological Association in Washington, DC, at the invitation of Said Amir Arjomand. I wrote this essay almost a quarter of a century after the publication of Edward Said's Orientalism and more than a decade after I had started teaching at Columbia and the commencement of my lifelong friendship and comradery with him. What is equally important today when I read this essay is the towering presence of Edward Said's thinking and particularly his Orientalism on my mind without even once mentioning him or his seminal text.[1] I was taking his insights in Orientalism forward into more deconstructive directions I was not sure he would have approved or even concurred. This is the reason I have always said Edward Said never turned you into a Saidian but enabled your own thinking on the premise he had mapped out. Taking his theoretical clues from Foucault, Nietzsche, and Gramsci, in Orientalism Said had theorized the relationship between knowledge and power in specifically an Arab and Islamic context. In doing so he had outlined the manner in which the Orient was invented in a way that made it subject to European colonial conquest. Such colonial acts of romanticism had become a form of cultural hegemony in which both European and non-Europeans were implicated. Taking my cues from these insights I went for a more radical dismantling of the East–West binary as a civilizational construct, and putting my habitual Marxist spin to postcolonial theory, I linked the formation of civilizational thinking to the global configuration of culture and capital. As will become apparent later in this volume in my essay on Rosa Luxemburg, this particular Marxist take on Edward Said and postcolonial theory would remain definitive to my work, enabled and anticipated by Edward Said but ploughing through its own particular blind spots and insights.

By the end of the millennium, a spirit of doom and termination pervaded the soul of the American Right, and there is no better text to see that sense of nostalgia and decay than in Jacques Barzun's *From Dawn to Decadence: 1500 to the Present: 500 Years of Western Cultural Life*.[2] As one of the most distinguished cultural historians of the century, Barzun wrote *From Dawn to Decadence* with a sense of prophetic doom. With a magisterial language at once celebratory and mournful, Barzun sets for himself the obituary task of grieving the demise of Western civilization. He declares early in his massive volume: "It takes only a look at the numbers, to see that the twentieth century is coming to an end. A wider and deeper scrutiny is needed to see that in the West the culture of the last 500 years is ending at the same time. Believing this to be true, I have thought it the right moment to review in sequence the great achievements and the sorry failures of our half millennium."[3]

To Barzun the present is decadent, corrupt, misguided, and a failure. The great achievements of Western civilization have been made and now is the autumn of its decline, its universal promises undelivered. Barzun notes with curiosity that it is not exactly clear for whom "our past" refers, but whitewashes over that fact as something "that is for each person to decide."[4] That is the first in a succession of narrative strategies to claim the West for the mighty and the victorious over the last five hundred years without as much as a hint at the catastrophic consequences of "Our Western civilization" at home and abroad. The text, as a result, is a nostalgic celebration of High European Culture, its art and music, philosophy and literature, sciences and technology. The result is a visit to the museum, guided by a world-class museum tour guide, knowledgeable of all the dead certainties.

Whence Civilization?

The reemergence of civilizational thinking in the last two decades of the twentieth century and at the heart of capitalist modernity is a defense mechanism, a futile attempt to salvage an outdated mutation of capital and culture at the commencement of the project early in the eighteenth century. At a time when the rapid globalization of capital has dismantled the very viability of national economies, at a time when postmodernism destroyed the cultural production of national cultures, and at a time when poststructuralism has deconstructed the very metaphysics of presence at the heart of the Enlightenment and all its categorical (e.g., civilizational) constructs, retrograde forces like Samuel Huntington, Allan Bloom, or Francis Fukuyama have put up feeble resistance to moral and material forces beyond their, or anybody else's, control.[5] More than anything else these feckless attempts make for rather pathetic scenes to observe, when outdated good and evil no longer recognize that the changing world has turned them into museum pieces. The phenomenon is not limited to malicious voices like Huntington's, outdated pieties like Bloom's, or vested political interests like Fukuyama's. Far more superior intellects like Richard Rorty and Jacques Barzun are missing the point, too. We are in the midst of massive subterranean changes in the material composition of the world and the moral correspondence to it is yet to come.

As Northrop Frye observed about a quarter of a century ago, the success of the Spenglerian conception of history and the very constitution of the West has been so thorough and so successful that it is now apparently very difficult not just for those who have a vested interest in the ideological construct but even for fairer and more liberal minds to see its historical fabrication.[6] But to us at the receiving end of the project in its colonial territories, there is no magic in seeing how the idea emerged and how it celebrated itself. To us it is quite evident that the very categorical constitution of "civilization" is an Enlightenment invention for very specific reasons and objectives, including its beneficiaries, excluding its victims.

The invention of civilizational thinking occurred at a very specific historical juncture in the rise of Enlightenment modernity. Neither the aristocratic nor the ecclesiastical orders of feudalism and scholasticism thought or practiced in civilizational terms. From Hegel's philosophy of history to Goethe's conception of *Weltliteratur* to Johann Gottfried Herder's idea of world history to Kant's groundbreaking metaphysics of morals, the very conceptual categories of civilizational thinking were coined and set in motion at the commencement of capitalist modernity. From the dawn of civilizational thinking in Hegel and Herder, to the wake of instrumental rationalism in Max Weber, the collapse of the polyvocality of what had not yet given birth to the very idea of "Europe" as a cultural contingency announced the supratribal formation of the "Western civilization."

The premodern configuration of power in medieval Europe had placed the aristocratic houses and the ecclesiastical orders as the bipolar centers of social structure, corresponding with a dynastic historiography (aristocratic) claiming Christendom (ecclesiastical) as its universal frame of reference. At the dawn of the capitalist revolution, the aristocratic and ecclesiastical nuclei of power gradually gave way to the rising bourgeoisie and as a result the dynastic histories yielded to conceptions of national cultures, while Christendom simultaneously yielded to the idea of Western civilization, with the rising Enlightenment philosophers replacing the clerical order as intellectuals organic to the new social order.

The idea of the Western civilization at the commencement of capitalist modernity was thus to the European national cultures what

Christendom was to dynastic histories during the medieval period. As the rising bourgeoisie replaced in power and prestige both the aristocratic and the ecclesiastical orders, dynastic histories and Christendom lost their conceptual legitimacy and epistemic credibility to those of national cultures and their enframing and emplotment in Western civilization. Because of its anxiety related to class legitimacy, and because it could not genealogically compete with either the aristocratic or the ecclesiastical orders, the rising European new class was intuitively drawn to such universal and universalizing abstractions as national cultures and universal civilizations. Formation of national cultures and the civilizational contexts of those cultures was the ideological byproduct of a specific period in the operation of capital. In that nascent configuration of forces and relations of production, the aggressive formation of national economies was the optimal unitary basis for the working of capital and its colonial consequences. National economies and national cultures were first concocted at the metropolitan centers of capital and then gradually extended into the colonial consequences of the project.

Civilizational thinking was therefore a European Enlightenment project to give its rising bourgeoisie a universal frame of collective identity. Western civilization gave universal identity to European national cultures. German, French, and British cultures were thought of as particular manifestations of, so the story unfolded, the Western civilization. While national cultures were concocted to distinguish one economic unit of capital from another, civilizational thinking was invented to unify these cultures against their colonial consequences. Islamic, Indian, and African civilizations were invented contrapuntally by Orientalism, as the intelligence arm of colonialism, in order to match, balance, and thus authenticate Western civilization. All non-Western civilizations were therefore invented exactly as such, as negational formulations of the Western, thus authenticating the Western. But there was much more to these non-Western civilizations than simply to authenticate the Western negationally. Hegel subjected all his preceding human history into civilizational stages leading to the Western civiliza-

tion, thus in effect infantilizing, Orientalizing, exoticizing, and abnor-
malizing the entire human history as preparatory stages toward their
implicated spiritual goal. As colonial nationalism aped and replicated
the nationalism of the capital at the European centers of the project, so
did Islamic or Indian civilizations mirror, though in a contorted image,
the inaugurating principality of Western civilization.

There thus developed a division of labor in the nature and function
of national cultures and their civilizational context. While national cultures corresponded to national economies as the analytical unit of the
economic working of capital, their constructed civilizational context
targeted the colonial consequences of the capital. European national
cultures were the domestic expressions of the national economic units
of the working capital, while the simultaneous construction of Western civilization identified and distinguished the constellation of these
national capitals and cultures from their colonial consequences. Islam,
like Africa, China, or India, were simultaneous abstractions invented
and animated by the project of Orientalism in the speculum of "The
West" as the Civilizational Self of all its colonial Others.

The European national cultures thus emerged as the ideological
insignia separating the European national economies as the currencies
of cultural exchange value, while the very idea of Western civilization
was to distinguish the accrued totality of those cultures and economies
from their colonial consequences. It is thus not accidental that practically the entire scholarly apparatus at the service of civilizational studies of non-Western civilizations was the handiwork of Orientalism as
the intelligence arm of colonialism. Islamic, Indian, and Chinese civilizations were concocted, crafted, documented, and textualized from scattered bodies of alternating evidence by successive armies of European
Orientalists negationally authenticating the simultaneous construction
of Western civilization. As from Hegel to Herder, the idea of Western
civilization was being crafted; far less illustrious but far more numerous
an army of Orientalists was mirroring its civilizational others as Eastern
civilizations in general and Islamic, Indian, and so on in particular. As

the colonial territories are mined to extract the raw material of a massive productive machinery switchboard in European capitals, the same exploitations are at work on the historical memories and evidence of colonized societies to serve the ideological foregrounding of Western civilization. Oriental texts were exploited by Orientalists to concoct Oriental civilization with the same tenacity and dexterity as the colonial territories were exploited for minerals by colonial officers. Practically all these civilizational mirrors are on the site of the colonial territories of European capital. They were all constructed to raise Western civilization as the normative achievement of world history and lower all others as its abnormal antecedents.

By the sheer force of European capital, conceptions of national cultures and civilizational constructs became the world picture of reality and were hegemonically adapted in colonial territories with the same force as their economies were being incorporated into the global order of capital. Very soon in the colonies too, dynastic, regional, and tribal histories were carved and renarrated into national cultures and placed within the civilizational constructs—Islamic, Indian, and Chinese. Iranian, Egyptian, and Turkish cultures were carved out of scattered memories and evidence and placed within the general rubric of the Islamic civilization, to match and contest, and thus to authenticate and superordinate, Western civilization. Thus, on the colonial territories, fabricated national cultures and civilizational contexts became the sites of hegemonic incorporation into the project of capitalist modernity, though from its colonial end. The more political nationalism functioned as a site of resistance to colonialism, the more cultural nationalism incorporated vast bodies of extraterritorial resistances to the project of capitalist modernity. We have launched nationalist movements against colonialism just to entrap ourselves ever so thoroughly in the project, having been modernized from the colonial end of the capital.

The people plotted into Islamic civilization (or Indian, Chinese, or African civilization) did not of course roll over and play dead to authenticate Western civilization. These colonial fabrications in turn became the sites of sustained ideological resistance to colonialism. In the case of Islamic civilization, as in others, the colonially constructed site began to mutate into a site of resistance to colonialism and called itself "Islamic ideology." The result was the production of a knowledge industry, a journalistic offshoot of Orientalism, that began to brand moral and material resistance to imperialism "Islamic fundamentalism" and use it as a ploy to authenticate the civilizational superiority of the West and the barbaric inferiority of the rest. Barnard Lewis became the doyen of this journalistic extension of old-fashioned Orientalism, and in a massive narrative output continued to authenticate Islamic civilization as the supreme civilizational other of Western civilization. Meanwhile native informers as varied as Fouad Ajami, Bassam Tibi, Fatima Mernissi, and Daryush Shayegan doubly authenticated the passivity of Islamic civilization by having it take, as Shayegan put it, a "vacation from history."[7]

Against all these feeble attempts, in the emerging globality of the working capital and its corresponding cultures, the metaphoric division of the world into civilizational boundaries, or center and periphery, are no longer valid. Whether invited for a dialogue or targeted for a clash, the very practice of civilizational thinking has received a new lease on life by Huntington's generation of nervous reactionaries to resist the uncharted consequences of globalization. The move is to pull the terms of engagement with our present predicament back to the early nineteenth century, when civilizational thinking was first launched in correspondence to the specifics of capital and colonial bifurcation of the world, enabling the beneficiaries of the capital, incapacitating its colonial victims. The move is thus to place the colonial cultures back where they belong and restore authenticity to the utterly discredited notion of Western civilization and all its false cousins. Civilizational dialogue, as indeed civilizational debates, clashes as indeed conversations, are therefore a latter-day collapse into the bare necessity of will to power disguising itself as will to truth, pragmatics of power selling itself as political theory. Reversing back to civilizational dialogue or debate, clash or conversation, is to resist ideologically the corroding power of the spiral capital that sells you a pair of Nike shoes whether you take them off before you do your ablutions and pray in a mosque or put them on to go for a jog in your bikini, as long as you wear them out quickly and go back for another pair.

Both the formation of national cultures and the civilizational framing of them corresponded to an age of capital in which the economic constitution of the European national economies and their colonial peripheries was the optimal unitary operation of economic production. At the threshold of the twenty-first century, the selfsame capital has evolved in the global logic of its operation and the unitary basis of national economies and their colonial consequences can no longer serve as the currency of its operation. The circular spiral of capital and labor has now so ferociously destroyed the artificial national boundaries (which themselves are of its own making not more than two hundred years ago) that it is no longer possible for any conception of national economy to have a legitimate claim on operation. The result is the aggressive acculturation of individuals from their national economies and national cultures, as they are being thrown into an entirely new configuration of capital and its ever-changing cultures.

A quick look at the United States, which is by far the most aggressively mutated national economy and national culture, reveals that we can no longer think of this country as having a claim over either side of the same coin. The influx of migratory labor into the United States has initially created a so-called "multicultural" society to which conservative thinkers like Huntington, Fukuyama, Bloom, Barzun, and others have violently reacted. Huntington's thesis of the clash of civilizations is a disturbed reaction to this phase of cultural confusion at the heart of the globalizing capital. What he and his cohorts do not understand is that they are quite late in responding, and that they are responding to something already on its way to change. Their real heartbreak is yet to come. This so-called multicultural phase to which Huntington and co. have responded so violently is only a transitory period in the modular reconfiguration of capital and labor. The real fireworks are yet to come.

This transitory multiculturalism we witness today in the United States
and in Western Europe will soon give way to the logic of the globalizing
capital that has already entered its electronic phase. Asians and Latinos
in the United States, South Asians in England, Turks in Germany, Indians and Koreans in the Persian Gulf—samples of a far more massive
migratory pattern of labor and capital—are now the prime examples of
a spiral movement that will utterly shatter not only the unit of national
economy but also its constituent conception of national cultures. From
the new configuration of global capital and labor, the material basis of a
new culture, which is neither nationally cultural nor recognizably multicultural, is already evident. That material reconfiguration of capital
and labor is generating its own culture, which is at once postnational
and as a result postcivilizational.

One

THE MOMENT OF MYTH

I wrote and published this obituary within days of the passing of Edward W. Said on September 25, 2003. It was initially published on the website of Asia Society in New York. But soon it disappeared from that site, by which time it had been picked up by Counterpunch. It is still on that website (dated October 2, 2003). What is peculiar to this piece is that I began writing it in Persian, for reasons entirely unconscious. A few sentences into my writing I stopped and asked myself "Why am I writing this in Persian?" I then code-switched and restarted writing it in English. I have always thought of this piece as my first public appearance far beyond my limited academic milieu and habitat.

C lose proximity to a majestic mountain is a mixed blessing—one is at once graced by the magnanimity of its pastures and the bounty of its slopes, and yet one can never see where one is sitting, under the shadow of what greatness, the embracing comfort of what assurance. The splendor of mountains—the Himalayas, the Rockies, Alborz—can be seen only from afar, from the safe distance of only a visual, perceptive, appreciative, awe-inspiring grasp of their whereabouts.

A very happy few—now desolate and broken—have had the rare privilege of calling Edward Said a friend, fewer a colleague, even fewer a comrade, only a handful a neighbor. The closer you came to Said, the more his intimate humanity, ordinary simplicity, the sweet, endearing, disarmingly embracing character—his being a husband, a father, a father-in-law, an uncle, a cousin—clouded and colored the majesty that he was. Our emails and voicemails are still full of his precious words, his timely consolations, anecdotal humor, trivial questions, priceless advice—all too dear to delete, too intimate to share. We were all like birds flying around the generosity of his roof, tiny dandelions joyous in the shade of his backyard, minuscule creatures pasturing on the bounteous slopes of the mountain that he was.

The prince of our cause, the mighty warrior, the Salah al-Din of our reasoning with mad adversaries, source of our sanity in despair, solace in our sorrow, hope in our own humanity, is now no more.

In his absence now it is possible to remember the time when he was not part of your critical consciousness, your creative disposition, your presence in the world—when he did not look over your shoulder watching every single word you wrote.

If remembering the time that he was not integral to you is not to be an exercise in archeological futility, then it has to account for the distance, the discrepancy, between the bashful scholasticism of the learning that my generation of immigrant intellectuals received and the confidence and courage with which we can stand up today in face of outrageous fortune—hand in hand with our brothers and sisters across races and nations, creeds and chaos—and say, "NO!"

Today, there is a solidarity of purpose among a band of rebels and mutineers—gentiles are among us and Jews, Christians and pagans, Hindus and Muslims, atheists we are and agnostics, natives and immigrants—who speak truth to power with the voice of Edward Said the echo of our chorus. How we came here—where we are, hearing with his ears, seeing with his eyes, talking with his tongue—is a question not for making a historical record but for taking moral courage.

Now in the moment of his myth, when Said has left us to our own devices and joined the pantheon of mythic monuments, is precisely the time to have, as he once said, a Gramscian inventory of our whereabouts—once with and now without him. Today the world is at once poorer in his absence and yet richer through his memory—and precisely in that paradox dwell the seeds of our dissent, the promise of our future, the solemnity of our oath at the sacred site of his casket.

I come from a generation of immigrant intellectuals who mark the origin and disposition of their critical intelligence from the publication of Said's *Orientalism*.[1] The shape of our critical character, the voice of our dissent, the texture of our politics, and the very disposition of our courage are all rooted in every nook and cranny of that revelatory text. It was in the year of the Iranian Revolution, 1979, less than a season after the publication of *Orientalism*, that Samuel Klausner, who taught us theory and method, first introduced me to Said's spectacular achievement in an utterly prosaic manner. I was a graduate student at the University of Pennsylvania, finishing a dual degree in Sociology of Culture and Islamic Studies. By the time I read *Orientalism* (inhaled it rather, in one deep, satisfying swoop—drank it like a glass of freshly squeezed lemonade on a hot summer day), I had already read Karl Marx, Max Scheller, Max Weber, and George Herbert Mead on the sociology of knowledge. What Said had argued in *Orientalism* was straight out of a sociology of knowledge angle—and yet with a globality of vision, a daring, defiant imagination, and with such an assured audacity that I remember I could not believe my eyes—that I was reading these words in that particular succession of reason and rhetoric.

By the mid-1970s, my generation of sociologists at Penn had already started reading Michel Foucault in a systematic and rather unusual curriculum given that the discipline of sociology was then being rapidly sold out to federally funded policy research and demography—a downward spiral from which a once-groundbreaking discipline never recovered. But at that time at Penn, Philip Rieff, E. Digby Baltzell, Samuel Klausner, Harold Bershady, Victor Lidz, and Fred Block were serious theorists with a relatively universal approach to their sociological concerns. I wrote my doctoral dissertation with Philip Rieff advising me on the sociological aspect of my work and with the late George Makdisi on the Islamic aspect. But the seed that *Orientalism* had planted in my critical consciousness never left my thoughts after that fateful fall semester of 1979 when we read it with Samuel Klausner in that dimly lit, tiny room on the fifth floor of McNeal Building off Locust walk on the Penn campus—smack in the middle of the hostage crisis in Iran, when I could hear a chorus of Penn undergraduates shouting in unison, "Nuke Iran, Maim Iranians!"

Take *Orientalism* out of that curriculum, Said out of our consciousness, and my generation of immigrant intellectuals would all be a bunch of dispirited souls susceptible to chronic melancholy, or else, *horribile dictu*, who would pathetically mutate into native informers of one sort or another—selling their souls to soulless sultans in Washington, DC, or else to senile patriarchs in Princeton.

I had no clue as to Said's work in literary criticism prior to *Orientalism*, and for years after my graduation I remained entirely oblivious to it. It was *Orientalism* that would not let go of the way I thought and wrote about modern or medieval Islamic or Iranian intellectual history. From then on, I began a journey, at once professional and personal, moral and intellectual, that brought me literally to his doorstep on the campus of Columbia University, where I now teach. To my dying day, I will cherish the precise spot next to Miller Theater on the corner of 116th and Broadway where I met Said for the first time and went up to him and introduced myself—the gratitude of a liberated voice in my greetings.

I discovered Said first from *Orientalism* and then from his writings on Palestine, and from there to his liberating reflections on the Iranian Revolution. From there I began an almost Jesuit training in every single book he ever wrote and the majority of his essays and articles, reading and rereading them like a dutiful student preparing for a doctoral exam, long after I was giving doctoral examinations.

Today, of the myriad of things I learned from Said, nothing matters to me more than the rhapsodic eloquence of his voice—the majesty, confidence, courage, audacity, and poise of his diction, without which my generation of immigrant intellectuals would have been at the mercy of mercenary academics and embedded journalists who have now flooded the gutters of the mass media—uttering their pathologies with thick Arabic, Persian, or South Asian accents and yet speaking with a nauseating "We" that sides with the bankrupt architects of this predatory empire. In Said's voice, in his princely posture and magisterial air of confidence, the fragile tone of our almost silent objections and the frailty of our say in the matter suddenly rose to the occasion.

Through Said we suddenly found comrades we never knew we had, friends and families we never suspected in our own neighborhood— Asia, Africa, and Latin America suddenly became the extension of our home away from home. José Martí I discovered through Edward Said, as I did Kojin Karatani, Chinua Achebe, Eqbal Ahmad, Tariq Ali, Ranajit Guha, Gayatri Spivak, Seamus Deane, Masao Miyoshi, and Ngũgĩ wa Thiong'o. Everyone else we thought we knew—Aimé Césaire, Frantz Fanon, Mahatma Gandhi, Mahmoud Darwish, Nazim Hikmat, Vladimir Mayakovsky, Faiz Ahmad Faiz—he made new sense of for us.

As the color of our skin began to confuse the color line drawn tyrannically between Blacks and whites in the United States—segregated in the respective corners of their misplaced confidence about their races—we Asians and Latinos, Arabs, Turks, Africans, Iranians, Armenians, Kurds, Afghans, and South Asians were instantly brought together beyond the uncommon denominator of our origin and toward the solidarity of our emerging purpose, the nobility of our handshake with Edward Said.

For years after I had come to Columbia, I could not quite reconcile the public, mythic, iconic Edward Said and the immediate Edward of my increasing acquaintance and friendship, camaraderie, and solidarity. It was as if there was an Edward Said the Magnificent for the rest of the world and then another Edward for a happy few. The two were not exactly irreconcilable; they posited a question, a distance in need of traversing—how could a mortal so fragile, frail, and accessible cut a global figure so monumental, metaphoric, parabolic?

When two years ago an infamous charlatan slandered me in a New York tabloid and created a scandalous website to malign my public stand against the criminal atrocities he supports, my voicemail was flooded with racist, obscene, and threatening messages by the lunatic fringe he had let loose. Smack in the middle of these obscenities, as if miraculously, there was a message from Said—a breath of fresh air, refreshing, joyous, reassuring, life-affirming: "Hamid, my dear, this is Edward . . ." Life was so amazingly beautiful. I kept listening to those obscenities just for the joy of coming to Edward's message. There was something providential in his voice—it restored hope in humanity. Today at Edward's funeral, the heartbroken few who could look over the shoulder of the pallbearers of Edward's coffin were witness to yet another sublime restoration of hope when Daniel Barenboim played Bach's Prelude in E-Flat from Part I of the *Well-Tempered Clavier* as a musical tribute to his deceased friend. Those in the vicinity of this miracle saw and heard that the Maestro's loving farewell was no longer just a virtuoso pianist playing a beautiful piece of music—they realized they were privy to Daniel Barenboim speaking with Edward Said for the very last time, in the common language of their choice, privilege, and transcendence.

Said was the walking embodiment of hope—one extraordinary incident that sought and detected an extraordinary sparkle in otherwise very ordinary people who happened on his watch. Years before, when I had open heart surgery and my dear, now departed, friend and colleague Magda al-Nowaihi was just diagnosed with ovarian cancer, Edward was extraordinary in his support: calling on us regularly, sending us his new books and articles, reading our manuscripts, making fun of what he called our postmodernisms—he was the sound of our laughter, the color of our joy, the shape of our hope. Magda fought her malignant cancer for years until her young children became teenagers; I defied my congenital fate and lived. Edward was the model of our endurance, the measures of our truth, the meaning of our daring to walk into a classroom.

The closer I became to Edward, the more impossible it seemed to tell what exactly it was that went into the making of his heroic character in such mythic measures—by now I was too close to the mountain, embraced by its grace, oblivious to its majesty. But even in public, the account of his life that Said published is no different. One reads his *Out of Place* in vain looking for a clue, a succession of historical or psychological causes and traits, as to what great or consequential events make for a monumentally moral life.[2] Everything about Said was rather ordinary, and yet an extraordinary adventure was made of the prosaic occurrences of this very life.

Born in Palestine in 1935, named Edward after the Prince of Wales, he lived a life of exile like millions of other Palestinians in the Arab world. Sent to Mount Hermon High School in New England, and subsequently to Princeton and Harvard for his higher education, Said reports no extraordinary event that one can identify, analyze, or theorize about the defining moment of the mythic figure that he cut at the time of his untimely death. Said was an ordinary man. Said was a giant. The distance was covered by nothing other than the glory of his daring imagination.

Knowing Said personally was a study in how heroes are made from the flesh and blood of the most ordinary and perishable realities. A Palestinian, an exile, an academic intellectual, a teacher, a scholar, a husband, a father, a friend: none of this common and abundant evidence of a disjointed world can account for the sum total of Said as a towering figure measuring the very definition of a moral life.

"Did you know Professor Said," I asked Chaplain Davis here at Columbia when looking for a place for Miriam Said to receive the flood of visitors who wanted to pay their respects last Friday. "I never met him," she said, "but I know he was a warrior," and then she looked at me with bright shining eyes and added "for justice." "It was just like a light going off on campus," another colleague said of Edward's death.

If one is to begin anywhere to place the particulars of Edward Said's moral and intellectual life together, it is not in the prosaic of his exilic life that he shares with millions of others, Palestinian or otherwise, but in the poetics of his creative defiance of his fate—where he was able repeatedly to give birth to himself. At his death, Said was the moral mandate, the volcanic outburst of a life otherwise wasted in and by accidents that accumulate to nothing. Exile was his fate and he triumphantly turned it into the fruit of his life—the gift he gave to a world now permanently cast into an exilic departure from itself.

We can find few places in *Out of Place* that reveal the creative concatenation of such moments better than the concluding paragraph of the book. Like his life, Said's autobiography has to be read from its endings and not from its beginnings. "Sleeplessness for me," he says, "is a cherished state to be desired at almost any cost."[3] He stayed awake when the world went to sleep—the insomniac conscience of the world, conversant with Minerva, observant with his eyes wide awake, like a wise owl, all-seeing, all-hearing, vigilant. "There is nothing for me as invigorating as immediately shedding the shadowy half-consciousness of a night's loss, than the early morning, reacquainting myself with or resuming what I might have lost completely a few hours earlier."

It is here, in the twilight borderline of repeated promises of a dawning light against the assured persistence of darkness, when it appears that the darker moments of our despair must yield to brighter hopes, that we always find Said waiting for the rest of us to awake, to arrive. "With so many dissonances in my life I have learned actually to prefer being not quite right and out of place." Right here, I believe, Said has rested his case and left his indelible mark on the rest of us, trying, as we are, to learn from him how to complement fatefully while remaining humanly incomplete. That, in my judgment, is the principal reason why so many people ordinarily at political and ideological odds with each other deeply loved Said without contradicting themselves or him. His was a spontaneous soul—he generated and sustained good will and moral purpose on the impulses of the premise he was given, not on the projected idealism of some metaphysical certainty.

What was paramount about Said is that in his utter solitude he was never alone. He always spoke for an otherwise muted possibility of living a moral life against all odds, a graceful David swinging his sling and launching his stones against the Goliath of a world so mercilessly cast in the logic of its own madness—to be the moral voice of a people, and to turn the tragic fate of that people into the tragedy of a global predicament in which we have all become homeless Palestinians. His virtue was to turn the vices of his time into momentous occasions for a more universal good that went beyond the specificity of one wrong or another. There was a catholicity to his liberating knowledge, a generosity to his moral rectitude, that easily transgressed boundaries and put to shame all territorial claims to authenticity. He was, as he rightly said, always slightly out of place, but that only brought out what was wrong with that place that could not completely accommodate him in the entirety of his character and culture.

In his legacy, Said has made a universal virtue out of the particular predicament that the world handed him at birth. Born in Palestine but denied his ancestral claims on that land, raised in Egypt but schooled with a British colonial education, dispatched to the United States by way of his father's claiming a more permanent part of his American dream but constantly driven to speak the truth of that lie to the powers that hold it, Said turned the inevitability of his fate into the defining moment of his stature as the iconic figure of an entire generation of hope—against a whole culture of despair.

Said's life has its most immediate bearing as an eloquent testimonial of a people much maligned and brutalized in history. His life and legacy cannot and must not be robbed of that immediacy. It is first and foremost as a Palestinian—a disenfranchised, dispossessed, disinherited Palestinian—that Said spoke. The ordinariness of his story—particularly in those moments when he spoke openly, frankly, innocently of his early youth, adolescence, sibling rivalries, sexual maturity, and so on— is precisely what restores dignity to a people demonized by purposeful propaganda, dehumanized to be robbed of their homeland in the broad daylight of history. No assessment of his multifaceted achievements as a teacher, a critic, and a scholar, no laudatory endorsement of his universal humanism, no perfectly deserving appreciation of him as a musician, an essayist, a subaltern theorist, or a political activist—nothing should ever detract from his paramount significance as a Palestinian deeply wounded by the fate of what he repeatedly and wholeheartedly called "my people."

But Said was not just a Palestinian, though a Palestinian he proudly was. Said also became an icon, a moral paragon in a time when taking desperate measures has cast doubt on the very possibility of a moral voice, and here the ordinariness of his life makes the extraordinary voice that he was even more enduring. Said was not just a Palestinian. But he made everyone else look like a Palestinian: made homeless by the mad logic of a brutal game of power that has robbed the whole world of any semblance of permanence.

How to remain an incessantly moral voice in a morally impermanent world, how to transfigure the disfigured mutations of the world into a well-mannered measure of truth, how to dismantle the power that false knowledge projects and yet insist that the just is right and the truth is beautiful—that is the legacy of Edward Said, right from the mountain top of his majestic peak visible from afar, down to the slopes of his bountiful pastures which few fortunate souls were blessed to call home.

Two

MOURNING EDWARD SAID

Soon after Said's passing on September 25, 2003, his widow Mariam Said asked a few of his close friends to contribute a short essay to a special volume she and Akeel Bilgrami edited for a limited edition. I was among these friends. This short piece was published in that volume and distributed to those attending Said's memorial.

Mourning Edward Said can never quite yield to a systemic act of ritual distancing—habitually seeking to mutate the painful loss of a creative core at the center of our critical character into a soothing memory. In the span of a lifetime, cut brutally short and yet left joyously fruitful, he saw to it that siding with him will always remain an incomplete act of moral defiance against whatever atrocity it is whose urgency on a particular day postpones and suspends any memorial ceremony of forgetful remembrance. Mourning Said will have to remain a permanently impermanent act for the community of his comrades—if we are to remain consistently true to the living memory of our fallen friend.

In becoming the defiant measure of a complacent community of professorial subservience to power, Said took his own cue from Antonio Gramsci who had once said that "The starting point of critical elaboration is the consciousness of what one really is." The Olympian oracle of "know thyself" thus became constitutional to Said's critical character—and with him that of anyone else graced by his friendship and borne by his caring intellect. But the critical inventory he took of himself was always morally inventive, politically contingent, socially spacious, globally intervening. He was never the past participle of anything—he is always the present tense of something else.

You could never locate him—except on the rainbow-arc trajectory of the precise, spectacular, and awe-inspiring moral choices he made. He was a progressive movement made of solid moral positions—and thus the contrapuntal logic of his principled defiance of conformity made him the dialectical embodiment of our will to resist power. To side with Said means to partake in his uncanny ability to sublate the moral impermanence of the world into a permanent measure of setting it aright. Said had the zeal of a Puritan pilgrim in the soul of a secular humanist.

It is now proverbial that Said made everyone who sided with him feel like a Palestinian refugee. But this was not a mere act of political solidarity with a comrade; this was by his consistently positing himself as the moral measure of the universe one had already inhabited. He was not a genealogist of morals. He was the manner of our moralities. In a world lost to all matters of moral permanence, he emerged as the normative reason of measuring the madness of any power—local or global—that sought to dominate it. For a man secular to the marrow of his bones, Said was the material simulacrum of an almost mystical conviction in a quintessential justice and a persistent beauty that he detected and proposed at the core of the universe. He never assured us. He was our assurance.

In by far the most brilliant act of taking an inventive inventory of his own critical character, Said planted the defiant character of the exilic intellectual right in the middle of the most conceited public space in the very heart of an Empire. He catapulted himself, as a permanent revolutionary, right into the middle of a moment when the figure of the public intellectual had been constitutionally compromised and institutionally privatized into subservience to power. As he projected it, the character of the exilic intellectual is neither culturally confined nor geographically dislocated. The space from which the exilic intellectual is permanently exiled is not just a homeland the colonial course of history can misappropriate. That space is primarily moral, not political. The exilic intellectual is not at home anywhere where injustice reigns supreme—and Said made that exilic condition blossom into a personal covenant rather than fade into a political commitment.

Siding with Said requires embracing the presence of an absence that has left no solid blueprint—only the moral memory of a voice that dared the elements of his own time, anticipating but not determining ours. There was a finesse about Said's moral rectitude that was at the root of his charismatic grace. He never acted from the doctrinal canonicity of a political pronouncement—he revived their ethical predicates. He sublated the specific political predicaments of nations at war with their colonial history into a graceful defiance of disgraceful atrocities at large. It is impossible to follow in his footsteps. He neither trailed nor left any. He made it impossible to emulate him—his prophetic soul—both by the gift of his own inimitable grace and by the glory of his own furious defiance of formulaic fantasies. To side with, honor, and mourn him in terms domestic to the dignity of his name is creatively to reimagine his critical intellect, cherish for the remains of our own days the sparkle of fire left in us from the lightning and thunder that he was.

Siding with Said is to have a lifelong conversation with him—as if you've just run into him on Columbia's campus on a beautiful autumn day—he on his way to his office, you on your way to some predestined point of irrelevance now made relevant only because you saw him on the way.

Said was a public intellectual not just in Columbia University, or New York City, the United States, Europe, or in the Arab, the Islamic, or the third world. The public space of his domain was amorphous—it could be your living room, classroom, the page you were reading, the paragraph you are writing, the melody you were humming, the thought that just occurred to you. Siding with Said is to think on your own feet, in a public space that is always somewhat off center and that pushes you slightly out of your element.

Siding with Said is an awakening. Mourning Said is a vigilance.

Three

FORGET REDS UNDER THE BED, THERE ARE ARABS IN THE ATTIC

I wrote the following essay at the invitation of Times Higher Education, *which noticed that my colleagues and I were under attack following a Palestinian film festival we had organized in January 2003. The essay was published on October 17, 2003, just after the celebration of the twenty-fifth anniversary of the publication of* Orientalism *that, as the chair of my department, I had organized, and was followed soon thereafter by the passing of Edward Said in September 2003. The actual harassment that came our way in those days now pales in comparison to the fact that Said was still with us when these events were taking place. In retrospect they may appear important. In the heat of the moment, we took them in stride.*

Late in June 2002, I came back to New York from a fortnight's trip to Japan to find my voicemail flooded with racist, obscene, and threatening messages. "Hey, Mr. Dabashi," bellowed an angry voice, "I read about you in today's *New York Post*. You stinking, terrorist Muslim pig. I hope the CIA is studying you so we can kick you out of this country back to some filthy Arab country where you belong. You terrorist bastard."

I subsequently discovered that on June 25, a certain Daniel Pipes had written an article in a New York tabloid attacking me and a number of other academics, identifying us as anti-American, anti-Israeli, and pro-terrorist. Among the charges that Pipes had brought against me was that I had cancelled one of my classes to attend a rally on behalf of the Palestinians. The rally was in connection with the April 2002 incursion into Jenin by Israeli forces. An Amnesty International expert had told the BBC that there was evidence pointing to a massacre.

Since the 2001 al-Qaida attacks, such reports do not find their way onto the major US networks. It is only through the miracle of the internet that ordinary people in the United States have a chance to transcend the rampant tribalism of the major networks, challenge the monolingualism of their culture, and search for a different angle on world events. Those who manage to do so then seek a more community-based venue to share what they have learned. It is in this context that I and a number of colleagues chose to speak at the rally.

As soon as I came back from the rally, I received an email from Rabbi Charles Sheer, who directs the Hillel Jewish Center at Columbia University, demanding that I submit to him the text of my speech. I answered that my speech was from scattered notes, and that I had published my views on the matter extensively elsewhere. I subsequently learned that the rabbi had gone on a rampage, calling the chairs and deans of my junior colleagues and demanding an explanation as to why the faculty had attended such a rally.

I wrote an article about Sheer for the students' newspaper, *The Spectator*, and a flood of messages from students and alumnae promptly clogged the emails and voicemail of the Columbia administration demanding that I apologize to him. I did not.

Instigated by the rabbi, some of my students went to the offices of the dean and the university ombudsman registering complaints against me. They were told I had done nothing wrong.

I spent the following May and the early part of June 2002 lecturing widely in the United States on Afghanistan and the terror of the US Empire. The rest of the summer was relatively calm, but the threatening voicemails flared up whenever something happened in Palestine. When on July 31 a bomb in the student cafeteria at the Hebrew University in Jerusalem killed seven people, the following message, dated August 1, 2002, was a typical example of voicemails I received: "I hope you are proud of your Palestinian heroes now, you fucking animal. Killing college students, OK. How do you like it, if someone ripped your fucking class, you pig!"

Late in August, I awoke to about 256 new messages. Startled, I opened my inbox and noted that the article Pipes had written about me in June was now emailed to me spasmodically hundreds of times, clogging my email account and preventing my account from receiving regular mail. This was the beginning of a nightmare that paralyzed my email communications at the busiest time of the academic year. I informed Columbia security and computer technicians. They massively increased my quota and blocked the server from which these emails were initiated. They also taught me how to save these spasmodic emails on a separate file, which they in turn burned onto a CD and gave to detectives in the New York Police Department. But the onslaught of emails was relentless. They were coming at a faster rate than I could file them. Our technicians created a fictitious email for me, but it wasn't much help because nobody knew me by that name.

I soon found out that every person named by Pipes in that June article in the New York tabloid was the target of this spamming. The mystery was solved when I received a phone call from a reporter with the *Chronicle of Higher Education* and then another from a reporter for the *New York Times*, informing me that I had been featured on a website that Pipes had created called Campus Watch.

Pipes was, of course, a bit late, because soon after September 11, Lynne Cheney, the wife of Vice President Dick Cheney, had created a list of what she called "suspicious professors," on which I was told that my friend and colleague Eric Foner and I had been posted for what she considered our anti-American views. But Campus Watch had added anti-Israeli and pro-terrorist charges, and now the spamming began to skyrocket and the voicemails turned positively nasty.

"Listen, you Muslim terrorist bastard," proclaimed one of the myriad emails I received subsequent to this website's launch, "we are watching you. We know who you support. We know you are the enemy of this country, and we are going to get you. We know where you live, we know where you work. Goodbye."

As the voicemail and email harassments proceeded apace in October and November, I was busy with a number of my colleagues at Columbia with a major divestment campaign urging our university to clear its portfolio of stocks in companies that sell military hardware to Israel. Our divestment campaign was squarely defeated by an anti-divestment campaign that mobilized hundreds more signatures from very wealthy donors to the university. Before we had even submitted our petition to the Committee for Socially Responsible Investment, before which Rabbi Sheer had appeared, Columbia's president dismissed our petition and killed the campaign.

Toward the end of the semester the spamming had subsided, replaced by the spammers subscribing me to every pornographic site in the cyber universe or ordering penis-enlargement medications, Viagra pills, and Rolex watches for me. This was not as bad and fairly entertaining to delete.

I spent the rest of the autumn semester preparing for the most comprehensive retrospective on Palestinian cinema ever. I invited a brilliant young Palestinian filmmaker, Annemarie Jacir, to help curate the festival, and, in preparation for our event in the first week of the spring semester 2003, we created a major website on Palestinian cinema.

To prevent the sabotaging of our festival, a small band of community activists and I waited until the night before the commencement of the spring semester and then flooded the campus with our posters and the email listserves with our announcements. We put an announcement in *The Nation* and the *Village Voice*.

The festival was one of the most spectacular success stories of my academic career and was attended by thousands of students and members of the community. In the course of the festival, we were able to screen thirty-three films, including three world premieres. Our website, dreamsofanation.com, meanwhile, had literally millions of hits, mostly from Palestine and Israel, followed by the Pentagon in Washington, DC. We never suspected movie fans in such militant quarters.

But the festival also brought more harassment. In January, our departmental administrator said she had received "an obnoxious phone call" from the Hillel Center about the festival, threatening to send a barrage of hate calls about the conference our way. Three days later, someone from the university development and alumnae relations office called to say that the office had received complaints about the festival from some of our alumnae. Two days later, my junior colleague Gil Anidjar, who had nothing to do with the festival, received a phone call from the university president's office asking about the event. The same day, Gil received a voicemail from an outside caller objecting to the festival.

In a matter of hours we learned that an organization calling itself the Conservative Club of Columbia University had issued a statement against the festival, calling on its members to call Columbia President Lee C. Bollinger (and President George W. Bush) to object to it. In this statement, the Columbia Conservative Club had misidentified the chairman of my department as Gil Anidjar.

On the morning of January 23, the day the festival began, I received a phone call from John Murolo of Columbia security, informing me that Rabbi Sheer had told him that Mordechai Levy was on his way from Brooklyn to disrupt the festival and the conference. Murolo claimed Levy was a criminal thug and suggested we increase security.

On the evening of January 23, I was interviewed for the *Jewish Week* newspaper about the festival. The reporter also spoke to Rabbi Sheer who, on an unrelated subject, said that "the appointment of Rashid Khalidi of the University of Chicago [as Edward Said Professor of Arabic Studies] affirmed his belief that Columbia's Middle East department is biased against Israel." He added that "Columbia is not a healthy place to study the Middle East" and said that the dean of the school for international and public affairs agreed that the problem of biased Middle East departments "is endemic to the field [of Middle East studies] and not just at Columbia." The dean categorically denies having ever said anything remotely resembling what Rabbi Sheer attributed to her.

Immediately after the publication of these lies about me and my department in the *Jewish Week*, the racist, obscene, and threatening voicemails increased dramatically. Columbia security brought a detective from the New York Police Department to my office for a long interview, and measures were taken to protect me.

In February, Bollinger's office called me to report a flood of phone calls objecting to the film festival and to ask what they should do. A week later, the office of public affairs rang with a similar query and asked if I could do something on Israeli cinema. The last week of February was the turn of the university secretary. I blew up and shot off a five-page email, promising to go public if they did not stop harassing me. They did.

But it didn't last. In March, during a formal university function, one of our alumnae singled me and my department out for a tirade against our perceived anti-Israeli positions and policies. Nobody in the upper administration raised an objection. I complained, but nothing was done.

I went about my business, preparing for a celebration for the silver jubilee of Said's *Orientalism*, which Said attended.

Over the summer, my activities were limited to a few radio or television interviews about US and UK involvement in Iraq.

September commenced uneventfully until the evening of September 24, when I learned that Said had gone into a coma. He died the following day. He was scheduled to give the keynote speech at the conference US Imperialism in the 21st Century, which I am helping to organize for early November and which is likely to spark further harassment. As I write, my department has once more come under attack after Campus Watch ran an article by a certain Greg Yardley.

Next year I go on sabbatical. I plan to spend my time in Palestine trying to set up a center for cinema studies. Our adversaries call Columbia Birzeit-upon-the-Hudson.

Four

For a Fistful of Dust

A Passage to Palestine

This account describes my one and only trip to Palestine, when Annemarie Jacir and I took our Palestinian film festival, "Dreams of a Nation," to six Palestinian cities in February 2004. During this visit I took a fistful of soil from a sacred gravesite near Al-Aqsa Mosque in Jerusalem to the Brummana suburb of Beirut and put it on Edward's gravesite. The travelogue first appeared on Al-Ahram Weekly, September 23–29, 2004, marking the first anniversary of Edward's passing. My dear friend Mona Anis was my editor at the time I wrote this essay for Al-Ahram. Soon after the coup in Egypt by General Sisi on July 3, 2013, all my essays disappeared from the Al-Ahram website; I later discovered they had all been collected and placed on a back-door of the website. At this writing, this essay is back on their regular website. This is the first of my two travelogues to Palestine; the second travelogue appears as chapter 7. These accounts capture the most precious memories of my beautiful visit to Palestine.

41

Ah, make the most of what we yet may spend,
Before we too into the Dust descend;
Dust into Dust, and under Dust to lie

—Omar Khayyam

E dward W. Said, for years a cherished friend and for a lifetime a towering comrade, died in New York at 6:45 a.m. on Thursday, September 25, 2003. After a funeral service at Riverside Church on Monday, September 29, 2003, he was cremated and his ashes taken to Lebanon by his widow, Mariam Said, and buried at the Quaker Friends cemetery in Brummana village in the Metn region of Mount Lebanon. Said was born in Jerusalem on Friday, November 1, 1935, before the colonial occupation of his homeland.

On Monday, February 23, 2004, I flew to Palestine and landed at Ben Gurion checkpoint. I went to Palestine as part of a collective to take an expanded version of our Palestinian film festival, "Dreams of a Nation," which we had initially organized in New York in January 2003, to four Palestinian cities—Jerusalem, Ramallah, Nazareth, and Gaza City. Our inaugural festival at Columbia University was a spectacular success. We had screened more than fifty feature, short, and documentary films, all made by Palestinian filmmakers in or out of their homeland. Said had delivered the opening address of our festival at a packed auditorium in Lerner Hall at Columbia University, to an audience that had come from all around the city, the state, the country—some from as far as Canada. Soon after, the festival assumed a life of its own, and began to travel around the United States, then to Europe and North Africa and other parts of the Arab world. Our small collective, however, thought it necessary we should take it to Palestine. A Palestinian cultural organization, Yabous, based in East Jerusalem, agreed to host our festival. I flew from Copenhagen, where I was invited by the Danish Cinematheque for a retrospective based on my book on Iranian cinema, via Zurich, and landed at Ben Gurion checkpoint.

My Palestinian friends could not pick me up from the checkpoint because I landed at 1:00 a.m. and they were all locked up inside occupied Ramallah. (In Tulkarem, now almost entirely encircled by a formidable wall, the Israeli army locks up Palestinians at about 6:00 p.m.) But they had arranged for a Palestinian cab driver to come from East Jerusalem to pick me up and take me to my hotel. The Christmas Hotel, where I was going to stay, is located just off Salah al-Din Street in East Jerusalem, about an hour drive from Ben Gurion checkpoint.

It took me about two hours to clear through the Ben Gurion security. When I exited the final interrogation hall, a young Palestinian cab driver was waiting for me, holding a piece of paper with my name on it. I approached him. We made quick eye contact and he smiled: "Professor Dabashi?" I nodded. "*Ahlan wa sahlan,*" he said and I smiled—"*Shokran habibi.*" We got into his cab and passed through yet another set of security stations patrolled by teenagers in military uniforms, with very long machine guns hanging from their necks. We finally entered a highway leading east toward Jerusalem. The highway was completely deserted. The surrounding landscape was wrapped in a black shawl, marked on its edges by dimly lit lampposts bending forward and turning their backs to the quiet darkness. On our way, when Ayman discovered that I am a Muslim, he showed me the spot where the highway had run through the mausoleum of one of the companions of our prophet, Muhammad, bulldozed and flattened for the concrete asphalt. He also showed me an apartment building that was built on the site of Deir Yassin—a Palestinian village whose inhabitants were massacred on Friday, April 9, 1948, by the commandos of the Irgun, headed by Menachem Begin, who later became the prime minister of Israel. We were mostly silent. It was dark—the highway lampposts now looked lost in a haze, shot like an oddly shaped bamboo shoot, out of place, bored, boorish, lighting as if nothing other than their own solitary stands, frightful of their own shadows. But the air was crisp, the night was cool, and the sound of asphalt under the wheel of Ayman's car was reassuring. "*Min wain anta?*" I said I was Iranian.

We entered Jerusalem about 5:00 a.m., as the sun was rising on the Dome of the Rock, gracing the blue sky watching over the old city. I asked Ayman to stop for a few minutes. I exited his cab. I looked at Qubat al-Sakhra. I had not prayed since I was eleven years old. The golden dome was marking the azurite cobalt of the expansive sky. Defiant. The entire universe was silent. There was a blueness in the sky over the golden dome. There was a humming sound in the air. I saw a few Hasidic Jews rushing to some unspecified destination. They seemed to be in a hurry.

I returned to the cab and Ayman drove me to the front door of the Christmas Hotel, off Salah al-Din Street. The door to the hotel was locked, but as soon as I stood at its threshold wondering what to do, a man appeared from inside the hotel, from the depth of its darkness, opened the door, and welcomed me in. I checked in and asked for permission to sit at a computer in the lobby to check my email. I sent a few emails to my friends and family, assuring them that I had landed safely in Palestine and that all was well. "Landed in thy homeland," I wrote to Rasha Salti, a Palestinian friend in New York, "its countenance valanced and yet still beautiful."

I took my backpack up to the second floor to my room, a modest but impeccably clean cubicle. I washed my face and brushed my teeth. I was too excited to rest. Insomniac. I came back down to the lobby, where the same man who had opened the door for me appeared again from the dark and asked if he could help me. I said I wondered if al-Haram al-Sharif was near the hotel. He said yes and pointed toward the direction on Salah al-Din Street where I had to walk for a few blocks to get there.

The streets were still quiet. It was now almost 5:00 a.m. The shops were closed. I saw a few Orthodox Jews rushing toward a determined destination. Then I saw two teenage Israeli soldiers with flashy sunglasses and two machine guns hanging from their necks. Their sunglasses were not necessary. The sun was not yet up. The street lamps were still lit. They looked tired. They paid no attention to me. They were busy talking to each other. I do not understand Hebrew.

At a street corner, I saw a bulletin board for public announcements. I noted a few prominent posters for our festival hanging on that board—"*Ahlam Ummah: Mahrajan al-Film al-Falastini.*" Annemarie Jacir, my principal partner in the "Dreams of a Nation" project, had been hard at work for months getting the festival moving in collaboration with our host, Yabous. "*Bravo 'aleyki, General Jacir!*" That's what we call her in our collective. She runs a very tight ship. A couple of our posters were torn down from that bulletin board. I fixed them.

From Salah al-Din Street I reached a major thoroughfare encircling the main citadel on which stood al-Haram al-Sharif. The early morning traffic was now getting crowded. I crossed the main street and walked toward what I later learned was called Bab al-Zahra. I did not know exactly where I was going. But I was drawn through the gate and into the market.

At the mouth of the market, there were three Israeli soldiers guarding the gate—one white soldier in a position of obvious authority and two Black soldiers beholden to him. I asked them, addressing no one in particular, just their constellation, if that gate led to the Dome of the Rock. No one answered me—as the gaze of the two Black soldiers gradually diverted from me and my question toward their white superior. The white officer did not look at me and did not move his upright and determined neck, holding his steadfast gaze away from my face and pierced beyond my back toward an unspecified direction. He had no sunglasses on—but he looked as if he did. I waited for an answer, as did the two Black soldiers, now circulating my gaze from one face to another—examining them under the surface of my unanswered question. These soldiers were slightly older than the ones I had seen at the airport and then near the hotel. They were perhaps in their early twenties—brandishing the same long machine guns from their necks. They looked tired—ready to go home and sleep. There was no answer. I could not move away because I had asked a question, the question was in the air, and I felt obliged to wait for even a hint, a suggestion of an answer so I could just leave. But no answer was coming my way. Nothing. The two Black soldiers threw a nervous look at me, and I at them—the three of us were now at the mercy of the white

Israeli officer—determined not to look at or answer me. We were like three mesmerized pigeons now under the spell of a cobra—waiting for his move. He did not move. He would not move. This may have taken no more than a few seconds, but it lasted an eternity—time had stood still, in a frozen frame: three frozen pigeons and one mighty cobra. The cobra finally moved, or did he, and his lips may have moved, or so I wished. I was not sure, but I took my chances, watched his lips, heard his voice—said, "Thank you," to no one in particular, just at the constellation of the two remaining pigeons and the cobra, and left.

The winding alley was fully covered with closed shops; very few shopkeepers were around, setting up their merchandise. The alleys were deserted, except for a few old men, walking aimlessly. I went down the winding alleys, until I saw a sign for the Dome of the Rock on an old arch. I followed it. I turned a few winding turns and then a sharp left and I headed down toward what I later found out was called Bab al-Usud, the Lions' Gate. At the bottom of the alley I saw a pack of Israeli soldiers, men and women (boys and girls, really), in riot gear, with long machine guns hanging from their neck. I did not look at them. They looked at me. I pretended I knew where I was going. I did not. I was nervous. Scared.

At the bottom of the hilly alley I saw an Israeli army station to my left, guarded by a teenage soldier with a very long machine gun hanging from his neck. Immediately to my right was the entrance to a graveyard. On a white board with black ink this graveyard was identified for having the mausoleum of two of the Prophet's companions—al-Sahabi al-Jalil Ibadah ibn al-Samit (d. 34 AH) and al-Sahabi al-Jalil Shidad ibn Aws (d. 58 AH). I had a pen in my pocket and a piece of paper. I took them out and wrote these names down. On the board they were written in *nasta'liq*. On my paper, I wrote them down in *naskh*. I entered the graveyard and began to whisper the *Fatiha*. A few steps into the graveyard I ran into an old Palestinian. "*Sabah al-kheyr*," I said; "*Sabah al-kheyr*," he replied and smiled and asked me if I were a Muslim. I said yes. "*As-salamu aleikum ya akhi*," he said. "*Wa aleikum al-salam ya akhi*,"

I said. He wondered where I was from. From Iran, I said, I am from Iran. He asked if I were a Shi'i. I said yes. He wondered if this was my first trip to Jerusalem and if I wanted to visit the sacred site of the two companions of our Prophet. I said yes it was, and yes I wanted to.

The old Palestinian Muslim led the way and I followed him. I could see a church down the hill to my left and a tall wall to my right. Halfway through the graveyard, my impromptu guide started climbing the rise from the narrow walkway up toward the wall. I followed him. At the foot of the wall we came across a modest gravesite. This was the grave of al-Sahabi al-Jalil Ibadah ibn al-Samit, as identified by a modest sign attached to an even more modest barrier constructed with metal around the grave. I touched the barrier and recited the *Fatiha* under my breath. The old Palestinian waited until I finished and then he walked away, toward the other side of the graveside where the mausoleum of al-Sahabi al-Jalil Shidad ibn Aws was located. We both stopped, and I said another *Fatiha*. The morning weather was cool, calm, and sedentary. The air smelled of freshly baked bread and dust and za'atar and olive trees. The light of Jerusalem was gray and the color of Jerusalem was light brown—and the soil of Palestine was ordinary.

The old Palestinian and I descended the rise and jumped from the last row of graves down on the narrow path. He asked me if I wanted to go to al-Aqsa Mosque. I said yes. He asked me if it was true that we Shi'is did not care for the *sahaba* of our Prophet. I said no. He asked me if I believed in the sanctity of the *al-'ashara al-mubashshara*, the ten most noble companions of the prophet to whom Paradise was promised while they were still in this life. I said no, we Shi'is did not believe in their sanctity or infallibility because they included the first three caliphs, whom we believe usurped the right of our *amir al-mu'minin*, Ali, who was the rightful heir to our Prophet. "*Shu ya'ni?*" He stopped abruptly and looked at me with a troubled hesitation creeping under his serene sense of hospitality to a fellow Muslim. He asked if I believed in the *khulafa' al-rashidun*, the four Rightly-Guided Caliphs who succeeded our Prophet. I asked if he knew where I could buy good Palestinian za'atar. He smiled and said most definitely and that he would take me to the best shop in Jerusalem for za'atar. I said, *"Shokran jazilan, ya akhi!"*

We exited the graveyard, turned left and walked toward the first entrance into al-Haram al-Sharif. A few Israeli soldiers were at the mouth of the long corridor leading to the gate. One of them asked me where I was going. I said to al-Aqsa Mosque. He asked was I a Muslim. I said yes. He let me and the Palestinian go. The Palestinian and I turned left, passed the Israeli soldiers, and walked toward the end of the alley, where a huge blue gate was guarded by yet another pack of Israeli soldiers. In front of us was now another older Palestinian in a dark brown *galabiyya*, walking with a cane slowly toward the gate. My Palestinian guide and I slowed down and followed him. He was whispering something as he passed through the first group of Israeli soldiers. I could not quite hear him. I thought he was uttering some prayers. But when we slowed down, I could hear him better. *"Ya ikhwan ash sharmuta!"* I heard him say, and I am quite sure I also heard a *"Ya hukkam al-'Arab!"*

The three of us slowly approached the big blue gate and the next pack of Israeli soldiers, who let the two Palestinians through but stopped me. One of them, an older soldier in blue anti-riot gear, asked me where I was going. Before I said anything, my Palestinian guide turned around and told him in Hebrew what I thought was something like I was going to al-Aqsa Mosque. The Israeli soldier disregarded the Palestinian and continued to look at and talk to me in English. The other two Palestinians entered through the gate and the gate closed—leaving me and the Israeli soldiers behind. "Are you a Muslim?" he asked.

"Yes," I said.

"Let me see your passport," he said. I reached for my passport but suddenly realized that I had left it in the pocket of my coat back in my room at the Christmas Hotel. I said I did not have my passport with me but that he would not be able to tell from my passport that I am a Muslim because I traveled with a US passport.

As this conversation between the Israeli soldier and I was progressing, suddenly the huge blue door to al-Haram al-Sharif opened and a tall and husky Palestinian came out, turned to the Israeli soldier, and told him in English, "Let him in, he is a Muslim." The Israeli soldier muttered something in Hebrew, to which the Palestinian answered, again in English, "No, he is a Muslim, let him in." The Israeli soldier turned away and left, and the Palestinian let me enter the vestibule leading to the huge courtyard. He closed the door behind me and said, "Are you a Muslim?"

"Yes," I said.

"Let me hear you recite the Qur'an," he said, smiling. I panicked and mumbled. All I could remember was the opening verses of *al-Baqara*.

"*Alif. Lam. Mim.*" I said, nervously, words barely audible even to myself, "*Dhalika al-kitabu la rayba fihi hudan li-l-muttaqin.*"

"That's too long," the Palestinian guard interrupted me. "Can you recite the *Fatiha*?"

"Yes," I said, "*Bism Allah al-rahman al-rahim,*" I said less nervously, "*al-hamdu li-l-ahi rabb al-ʻalamin, al-rahman al-rahim, malik yaum al-din.*" He listened reverently, whispering the verses with and after me under his breath, just like a father looking over his son performing in public something rehearsed before, nervous that he may go wrong, that he may forget a memorized verse. But I made no mistake, until I finished the *Fatiha* chapter by heart, "*ghayr al-maghdhubi ʻalayhim wa-l-al-dhalin,*" as with every trembling verse out of my mouth his wise and generous face opening up with an expansive embrace, a glitter in his eyes confirming his intuition.

"*Ahlan wa sahlan ya akhi,*" he said as soon as I finished, "Welcome to Palestine! You are not only a Muslim, you are also an Iranian because you don't know how to pronounce *qaf*. It is *qaf*, habibi, not *ghaf*—so it is *mustaqim*, not *mustaghim*." I smiled back with embarrassment and tried to say *mustaqim* as best as I knew how. Then I turned around and saw that my old Palestinian guide from the gravesite was watching over this whole proceeding approvingly, totally bemused and exonerated by my claim, though a shade Shiʻi, to our faith.

The courtyard of al-Haram al-Sharif was vast, flat, and full of olive trees. Two other Palestinian guards of the sacred site, with special green uniforms, appeared and asked me where I was going. My Palestinian guide said that I was a Shi'i going to al-Aqsa Mosque. These ones did not ask me to recite the Qur'an and let us go. As I was talking to the guards I noticed that my Palestinian guide sat on the edge of a border defining the boundaries of the olive groves and wrote down his name, the name of his son, and his cellular phone number for me to call him to go and buy za'atar. I thanked him for it, and I followed him toward the Dome of the Rock, which was now visible to our right on a raised platform overlooking our approach.

It was a Tuesday morning and the site around the Dome of the Rock was completely deserted. As we approached it I noticed that its doors were closed. *Cho beyt al-moqaddas darun por qobab* was the first thing that came to my mind, a famous line of Sa'di in his *Bustan*, describing the Sufis, "Just like the Dome of the Rock, their interiors fully sculpted," *Raha kardeh divar birun kharab*. He had visited this site in the seventh Islamic century (thirteenth on the Gregorian calendar), "while they have left their exterior to ruins." Apparently when Sa'di had visited this site, the exterior of the Dome of the Rock was in a state of disrepair. I approached the exterior wall of the Dome and gently kissed its checkered blue and yellow ceramic tiles. My Palestinian guide looked at me bewildered and said that what I did was not necessary. I thought it was. I circumambulated the Dome, where we believe our Prophet ascended to the Seventh Heaven, and then went down from the steps on the other side and walked toward al-Aqsa Mosque. Behind me was now the central site of the Islamic cosmogonic imagination—ahead of me the most famous mosque affiliated with it—and I felt I was home.

My Palestinian guide explained to a guard sitting inside a cubicle at the door of the al-Aqsa Mosque that I was a Muslim, that I was a Shi'i, and that I was an Iranian and wanted to enter the mosque. The guard smiled and welcomed me. My guide at this point said he had to return to the market to attend to his business. I thanked him and said goodbye. As he was leaving, I approached the mosque, took off my shoes, placed them inside a small cubicle at the entrance, very much like those

I remembered from Qom and Mashhad of my childhood, and entered the mosque—vast, spacious, welcoming, reassuring, covered, wall to wall, by soothing layers of carpets, a sudden, almost surreal silence exuding from its spatial confidence. I walked slowly toward a pillar at the left side of the mosque. There were not that many people inside. Both men and women, without any marked barrier or even distance between them, were either performing their ritual prayers or reading from the Qur'an. This was markedly different from Iranian mosques where men and women are not allowed in the same space. I went and sat at the foot of a pillar, picked up a copy of the Qur'an, and began reading from the first and the second chapters—*al-Fatiha* and *al-Baqara*—trying to pronounce my *qaf*s properly. Then I just sat there and looked around. Nobody was paying any attention to me. I had long since forgotten that silence had a resonance, that peace had a presence, that there is a deliberate consciousness to motions, that absolute and definitive serenity could fill a space so voluminously. Whence so much peace? How many Palestinians had been murdered here, trying to prevent its desecration, destruction—the eradication of the center site of a world religion? Wherefore this silence?

After a few minutes I got up and gently left the mosque, put on my shoes at the door, thanked the Palestinian guard in his cubicle, and headed back toward the Bab al-Faysal exit of al-Haram al-Sharif. Exiting, I crossed yet another two or three layers of Israeli soldiers with machine guns hanging from their necks and headed back toward my hotel.

My repeated traffics between Jerusalem and Ramallah, with trips to Bethlehem, Beit Sahhur, Nazareth, Nablus, and of course the myriad of Israeli checkpoints in between, kept me busy for the next few days, and I was not able to return back to al-Haram al-Sharif until Friday, February 27, when I had cleared my morning for that purpose. I had an early breakfast on that Friday in the backyard of Christmas Hotel and headed toward the Lions' Gate at about 8:00 a.m. There was a much more heavily armed Israeli presence on that occasion in obvious anticipation of the

Friday noon prayer. I passed through a few congregations of Israeli soldiers and entered al-Haram al-Sharif fairly easily. It was still too early for
the noon prayer and not that many people were around. I went straight
to the Dome of the Rock and found its doors open, with a Palestinian
older gentleman sitting on a small stool at the main entrance. I greeted
him, took off my shoes, and entered the compound. Not more than a
hundred people or so, men and women, were praying in various parts of
the interior. I circumambulated around the rock and finally approached
it from an angle where a group of pilgrims had gathered around a man
who was giving a historical account of the significance of the rock. I
stood by the rock and watched it closely as I listened to the man discussing the Qur'anic verse pertinent to the Prophet's nocturnal *Mi'raj:* "Glo-
rified be He who carried His servant by night from the Masjid al-Haram to the Masjid al-Aqsa."

  After a few minutes, I turned around and went to a corner and looked
up toward the ceiling. There was a sustained serenity in the air of the building, a miasmatic permanence about its architectural confidence—as if the
rock that lay bare and exposed at the heart of it had a knowledge of itself.
I noticed a group of women praying, reading the Qur'an, chatting silently,
and I saw a few children holding the hand of their fathers—silent, quietly
playful, one of them a bit bewildered. People looked neither rich nor poor,
neither old nor young, neither black nor white—men and women were almost indistinguishable in their long *galabiyya* or *'abaya*. A streak of trans-
lucent light entered the arena from the main gate almost in a rush, and its
shades and shadows spread around. I could not hear anything.

  I eventually left the Dome of the Rock, picked up my shoes from
the small cubicle by the door, and sat down and put them on before
I descended the plateau on which the Dome is located. There was a
small market inside al-Haram al-Sharif where they were selling various
religious items, but the shopkeepers were also selling pirated copies of
movies of Arnold Schwarzenegger and Tom Cruise. I bought a small
key chain with a replica of the Dome of the Rock on it. It was much
cheaper than the DVDs of *Terminator II* and *Mission Impossible.*

I wandered around in the space between the Dome of the Rock and al-Aqsa Mosque for a while. It was a beautiful and sunny day in late February. The light was grayish, the walls around me luminous. I gradually exited al-Haram al-Sharif through Bab al-Faysal and turned right toward Bab al-Usud, crossed the Israeli army station to my left, and entered the cemetery. I whispered a *Fatiha* as I went straight to the mausoleums of the two companions of the prophet. First I climbed the rise toward the site of al-Sahabi al-Jalil Ibadah ibn al-Samit. I stood in front of the grave, held onto the metal barrier, and recited another *Fatiha*. Then I took out from my pocket a small plastic Ziploc bag that I had brought with me from New York, bent over the grave and started digging a small hole with my fingers, extracting the soil and placing it inside the bag. About half a fistful of dust into the bag, I got up and approached the grave of al-Sahabi al-Jalil Shidad ibn Aws. Again, I whispered a *Fatiha*, bent over, made a small hole with my fingers, picked up the soil and added it into the bag. Now I had about a full fist of earth from both the gravesites of the Prophet's companions buried in Jerusalem.

I got up, placed the plastic bag and the soil inside it into my pocket, and headed back down the slope over, away from the wall, and toward the last row of graves. As I was jumping down from the small rise onto the narrow path I saw a small pack of Israeli soldiers, all except their commanding officers' teenagers, boys and girls, in full riot gear and heavily armed with machine guns hanging from their necks—some in greenish and others in bluish uniform. Their commanding officer looked at me, smiled, and said *"As-salamu aleikum."*

I said, *"Wa 'aleikum al-salam,"* lowered my head, and dusted my jeans. When I raised my head, my eyes caught the eyes of a very pretty Israeli girl in military uniform in the company of her fellow soldiers, with a machine gun hanging from her neck. Her eyes were green. Her hair was light brown. She was medium height, a bit husky, holding her helmet in one hand, and with the other caressing her machine gun. She looked at me for a few seconds and I dropped my eyes and fell behind their march. From behind they looked quite playful, giggling even.

I slowly followed the Israeli soldiers out of the cemetery. At the gate of the cemetery I saw the same group of soldiers sitting at a corner and chatting with each other. Except for their uniforms, riot gear, helmets, and machine guns (still hanging from their necks, even while they were sitting), they looked like a group of high school kids out on a field trip. I got a glimpse of the same pretty young girl chatting with a fellow soldier as I turned left and headed back to the winding market. It was Friday and all the shops were closed. I exited the compound from Bab al-Zahra and went back to Salah al-Din Street to do some shopping before the Friday noon prayer. Some of the shops in the main square in front of the old city were open. I bought a few red and blue scarves, a gold bracelet, and a kilo of za'atar. The Palestinians do not have their own money. They have to use Israeli money—even in Jerusalem and Ramallah. I did not have Israeli money. I had to exchange US money for Israeli money at a Palestinian currency exchange outlet on Salah al-Din Street, right in front of Bab al-Zahra gate to al-Haram al-Sharif.

By about 11:00 a.m. I had deposited my za'atar and other purchases in my room at the Christmas Hotel and headed back toward al-Haram al-Sharif because I wanted to attend the Friday noon prayer. I kept the Palestinian soil I had collected from the gravesite of the Prophet's companions in the Ziploc bag in my pocket. Within the two hours or so that I had left the area to do my shopping, it seemed like the entirety of the Israeli army had moved into the surrounding streets of al-Haram al-Sharif. I ran into literally hundreds of teenage soldiers in an uncanny combination of military readiness and juvenile playfulness. They looked like they were excited by a kind of picnic outing, relentlessly talking and laughing with each other, while sporting an assortment of machine guns hanging from their necks, all in riot gear. There was an influx of an ostensibly Palestinian crowd moving through the alleys of the market toward al-Haram al-Sharif. I walked in their midst. No Israeli soldier stopped me or asked me any question and I avoided all eye contact until I reached the very last right turn into the alley that led to the Bab al-Faysal vestibule. The flow of the crowd carried me with it all the way to the main compound, which was completely covered with worshippers ready for the Friday prayers. The crowd was ostensibly young—though many middle-aged and older men were also among them. There was running water at a corner by an olive tree, where I joined a group of young men and did the ritual ablutions. I could not quite remember how to do it. So I followed other people around me. They were doing it slightly differently than the way I remembered it from my childhood when my mother used to take us to the Eighth Shi'i Imam shrine in Mashhad, in the Khurasan province of Iran. I followed the crowd of Palestinians ready for Friday prayers toward al-Aqsa Mosque. I could not get any closer than a few steps down from the Dome of the Rock and could not see the end of the prayer rows extended into the mosque itself. I was now standing between the Dome of the Rock and al-Aqsa Mosque—two of the most sacrosanct sites in the sacred geography of Islam.

I began my prayers with others—remembering when my mother first taught me how to recite the Qur'an in the Goharshad Mosque in Imam Reza Mausoleum in Mashhad. I must have been seven or eight years old. I remembered my parents, and I remembered my children, and I remembered everyone else near and dear to me, on this hallowed ground—the sacrosanct site of the faith that claims my conscience, where we believe our prophet ascended the heavens. I had not prayed since I was eleven years old. I was now fifty-two, and I had a fistful of Palestinian soil in my pocket that I wanted to take to Lebanon, go to Brummana, and pour on the last resting place of my fallen friend, Edward Said. This soil belongs to him, and he belongs to this soil, and he would not rest in peace until he was under this soil. "I testify that God is one," I said in the company of my Palestinian brothers, "and I testify that Muhammad is the prophet of God," and then I added in my mind, "*wa ashhadu anna Alian wali Allah.*"

As the prayer was nearing its end, I suddenly heard shouts of *Allahu akbar*, interspersed with sounds of explosions and bullets, from various corners of the compound. They were haphazard and nervous. I eventually noticed a commotion from behind me. I turned around and saw crowds of worshippers in disarray. From behind them, down from behind the Dome of the Rock, I could now see rows of Israeli troops storming into al-Haram al-Sharif in riot battle formations, coming, it seemed, from Bab al-Maghariba. They started hurtling canisters at us without breaking their ranks. Columns of white smoke began to separate their advancing rows from our confusing formations. Suddenly I heard explosive sounds; I had no idea what they were and where they were coming from. My eyes began to burn and I became frightened. A young Palestinian noticing my fear and bewilderment smiled widely: La takhaf habibi," he said. "Qanabil sawtiyya," sound grenades, he said. I had no clue what he meant. I did not see any sign of people throwing stones at the Israeli soldiers around me. In fact I saw no pebbles or stones on the compound anywhere—except behind me to the left of al-Aqsa Mosque (when facing it with our back toward the Dome of the Rock) where some sort of construction, excavation, or restoration (I could not tell) was in progress. I had already seen a stone-throwing occasion on Wednesday, February 25, early in the afternoon, when the Israeli army was robbing the Arab Bank in downtown Ramallah. This was an entirely different situation. There was something calm and even relaxed about both sides, as if they were two sides of a game they were playing. There was no physical contact between us and the Israeli soldiers, but a shuddering rush of people at the front row facing the army. Suddenly from my back, toward the mosque, I heard an abrupt burst of firing of what I presumed (hoped) were rubber bullets ("na'am ya akhi, al- rasas al-matati"). I thought there were soldiers coming at us from that direction, too. But I think I was hearing the echoes of rubber bullets being fired from the front. At one point, the crowd around me became quite jittery and nervous and I was knocked over and lost my control. There were a few seconds of panic when I did not know what was exactly happening over my head. But I got up and walked toward Bab al-Rahma Cemetery and Musalla Marwan, to the left side of the Dome of the Rock when facing al-Aqsa Mosque. The space there was a bit wider and safer, I thought.

After catching my breath and reassessing where I was in relation to the rest of the compound, I moved back toward al-Aqsa Mosque and the Dome of the Rock and noticed that the crowd was getting more relaxed and even conversant, as the rows of Israeli soldiers began to retreat and move out of the compound. The remarkable thing about this whole affair was that there was a festive spirit about the crowd, at least those around me. The older people were far more angry and agitated. The younger Palestinians had a cheerful and jovial disposition—their *ya akhu al-sharmuta!* thrown at the Israeli direction with an almost choral choreography in diction and disposition. I looked up toward the heavens. There was a certainty about the cloudless sky, a grayish indifference, and I could hear a faint humming of a distant traffic encircling the sacred citadel. I reached for my plastic bag in my pocket, full of soil from the mausoleums of the Prophet's companions. I did not take the bag out of my pocket. I just felt the earth between my fingers. The crowd eventually began to thin out as the Israelis started pulling out and leaving al-Haram al-Sharif. I followed the crowd and entered the winding streets around the compound, and headed back to my hotel. It was getting late. I had to go back to my hotel, where Hany Abu-Assad was sending his producer to pick me up and take me to Nablus, where he was getting ready to shoot his next film.

I had no other occasion to visit al-Haram al-Sharif during that trip and spent most of my time between Nablus, Nazareth, Ramallah, and Jerusalem. I left Palestine via Ben Gurion checkpoint on Monday, March 1, in order to be back in New York for the memorial service that Columbia University had organized for Said. Before I had left for Palestine, Mariam Said and Akeel Bilgrami had asked me to write a short memorial essay to be included in a small volume they were putting together to commemorate the occasion. I wrote a short piece, called it "Siding with Said," and emailed it to Akeel Bilgrami before I flew to Palestine. I was anxious to attend this memorial.

Exiting the Ben Gurion checkpoint is far more difficult than entering it. Ihsan, a Palestinian cab driver friend of Ayman, drove me and Fayçal Hasaïri, a producer with the Orbit satellite television and radio network who had come to Palestine to do a documentary on our "Dreams of a Nation" film festival, from the Christmas Hotel to Ben Gurion. At the very first checkpoint entering the airport, the Israeli soldiers stopped us and asked us to pull over. They checked our passports and looked at our bags. They asked me to pick up my green backpack and go and sit on a bench at the side of their station. I did so. They asked Ihsan to open his trunk and front hood and the four doors of his car and go and sit next to me. Fayçal they asked to go inside their station with all his camera equipment. While Ihsan and I sat on that bench and waited and watched, two Israeli soldiers brought a couple of German Shepherd dogs and all sorts of equipment and began checking Ihsan's cab inside and out.

After a thorough examination that took about an hour, we were let go. Ihsan stopped his car at the entrance to the departure area. We said good-bye, and he left. Fayçal and I also said goodbye as soon as we entered the departure lounge because he needed to find a cart to carry his equipment and I was anxious to catch my flight. Fayçal's flight to Rome was later than mine to New York via Zurich.

Numerous and interminable serpentine lines await bewildered travelers as soon as they enter the departure lounge. After waiting for almost two hours to get my small backpack, passport, and ticket checked, the Israeli teenager in charge of security was visibly troubled when I submitted to his inspection my belongings. I do not know whether it was the word "Iran" in front of "Place of Birth" in my passport or the whitish beard I was sporting, or my Arabic first name, or undecidable last name, or signs and stamps that showed I had visited Lebanon, Syria, Egypt, United Arab Emirates, and Morocco that did it, but he left me standing in front of the huge electronic security belt and disappeared into a crowd of other security teenagers to ask what level of security he had to assign to me. The security hazard that people like me posed to the world at large was properly color-coded, I soon realized. The only problem was that the teenager could not decide if I were of a yellow or a red status.

After consultation with his companions, he decided that I was security hazard level yellow, meaning I was assigned only two teenage ninjas and a German Shepherd to make sure I was not going to cause any trouble.

The two teenagers, followed by their diligent German Shepherd, grabbed my green backpack (it is actually my daughter Pardis's, which I picked up when she threw it away and bought a new one), sent it through the belt of electronics checking for explosives, weapons of mass destruction, and such, picked it from the other side, and asked me to join them at a counter where they placed my backpack very carefully, unzipped all its pockets, and took out every single item of my belongings, half of which was my collection of various sized packs of za'atar that I had collected from different Palestinian cities, and the other consisted mainly of my clothing items and such, a copy of John Steinbeck's *East of Eden* that I was reading, and the bag of my toothbrush, toothpaste, and the collection of my medicine, including the precious Lipitor 20mg that I take for my cholesterol after my open heart surgery.

The teenagers spread all my belongings widely and generously on the counter for the whole airport to see and their suspicious German Shepherd to sniff and investigate. One of the teenagers produced a metal detector, with some sort of sanitary earmuff attached on the top of it, and applied the contraption to all my belongings, randomly reaching for one of my colorful underwear shorts. A considerate third teenager, not initially assigned to me, asked me where I was going, and as soon as I said New York, she realized that given the color-coded level of my security danger to the world I was about to lose my flight. She grabbed hold of my passport and ticket while her comrades were sniffing at my underwear and squeezing my toothpaste, and rushed to get me checked in.

I stood there watching as one of the teenagers, also a girl, reached for the small pocket of my backpack and took out the Ziploc plastic bag in which I had deposited the earth of Palestine. She offered it to the German Shepherd who sniffed at it suspiciously and looked a bit baffled and undetermined. She opened the built-in zipper and reached for the earth I had collected with her gloved fingers and asked me what it was. I said it was the soil from the mausoleums of the two companions of the prophet of Islam. She zipped the bag back up and took it away and disappeared behind a closed door, while her comrade reached for my white iPod and asked me what it was; an iPod, I said. What's in it, he asked. Umm Kulthum, I said, and lots of Bach cantatas if he cared to listen, plenty of Abd al-Basit, I said, then the songs of Mohammad Reza Shajarian and Abd al-Halim Hafiz, Ella Fitzgerald I had in there with Kiri Takanawa, Billie Holiday and a few Shahram Nazeri, plus lots of Muddy Waters, Fairuz, Mozart's piano concertos and a complete *Don Giovanni*, Herbert Von Karajan conducting the Berlin Philharmonic, with Samuel Ramey in the lead role and Ferruccio Furlanetto as Leporello, and that I had Jessie Norman in there singing Strauss's *Vier letzte Lieder*, and a few John Lee Hooker songs, John Coltrane was in there, I said, and Howlin' Wolf, Nusrat Ali Khan and Cecilia Bartoli, Esma'il Kho'i reciting his poetry, Marziyeh and Banan singing "Bu-ye Ju-ye Mulian Ayad Hami," Stan Getz and Dizzy Gillespie, and . . .

He thought I had uttered enough. He took my iPod and went in the direction that his colleague had disappeared with my bag full of Palestinian soil. I stood there with all my za'atar collection and clothing items spread all over the counter—one teenager running away with my passport and ticket, another with my iPod, and a third with my fistful of Palestinian earth. I stood there aimlessly, not knowing what to do. I picked up my copy of *East of Eden* and started reading randomly from a page. It was where Cathy Ames had just drugged her husband Adam Trask on their wedding night and was about to sleep with her brother-in-law Charles. I have always thought that the sappy obsequiousness of Adam Trask was a kind of penance he was paying for all those Native Americans he had joined in murdering—a premonition of the guilty conscience of a nation that had all but repressed Custer at Wounded Knee. I closed the book and looked around. I missed Jerusalem.

I sat on the edge of the counter and awaited my fate. I looked around me. The place had an uncanny similarity to an airport, but the garrison was a fully fortified barrack, with its battalion of security forces treating all the transient inmates with equal banality. It was not just colored Muslims like me that they treated like hazardous chemicals. It was everyone. "One," as in our quintessential humanity, melted in this fearful furnace into a nullity beyond human recognition. What they call "Israel" is no mere military state. A subsumed militarism, a systemic mendacity with an ingrained violence constitutional to the very fusion of its fabric, has penetrated the deepest corners of what these people have to call their "souls." What the Israelis are doing to Palestinians has a mirror reflection on their own souls—sullied, vacated, exiled, now occupied by a military machinery no longer plugged into any electrical outlet. It is not just the Palestinian land that they have occupied; their own souls are an occupied territory, occupied by a mechanical force geared on self-destruction. They are on automatic piloting. This is they. No one is controlling anything. Half a century of systematic maiming and murdering of another people has left its deep marks on the faces of these people, the way they talk, the way they walk, the way they handle objects, the way they greet each other, the way they look at the world. There is an endemic prevarication to this machinery, a vulgarity of character that is bone-deep and structural to the skeletal vertebrae of its culture. No people can perpetrate what these people and their parents and grandparents have perpetrated on Palestinians and remain immune to the cruelty of their own deeds.

I sat there frightened—frightened not by any specific danger, not by the massive machinery of death and destruction that surrounded me in that checkpoint and beyond that checkpoint into every nook and cranny of the occupied Palestine I visited, not by any specific machine gun hanging from a thin neck, frightened by the miasmatic mutation of human soul into a subterranean mixture of vileness and violence that preempts a human being from the simplicity of a human touch, of a human look, of a human voice. Where did humanity end and this colonial settlement and machinery begin? Is this the reason why Israel as a collectivity is so indifferent to what the rest of the world thinks of it? Is Ariel Sharon accidental or integral to these people? They were not

subjecting just me to this subhuman behavior. They were indiscrimi-
nate to names, passports, identities, nationalities. All humans to them
were not just potential but actual bombs, with different timing devices
set to trigger their explosions at varied, but certain, intervals. How can
a people live with such fear without becoming fear incarnate? Not a
single sound of laughter, not a single sight of a leisurely walk, no one
crying for a departing loved one, no one joyous at the arrival of a friend,
no human rush to catch a flight, no two strangers exchanging flirtatious
glances. Before I had left New York, I had just watched Orson Welles's
adaptation of Kafka's *The Trial* (1962)—and I felt I was in the midst of
that nightmarish labyrinth of deceased shadows and sinuous insanity. I
lifted my right hand and touched my left elbow, while looking at myself
doing so. I was dead cold.

I was now almost sure that I would miss my flight to Zurich. The
teenager who had taken my iPod came back empty handed and asked
me to step into a cubicle at the corner of that counter. I left my belongings and my backpack on the counter and followed him there and he
asked me to take off my belt and lower my pants. I did. The boy reached
for my groins. I looked at my shoes. They needed some serious clean-
ing. They looked miserable. I had bought them almost a year ago in
Carmel, California, in March 2003, when President Bush attacked Iraq
and I interrupted my spring break at Big Sur to look for Amy Goodman and Radio Pacifica to follow the news. The boy—he looked like
my son Kaveh, though a bit younger and yet his skin thicker than his
young age warranted—bent my belt and kept it close to his eyes. His
eyes looked tired. They were not green like that pretty Israeli soldier I
had seen at al-Haram al-Sharif. His eyes had no color. They were just
tired. His bony cheeks and drawn face showed he had been at work for
a long time. His white shirt was sticking out of his gray pants. His belt
was shiny black. His shoes did not need any shining. He gave me back
my belt and asked me to take off my shoes. I bent, while trying to hold
onto my pants, and untied my shoes and gave them to him. He started
examining them. I was about to put my belt back when the teenage girl

who had taken my bag full of Palestinian earth stuck her neck from behind a curtain and peeped inside the cubicle and told me to follow her.
I followed her, while holding my pants with one hand and with the other holding onto my belt, my shoes left behind for further examination
with the tired teenager inside the cubicle. The floor of the airport was
chilly, and now I had nasty nausea and a pounding headache.

I went and sat on the edge of the counter with my belt in my hand,
while trying to hold my pants from falling down, looking at the scattered
bags of za'atar, my shirts, toothbrush, and toothpaste. I had forgotten to
take my vitamin E, and I think that the *knafeh* I had at Nazareth was
too fattening for me. The teenager was now thumbing through Steinbeck's *East of Eden*, examining very closely the page where Cathy Ames
sets her parent's house on fire. What a troublemaker that Cathy Ames
was—mayhem and destruction following her wherever she went. The
teenager with tired eyes and bony cheeks came out of the cubicle and
brought me back my shoes and encouraged me to put them back on. I
thanked him and bent and put my shoes on. It took me a few minutes to
do so. When I got up my head began to spin and I had a black out. This
usually happens to me when I have sat down for a while and then get
up. It took me a minute to get back my sight and stability. I now noticed
that all my belongings, za'atar and all, had been put back inside my bag.
"Where is my soil from al-Sahabi al-Jalil Ibadah ibn al-Samit and al-Sahabi al-Jalil Shidad ibn Aws?" I asked. "It is in your bag," she said; "and
my iPod?" I continued, "It is in your bag." I had no way of knowing, but
she looked like a trustworthy ninja. I was putting my belt back when the
third, quite considerate, teenager walked fast toward me with my passport and boarding pass. "Please follow me," she said. I thanked the other two teenagers, collected my green backpack, looked at the German
Shepherd attending his comrades faithfully, and followed the conscien-
tious teenager. There were three or four more security points still ahead
of me. But she saw me through all of them while I was trying to button
up my pants and put my belt back where it belonged. At the very last
checkpoint, the teenager gave me my passport and boarding pass, and

said something like "Have a safe trip!" (or that's what I thought or hoped she said). I said thank you and rushed to get through the last check-point. A family of seven people—a young couple and their five children, all boys and all with yarmulke on their heads—was in front of me. The mother was pregnant, the father was murmuring something under his breath, the children were each eating a McDonald's hamburger. I presume McDonald's makes kosher hamburger. I was quite nauseous.

Fortunately, my gate was very close to the very last security check. As I finally entered the plane, everybody was giving me dirty looks for having kept them waiting. I wish I knew how to say I am sorry in Hebrew. But half of the passengers I thought looked like they were from Brooklyn.

In about an hour we were all safely flying over the Mediterranean and I panicked. Where was the Ziploc plastic bag full of soil I had collected from the mausoleums of the two revered *sahaba*? I got up and gently took my daughter's green backpack down from the overhead compartment. People around me were looking at me suspiciously. I sat down and opened the main part of the backpack. It was a mess. I found a bag of za'atar stuck in the middle of chapter twenty of John Steinbeck's *East of Eden*, right were the treacherous Cathy Ames was busy poisoning the goodhearted Miss Faye to inherit her whorehouse. What a troublemaker was that Cathy Ames. To me Miss Faye is the model of gentility and unsurpassed moral rectitude—and yet with what methodic cruelty did Cathy Ames poison and kill her. I have no patience for those who are trying "to understand" Cathy Ames. There is nothing to understand. She is just plain demonic. That's all. What a mess—and no sign of my bag full of soils from Palestine. I reached for the smaller side bag of the backpack and unzipped it, and there, tucked away gently among my bags full of za'atar from Jerusalem and Ramallah, Nazareth and Nablus, was the bag of Palestinian soil. I opened it gently and smelled it. It smelled of moist soil and of aromatic za'atar. I closed it, put it back where it was, closed my eyes, and tried to rest. The other passengers around me were talking relentlessly, almost all at the same time, to my tired ears and nauseous headache, in an indecipherable combination of Brooklyn English and relentless Hebrew. I reached for my iPod and turned it on. There was no sign of any of my recordings. I turned the knob up and down. Nothing. My iPod was completely cleaned of all its musical memories. I turned it off and put it back into my bag, closed my eyes, and tried to fade out all the surrounding sounds. "We are now cruising at an altitude of 35,000 feet," said our captain in Brooklyn English.

I arrived in New York in time for Said's memorial at Columbia University on March 3, 2004. A huge crowd had gathered and many of Said's friends were there. Nadine Gordimer was there, as was Danny Glover, Vanessa Redgrave, Salman Rushdie, and Daniel Barenboim. But all through the service, presided over by our university chaplain, Jewelnel Davis, all I could think of, especially when I saw Edward's face on a huge screen where they were showing a documentary on him, was the bit of an unfinished business I had with the soil I had collected from Palestine, now safely tucked away in the smallest pocket of my green backpack.

On Tuesday, July 20, 2004, I flew from New York to Beirut. I had joined a small group of young Lebanese and Palestinians who were active in Palestinian refugee camps in a variety of ways but particularly in establishing youth cultural centers. They had invited me to explore with them the possibilities of taking a portion of our Palestinian film project, "Dreams of a Nation," to the camps. This was more of a reconnaissance mission for us to find out what our needs were and what sort of equipment and infrastructure would be required. Locarno Film Festival had invited me to be a member of their jury in August, and they had generously agreed to finance my trip to Lebanon and Syria to visit Palestinian refugee camps for this purpose. I left Newark Liberty International Airport early in the evening of Tuesday and landed in Beirut the following Wednesday, after a short stop in Paris, at about 1:30 p.m. local time. I traveled with my usual green backpack, and in one of its smallest pockets I had brought with me the plastic bag that contained the soil of Palestine. Before I left New York, I had sought from Mariam

Said, and she had graciously granted me, permission to put this soil on Edward's grave.

A Palestinian friend, Rasha Salti, picked me up from the airport and for about two weeks we traveled around Lebanon and Syria, visiting camps, showing films, and making a preliminary assessment of what we needed to do. While in Lebanon and in between our trips to camps around Beirut—Sabra and Shatila, Mar Elias, and Burj al-Barajna—on Sunday, July 25, 2004, at about 3:30 p.m., Rasha Salti and I hired a cab in front of Mayflower Hotel in downtown Beirut and drove to Brummana village. In the right pocket of my jacket I carried with me the Ziploc plastic bag that contained the soil I had brought with me from Palestine.

The cab navigated its way around Ras Beirut in the early afternoon light that was about to lose its midday alacrity and ease into a gentler version of itself. There is something suspended in the bared soul of Beirut that has survived the end of the Lebanese civil war. The day I arrived in Beirut, the Israeli fighter jets had flown over the city and broken the sound barrier. "It is like raping the sky," Rasha told me that day. In my naked eyes, entirely empty of the miasmatic memories the native Beirutis have of their own history, Beirut is a mille-feuille pastry of enduring miseries interlaced with creamy layers of sweet hopes. A bite into Beirut, and you don't know whether to laugh with their joy or to cry from their pain. Beirut remains pathologically sectarian, but something in the heart of that sectarianism wishes to flower and fruit into religious tolerance. From private parties to the staff of a modest hotel, one sees conversant a cross-section of Lebanese society—Sunnis, Shi'is, Christians, and blessed atheists, sharing the same food, defying the same fate, remembering the same fears, nourishing the same hopes, the making of the same destiny, and yet speaking of sectarian identities as if they were talking about some other people in some distant planet.

As a city, Beirut is a bizarre combination of postmodern banality and a deep sense of irascible tragedy written all over its face. The archaic memories of the civil war—rundown buildings, bullet holes zigzagging on the dilapidated facades of abandoned buildings, portraits and statues of iconic sheikhs and charlatans, Palestinian refugee camps replete with unconscionable poverty, Lebanese yuppie intellectuals organizing art festivals in French—compete with Prime Minister Rafic Hariri's downtown Beirut, made up in vain and vanity to divert lucrative business and Saudi attention from the Gulf States. Secular Beirutis detest being asked to what religious denomination they belong. They believe their secular and progressive politics are beyond the religion of their birth and breeding—and by and large they are. There is a universality of learning about their prominent public intellectuals, people like Fawwaz Traboulsi or Elias Khoury, that defies all sectarianism and articulates a vision of the Arab and the Muslim world, and beyond them of the world at large, extraordinarily expansive and embracing in its cultivated cosmopolitanism. And yet constitutional to the discursive disposition of the Lebanese is an almost instinctive identarian politics far beyond the pales and forts of their own reason. The Druze did this, the Maronites did that, the Greek Orthodox are this way, the Shi'is, the Sunnis, the Armenians. But if you were to bear with this for a few minutes until they are let all loose in an Armenian restaurant, then the best in them (which is their food) overcomes their worst (which is their sectarian politics). Beirut always reminds me of the Shah's Tehran—rampant poverty ravaging the soul of the city on one side and obscenely rich shopping quarters, marked and monitored by a phantasmagoric construction of a huge mosque—paid for by Prime Minister Hariri himself—pretending to hint at Aya Sofia, on the other—while claiming the tallest minaret in the world! (Hariri and the late Shah of Iran seem to share not just their short height but their phallic propensity for architectural overcompensation.) I believe when this mosque is completed, the pompous absurdity of Hassan II Mosque in Casablanca will have found its match. Beirut is full of exceptionally beautiful mosques, churches, and a synagogue. This monstrosity, as the rest of Hariri's Saudi money, will dwarf them in size and cast an unseemly shadow over their exquisite souls.

The sun was much gentler as we began to exit the city limits of

Beirut toward the mountains. Though exceptionally clean for a major metropolis, Beirut is not a healthy city. It looks like it is going to explode any minute. But the life that it does manage to sustain in the midst of that lurking danger and in the minutiae of its small and modest (not expensive and vulgar) restaurants are the very definitions of poise and grace. The road out of Beirut to Brummana passes through some of the oldest and poorest neighborhoods of the city, and Rasha knows Beirut better than her own kitchen in her apartment in East Village in New York. We first passed by Suq al-Ahad, a Sunday market where, Rasha said, the most recent waves of migrant laborers from Syria and Sri Lanka go shopping. Migrant laborers abound in Lebanon. Shatila, for example, is no longer limited to Palestinian refugees. The migrant poor from Syria, Egypt, Iraq, and as far as Bangladesh have moved to Shatila and share the fate of the homeless Palestinians (minus their having been massacred by the Phalangists on behalf of the Israelis, of course). From Suq al-Ahad, we crossed Jisr al-Basha (over the Beirut river), and then we took the road that separates an old industrial zone called Sin al-Fil ("The Tooth of the Elephant," because someone had apparently found the remains of a prehistoric mammoth from antiquity there), and al-Naba'a. For native Beirutis, al-Naba'a is reminiscent of yet another industrial zone before the civil war, where the poor working class used to congregate, a mixture of Lebanese and Palestinian laborers in particular. Here is where the Leftists did most of their organizing and here is where there were systematic massacres of poor people at the beginning of the Lebanese civil war. Immediately after al-Naba'a, the *mille-feuille* began to change color and taste and we reached Horsh Tabet, an extremely posh residential area where the Lebanese political and economic elite own villas.

At the Mkalles roundabout we turned toward al-Mansourieh, a new industrial zone, which is now home to a new Hotel Management School, and then drove up to the valley where Tall al-Za'atar, the site of a major massacre of the Palestinians, was once located. But right before you can completely remember or barely forget the memory of Tall al-Za'atar, immediately next to it is Beit Merry, yet another luxurious residential and summer home area. The weather by now had noticeably changed—much cooler, fresher, and far less polluted. This is a primarily Christian neighborhood, Rasha said, recently flooded by the Saudis and the Khalijis.

Immediately after Beit Merry we reached Roumieh, home to one of the biggest jails in the country, where kids and adult felons are incarcerated. Soon after Roumieh is Brummana, a summer resort area about an hour from downtown Beirut. The physical expansion of Beirut has gradually reached all the way up there, so that people live in Brummana or Roumieh all year around and commute to Beirut. Just before we entered Brummana, a very expensive Mercedes with a Saudi plate was speeding and taking over a row of cars coming from the opposite direction, and by the skin of our teeth our driver managed to prevent an accident, right in front of the Quaker Friends School where Edward, Rasha said, gave its 1998 convocation speech.

I had already called Sami Cortas, Mariam Said's brother, from Beirut. He had graciously offered to pick me up from Beirut but I did not wish to impose more than I already had and said that we would take a cab. We called Sami when we entered Brummana area and arranged to pick him up from near Grand Hills Hotel, just off the main road, and he guided us toward the Quakers Friends Burial Ground (Madafin Jam'iyyat Ashab al-Quakers), a modest, almost inconspicuous, burial ground, just off the main winding road in Brummana. The gate to the cemetery was locked, and Sami Cortas had the key. He opened the gate, and Rasha and I followed him down a stairway into a small, enclosed, beautifully kept garden. The garden is full of pine trees, native to the Metn Mountain. In between the pine trees, there was an assortment of various vines, shrubs, and flowers. There were graves scattered all around the garden, in no particular order that was immediately evident to a pilgrim's eyes. We followed Sami Cortas for a few steps until he stopped at a grave located immediately to the left of the stairs as we entered the garden. He motioned with his right hand toward the grave and said, "Here it is." The gravesite is simple, elegant, gracefully minimalist. It is marked by two black granite stones—one horizontal and one vertical, with the birth and death dates of Edward Wadie Said carved on it in both Arabic and English. The first thing that I noted about the grave was that it faced east. It was properly oriented. To the left of the grave, when facing it, there is an extraordinarily beautiful and old olive tree, looking almost like an oversized bonsai, which is sitting in a bed of dense orange and yellow flowers in full bloom in July when we visited it. Sami Cortas told us that Mariam Said had planted this singular symbol of Palestine on Edward's gravesite. The grave is immediately distinguishable from others because of its vertical and horizontal black granite, separating it from others, which are mostly in alabaster white and laid horizontally. "With so many dissonances in my life," I remembered the concluding sentence of Said's autobiography, "I have learned actually to prefer being not quite right and out of place." To the left of the olive tree and fencing the stairs from which we had descended into the cemetery is an expansive and generous fig tree that carried unripe fruit in thick bunches when we were there; and at the foot of the stairs on the other side was a lush vine. I turned around and looked behind me, from the angle of Edward's grave, and there was an expansive panorama of Mount Lebanon—calm, reassuring, permanent.

It must have been five or six o'clock in the afternoon by now, and the three of us stood there on top of Edward's grave, under the shade of a constellation of memories and emotions too precious to disentangle. All I remember now from that moment is Sami's gentle hand motion and his soft voice, "Here it is." And here it was. I took the Ziploc plastic bag from my pocket, opened it, took some of it out and gave it to Sami. My hand was shivering. His was stable. We thought it best to put the soil in the flowerbed under the olive tree over the grave. Sami poured the soil on the flowerbed. I gave another pinch to Rasha and she did the same. The rest I emptied into my hand and poured it in between the flowers and the olive tree, and then shook the plastic back over it so that all of it landed on earth. I put the plastic bag back into my pocket and looked at Edward's grave. I asked him to forgive this piece of my Muslim antiquity. I know he would have laughed at me. "Professor Dabbashi" (he always put a couple of extra Bs in the middle of my last name), "you are a postmodern *muthaqqaf*." And as soon as I protested, he would say, "Don't worry, I invented their vocabulary." His gravestone was so clean. It exuded confidence, a life well-lived. "There is, here, a present not embraced by the past," I remembered Mahmoud Darwish:

> A silken thread pours letters of the page of night from the
>   mulberry tree.
> Only the butterflies cast light upon our boldness
> In plunging into the pit of strange words.
> Was that condemned man my father?
> Perhaps I can handle my life here.
> Perhaps I can now give birth to myself
> And choose different letters for my name.

I bent forward and kissed the tip of his gravestone, and then I sat down and whispered my prayers. I missed him. I thought something was amiss in the wandering walkabout of my universe, like having lost a cane, a compass, a guiding star, the Milky Way. "For me, sleep is death," I remembered his invective in *Out of Place*. I got up and followed my friends out of the garden. "Do you want to take any pictures?" asked Rasha. "No," I said, and we ascended the stairs.

Five

Dreams of a Nation

In 2006 I edited and published a book on Palestinian cinema, Dreams of a Nation: On Palestinian Cinema *(Verso, 2006). The volume was based on a major film festival I had helped organize at Columbia University in January 2003, which we subsequently took to five cities in Palestine in February 2004. The project that had ultimately culminated in these two festivals in the United States and Palestine and then the volume of essays I had edited and published had started in the early 1990s when I had commenced collecting Palestinian films to screen for my students at a course I was offering on world cinema at Columbia University. Edward Said was a key figure in helping me collect those films, and the keynote he delivered at our festival appeared as a preface to our edited volume. Here I reproduce the introduction to the edited volume as a record of what Said had enabled us to do at Columbia. He was initially incredulous of our ability to hold such a festival at Columbia. "You are one crazy Iranian comrade," he would say half-jokingly and affectionately. "We are part of a window dressing here. They will not let you do it." He was deeply entangled with chemotherapy at the time. When I saw him after a chemotherapy session he'd say, "I am a public hazard right now." When he, his wife Mariam, their children Wadie and Najla, and their daughter-in-law Jennifer came through the winding line of people trying to*

*get to the Walter Reade Theater for the opening night, I met them at the door.
I led them to their seats. He walked heavily. He had just been to a session
of chemotherapy. I gave my opening remarks, he delivered his keynote. We
screened Michel Khleifi's* The Tale of the Three Lost Jewels *(1995). The
following day I woke up to his email. He had woken up early that morning,
as he habitually did, making sure his comrades were aware of his affection.*

> *Here, on the slopes before sunset and at the gun-mouth of time*
> *Near orchards deprived of their shadows*
> *We do what prisoners do: We nurture hope.*
>
> —**Mahmoud Darwish**

PALESTINE: THE PRESENCE OF THE ABSENCE

Making a case for the cause and consequences of Palestinian cinema as
one of the most promising national cinemas cannot stop at the door-
steps of simply proposing that its local perils and possibilities are now
transformed into a global event. The proposition itself is paradoxical and
it is through this paradox that it needs to be articulated and theorized.
How exactly is it that a stateless nation generates a national cinema—
and once it does, what kind of national cinema is it? The very proposition of a Palestinian cinema points to the traumatic disposition of its
origin and originality. The world of cinema does not know quite how to
deal with Palestinian cinema precisely because it is emerging as a stateless cinema of the most serious national consequences. I have edited this
volume in part to address the particulars of this paradox—at once enabling and complicating the notion of a "national cinema."

The most notorious recent case that has dramatized this paradox is
the refusal of the Academy of Motion Picture Arts and Sciences to consider Elia Suleiman's *Divine Intervention* (2002) for the Oscars, objecting
that he is a stateless person. This happened in a year that the Cannes Film
Festival had accepted three Palestinian films in its various venues. As for

Elia Suleiman's nationality, well, he is officially an Israeli citizen—and the fact is that he would be accepted into the Academy if he were to submit his film as an Israeli, except that he was born into a Christian Palestinian family and does not have equal citizenship rights in the Jewish state. "The Academy does not accept films from countries that are not recognized by the United Nations," an official of the Academy told reporters. The same UN resolution that recognized the formation of the state of Israel, however, partitioned the historical Palestine into two states, and the other one is Palestine. So if Palestine is not a state, the same is true about Israel. The Academy further stated that to be eligible for the Best Foreign Film category, a film must first be released in the country of its origin. But how would that be possible in the case of Palestine? With East Jerusalem, the West Bank, and the Gaza Strip—as indeed the rest of Palestine—under full Israeli military occupation, and most of the population under curfew, there are almost no functioning cinemas left, and few Palestinians have the financial means to attend them. With the systematic destruction of Palestinian civil society and cultural institutions, and decades of Israeli military censorship, how could such a demand be met?

In February 2004, when I helped organize a Palestinian film festival in Jerusalem, the Palestinian cultural organization that hosted us (Yabous) had to transform the lobby of a YMCA into a makeshift movie theater—with foldable chairs, a rented projector, and a pull-out screen. Our audience had to negotiate their way through a labyrinth of Israeli military checkpoints to get to the festival. During the following summer, I traveled through a series of Palestinian refugee camps in Lebanon and Syria, with a backpack full of Palestinian films, showing them to Palestinian refugees on the rooftops of dilapidated buildings—projected on walls from a mismatched constellation of equipment running on stolen electricity. Which of these "movie theaters" did the Academy have in mind in order for *Divine Intervention* to be seen by Palestinians in "their country"?

Today we are witnessing the spectacular rise of a national cinema—predicated on a long history of documentary filmmaking in pre-

1948 Palestine and a subsequent dispersion of Palestinian filmmakers throughout the Arab world—precisely at a moment when the nation that is producing it is itself negated and denied, its ancestral land stolen from under its feet and militarily occupied by successive bands of white European and American colonial settlers. That paradox does not only preface the case of Palestinian cinema, it occasions it and gives it a unique and exceptionally unsettling disposition. What precisely that disposition is will have to be articulated through a close reading of its films—a principal reason behind the compilation of this volume. Palestinian filmmakers dream their cinema—the visual evidence of their being-in-the-world—in a forbidden land that is theirs but is not theirs. These dreams, as a result, always border with nightmares—hopes transgressing into fears, and at the borderlines of that im/possibility of dreaming and naming, the Palestinian cinema is made im/possible.

It is crucial to keep in mind that the origin of Palestinian cinema predates the dispossession of their historical homeland. The first Palestinian film to have ever been made was a short documentary by Ibrahim Hasan Serhan, which recorded the visit of King Abd al-Aziz bin Abd al-Rahman bin Faysal al-Saud (1875–1953; reigned 1932–53) to Palestine and his subsequent travels between Jerusalem and Jaffa. In the history of Palestinian cinema there dwells a sense of continuity that outlives the current political predicament of Palestinians and the disrupted course of their nationhood.

At the end of the nineteenth century, groups of white European settlers—escaping persecution from acts of religious, racial, and ethnic violence endemic to Europe, or else colonial opportunists taking advantage of that fact—began to move into Palestine and gradually took it over, forcing its native inhabitants to live in exile or be crammed into refugee camps, or else subjugated into second-rate citizenship in their own homeland. Mobilized by the memories of their pogroms and then a genocidal Holocaust perpetrated against millions of European Jews, white Europeans sought to assuage their guilty conscience by granting the descendants of those they had sought to exterminate a state that was built on the broken back of another nation, which had absolutely nothing to do with the criminal atrocities committed by one group of Europeans against another. Thus, the Palestinians were robbed of their ancestral homeland and the State of Israel—the first religious (Jewish) state in the region (preceding an Islamic Republic by more than a quarter of a century)—was born in 1948. Palestinians call this event Nakba or "Catastrophe," and to this day it remains the central traumatic moment of their collective identity.

At the beginning of the twenty-first century, Israel has mutated into a military machine no longer even true to the original design of pioneering Zionists in the nineteenth century, who dreamt of an exclusively Jewish state. Today, Israel is a military camp completely given over to the imperial designs of the United States. Most cases of colonialism have ended in indignity: the French packed up and left Algeria, the Italians Libya, the British India; so did the Portuguese, the Spaniards, the Belgians, and the Dutch. Those such as the Afrikaners who did not leave and stayed put with a shameless insistence on apartheid were finally swept away by the force of history and had to abandon their racist practices and concede to the will of the nation they had subjugated. But the Zionists remain. The fact that Jewish communities have lived in Palestine since time immemorial is as much an excuse for the formation of a Jewish State in Palestine as the equally historical presence of Muslim or Christian Palestinians is an excuse for the creation of an Islamic or Christian republic. Palestine belongs to Palestinians—whether Jews, Christians, or Muslims.

At the core of the Palestinian historical presence is thus a geographical absence. The overriding presence of an absence is at the creative core of Palestinian cinema, what has made it thematically in/coherent and aesthetically im/possible.

Abdel Salam Shehada's gut-wrenching film *Debris* (2002) is an example par excellence of the active mutation of body and soil in Palestinian cinema. "Every time I saw a tree being uprooted," says the young Palestinian boy to the camera as he remembers the scene of Israeli bulldozers razing his parents' olive grove, "I felt a part of my body was being ripped out." The elders claim the land with their memory, as their children and their olive trees grow on it. Populating the land with Palestinians becomes the key element in preventing the question of Palestine to remain a question, or to become only a metaphor. "Palestine is an issue," interjects Mahmoud Darwish at one point in the course of a conversation with Said in Charles Bruce's *In Search of Palestine* (1998), "not an essence."

In most world cinema, the active formation of such globally celebrated traditions as Soviet Formalism, Italian Neorealism, French New Wave, or German New Cinema has taken place in the aftermath of a major political upheaval and national trauma. The Russians discovered and articulated their cinema in the aftermath of the Russian Revolution of 1917; Italians did the same in the immediate decades after the Mussolini era and in the throes of massive poverty caused by the war; the French followed suit in the aftermath of their colonial catastrophes in Africa, while the Germans did the same in the aftermath of the Holocaust. Hiroshima was as definitive to Akira Kurosawa's cinema as the Chinese, Cuban, and Iranian revolutions were to the Chinese, Cuban, and Iranian national cinema. The central trauma of Palestine, the Nakba, is the defining moment of Palestinian cinema—and it is around that remembrance of the lost homeland that Palestinian filmmakers have articulated their aesthetic cosmovision.

TRAUMATIC REALISM

In what particular way can a Palestinian cinema have a claim to an aesthetic that corresponds to or transcends the fact of its politics? The paramount feature in Palestinian cinema is a subdued anger, a perturbed pride, a sublated violence. What ultimately defines what we may call a Palestinian cinema is the mutation of that repressed anger into an aestheticized violence—the aesthetic presence of a political absence. The Palestinians' is an aesthetic under duress—and this book is a preliminary attempt at navigating its principal contours.

What happens when reality becomes too fictive to be fictionalized, too unreal to accommodate any metaphor? Palestinian filmmakers have taken this mimetic crisis and turned it into one of the most extraordinary adventures in cinematic history.

The Palestinian cinematic will to resist power, ranging from Michel Khleifi, Rashid Masharawi, and Mai Masri at one end to Elia Suleiman, Hany Abu-Assad, and Annemarie Jacir at the other, is the crowning achievement of its traumatic realism. That traumatic realism is integral to its cinematic mannerism—whether factual or fictive. What we witness in Palestinian documentaries, for example, is not a plain act of certificating a past history. A certain fear of loss, a worrisome look at the historical evidence, and keeping a sustained record of an endangered memory inform much of what we see in Palestinian documentaries. Documentaries, as a result, are also a form of visual "J'accuse"—animated by a tireless frenzy to create an alternative record of a silenced crime, to be lodged in a place that escapes the reach of the colonizer as occupier. There is an obvious anxiety about the narrative pace of these documentaries, a traumatic documentation of events beyond the pale of memory. Consider, for example, Kais al-Zubaidi's *Palestine: A People's Record* (1984) and its compulsive meticulousness in safeguarding and narrating the archival footages of the earliest history of Palestine in moving pictures. To overcompensate for that traumatic anxiety, notice the polished accent of the voice that narrates the documentary—a feature of Palestinian documentaries now completely taken over by the accented voice of the filmmakers themselves narrating their own stories. The formality of this official voice—about Palestine but not of a Palestinian—is matched by the formal attire of the interviewees—invariably wearing ties and suits—adding authority and authenticity.

Orality is a strong element in the making of this documentation because it gives it immediacy and urgency. We see old people reminiscing, "I can remember . . ." The underlying meaning is, "Let me tell what the books won't tell you," or "I hold the truth, I was there." The people delivering their *shahada,* or testimonial reports, convey what took place when the world had its back turned. Their account serves to redress the record in the hope of redressing the injustice. The absence of a Palestinian state does not imply amnesia. In fact, the documentary film itself becomes that ledger, the document of these crimes.

Most Palestinians who are interviewed in these documentaries are old people, evidence of memory on the edge of disappearance. What factually emerges from the documentary—that Zionism was integral to European colonialism as it is now to US imperialism and that the Ottoman, Syrian, and Lebanese absentee landlords sold their lands to Zionist settlers entirely unbeknownst to their Palestinian tenants—is almost secondary to the urgent necessity of preserving the fading memory of a people and their material culture.

The mutation of the politically repressed into the aesthetically representational becomes a defining moment of Palestinian cinema. This representational impossibility is deeply rooted in Palestinian realism and constitutional to its crisis of mimesis. Integral to Palestinian realism is its particular fascination with turning rural landscape into urban legends. Films such as Michel Khleifi's *Fertile Memory* and Abdel Salam Shehada's *Debris* have an obsession with Palestinian rural life—with open air, fertile land, and olive trees at their centers. But in films such as Elia Suleiman's *Chronicle of a Disappearance* (1996); Alia Arasoughly's *This Is Not Living* (2001); Hazim Bitar's *Jerusalem's High Cost of Living* (2001); Akram Safadi's *Songs on a Narrow Path: Stories from Jerusalem* (2001); Muhammad al-Sawalmeh's *Night of Soldiers* (2002); and Hany Abu-Assad's *Ford Transit* (2002) and *Jerusalem on Another Day: Rana's Wedding* (2002), we also see a common concern with Palestinian urbanity. To see the rhyme and reason behind this sustained gaze at Palestinian cities, we need first to visit a Palestinian refugee camp.

In Mohammad Bakri's *Jenin, Jenin* (2002), the camera follows the director from behind as he walks over the ruins of this camp. The camera does not come anywhere near his face. This device is reminiscent of Handala, the central character in Naji al-Ali's cartoons. Before he was murdered on July 22, 1987, Naji al-Ali had crafted an extraordinary body of work about the brutal predicament of Palestinians. In all of these cartoons, Handala is defiant, angry, and bitter (and thus his name "Handala"), with his back turned to the people watching Naji al-Ali's cartoons. This gesture has two important functions: (1) he turns his back in anger on a world that refuses to watch, wonder, and respond; and (2) he acts as the unflinching conscience of his people, as an eyewitness to a systematically denied and denigrated history. Mohammad Bakri pays homage to Naji al-Ali, mutates into Handala, and thus partakes in the iconography of his people.

Throughout the Sabra and Shatila Palestinian refugee camps, when I visited them in July 2004, there were myriad murals ranging in subject matter from defiant cries for a return to Palestine to asking the inhabitants of the camp to keep it clean, and they were all written and articulated from the position of Handala, with his tiny little figure at a corner of the mural encouraging his fellow Palestinians to do one thing or another. One may also read in a similar way the silent and observant figure of ES, the screen version of Elia Suleiman himself in his cinema.

Leading Mohammad Bakri into the Jenin refugee camp is a deaf and dumb man who has witnessed the massacre and yet has no language to speak out about it. The man motions, pleads, leads, moves, gestures, and gesticulates to express the dread he has witnessed. In a sense, that deaf and dumb man is Palestine: having witnessed but not able to bear witness to the crime he has seen. He has to invent, to *will*, a language, to speak out against a massive propaganda machinery that denies its very existence. "I am a dumb man who has seen a nightmare," goes a proverbial poem in Persian. "Facing a crowd both blind and deaf / I cannot tell the terror I have seen / And the crowd incapable of comprehension."

The Jenin refugee camp was established to house the residents of Lydda, once a thriving port city with a long and thriving history of urbanization. The inhabitants of Lydda were expelled by the Zionists and shipped to a concentration camp for a few years then settled in Jenin, while the old city itself is today hailed as a gem of architectural preservation and restoration, marketed to Yuppie Zionists. What is a refugee camp other than the negation of one's claim to urbanity? Mohammad

Bakri's *Jenin, Jenin* encapsulates the trauma of Palestine's arrested urbanity in the ruins of a refugee camp—the brutal irony of being robbed of one's urbanity, condemned to a refugee camp, and subjected to even more destructive terror in the middle of that deprived urbanity.

The Palestinian claim to a stolen *civitas* in the broad daylight of history creates a traumatic amnesia, a phantom pain. Sawalmeh Mohammed's *Night of Soldiers* (2002) is a deeply moving reflection, this time on Ramallah. Sawalmeh Mohammed's camera stays behind closed doors and nervously looks through windows, creating a mood of claustrophobia and fear. *Night of Soldiers* is a mournful elegy, adopting the gaze of a lonely young woman sitting and remembering.

The traumatic realism at the heart of Palestinian cinema weaves its agitated rural and denied urban imagination together, at once suggestive and arrested. Consider Rashid Masharawi's *Haifa* (1995), a successful experimentation with the trope of madness—narrated around a village idiot—by way of defying the limits of representation in a deliberately rambunctious way. Haifa, the lead character, is the schizophrenic displacement of Haifa, the city. In Haifa's madness dwells the insanity of dispossession, and in his representation of Haifa as occupied territory the ravages of colonialism. Everything in Haifa is misplaced—Haifa lives in Gaza; Gaza dreams of Haifa; Haifa is a madman; Haifa is an occupied urbanity depleted and deprived of its rightful inhabitants. In the ravaged mind, depleted body, and emptied gaze of Haifa, Rashid Masharawi maps out the history and geography of the dispossessed Palestinians—of Palestine.

The traumatic realism at the heart of Palestinian cinema breaks through the history that has been mandated. History cannot be reversed, but it can be reimagined.

TOWARD AN AESTHETICS OF THE INVISIBLE

This volume begins with a short reflection by the late Said on the problem of visibility for Palestinians. His preface is the text of the keynote speech that he delivered at the opening night of our "Dreams of a Nation: A Palestinian Film Festival," on Friday, January 24, 2003, at Roone Arledge Cinema of Lerner Hall, Columbia University.

Next is a short chapter by Annemarie Jacir, who curated the film festival. Very few people, in my judgment, know Palestinian cinema better than Annemarie Jacir, herself an accomplished filmmaker. In this chapter she reflects on the trials and tribulations of putting a project of this sort together, as well as making and archiving films.

Joseph Massad's scholarship, over the last decade, has facilitated a critical conversation about the vagaries of politics and the transformative power of culture, toward which he sustains an unflinchingly critical perspective. His wide range of writings on the modern Arab artistic and intellectual disposition uniquely qualifies him to place Palestinian cinema in the context of the Palestinian national liberation movement. In his chapter, Massad makes a persuasive argument about the integral function of Palestinian art in general and cinema in particular in the historic struggle of the Palestinian people to liberate their country from colonial occupation.

Michel Khleifi is widely considered the founder of contemporary Palestinian cinema. Born in Nazareth in 1950, two years after the Nakba, Khleifi entered the world a disinherited Palestinian. In 1970 he left his occupied homeland for Europe and settled in Belgium, where he turned to theater and cinema as the principal mode of his creative reflection on the predicament of his people. Beginning in 1978 he made a succession of documentaries in and on Palestine. But it was his first feature film, *Wedding in Galilee* (1987), that garnered him and Palestinian cinema global recognition. In his chapter, published in its Spanish translation for the first time in February 1997 in *El Pais* and now translated from the original Arabic into English for this volume by Omar al-Qattan, Khleifi gives his own reflection on the causes and consequences of the aesthetics and politics of a Palestinian cinema.

Khleifi's documentaries and feature films have crafted a microcosmic universe in which the Palestinian national liberation movement finds its universal texture and dexterity, to reveal and to intervene in the historic fate of his people. Particularly important in Abu-Manneh's chapter is the link that he establishes between Khleifi's cinema and the rise of the intifada—the popular uprising of Palestinians against the colonial occupation of their homeland.

One of the principal concerns I had in editing this volume on Palestinian cinema was not to isolate it within its immediate cultural confinements and to link both its liberating forces and particular predicament to a larger—more emancipatory—frame of reference. I asked Ella Shohat, a feminist critic of nationalism, to contribute a chapter. She offers a critique of a nationalized cinema that is quite relevant to Palestinian filmmaking.

Years ago I had read Hamid Naficy's pioneering essay on Palestinian cinema as a form of epistolary narrative. When I was putting this volume together, I asked Naficy to update and expand it as a chapter to be included here. Particularly important is his placing of Palestinian cinema in the context of what he calls "accented cinema," namely a cinema produced by artists accompanying massive labor migrations around the world, particularly from the former European colonies such as Algeria into France. As Naficy notes, the case of Palestinian cinema is a unique historical example in which the condition of exile is "structural" to its narrative and is not caused by forces of global labor migration.

Nizar Hassan is a distinguished Palestinian documentary filmmaker, born in Nazareth, Palestine, in 1960. His short chapter, written originally in Arabic and published in *Al-Ayyam al-Iliktruniyya* on July 20, 2004, and now translated into English for the first time by Taoufiq bin Amor, speaks directly to the predicament of Palestinian filmmakers and national identity. Nizar Hassan's hilarious yet resolute take on a certain incident shows his determination to be identified as a Palestinian filmmaker and the wider range of implications for the fate of this national cinema.

First-person narratives by Palestinian filmmakers are rare. I was very happy that Omar al-Qattan agreed to join us in this volume not only by translating Michel Khleifi's account of his career as a filmmaker but also by writing his own. These two statements, plus those of

Annemarie Jacir and Nizar Hassan, provide an exceptionally important account of the extraordinary challenges and opportunities faced by Palestinian filmmakers and producers.

In the final chapter of this book, I discuss what I believe to be the quintessential force of Elia Suleiman's cinema—his uncanny visual command of cinematic frivolity, exceptionally rare in world cinema. I believe Elia Suleiman is the most creative Palestinian filmmaker of his generation and one of the most brilliant filmmakers anywhere in the world. Aspects of his cinema can be (and have been) traced to the French filmmaker Jacques Tati or even to the American comedian Buster Keaton. But such similarities, I believe, are superficial. There is something unique about Elia Suleiman's cinema and the visual vocabulary he is creating. I believe what James Joyce said about his *Ulysses* (1922)—that he "put in so many enigmas and puzzles that it will keep the professors busy for centuries arguing over what I meant, and that's the only way of ensuring immortality"—is also true about Elia Suleiman's cinema. My purpose in this introduction is to offer a manner of reading Elia Suleiman's visual vocabulary, and thus his cinema, that is rooted in the crisis of mimesis in Palestinian cinema—how is a Palestinian filmmaker to attend to the impossibility of representing his or her national trauma? What I have termed "traumatic realism" as the defining moment of Palestinian cinema assumes a particularly creative effervescence when we come to Elia Suleiman's cinema, and the manner in which he has sought to tell the trauma at the fractured center of his nation.

In the summer of 2004, I met a young Palestinian cultural historian in Damascus. His name is Bashar Ibrahim and he has written an excellent book on the history of Palestinian cinema, *al-Sinama al-Filasatiniyyah fi al-qarn al-'ishryn* (Palestinian Cinema in the Twentieth Century), published by the Syrian Ministry of Culture in 2001. He lives in a Palestinian refugee camp on the outskirts of Damascus and devotes his life to collecting and archiving Palestinian film. It was after getting to know about Bashar Ibrahim's archive that I realized that putting together a comprehensive filmography of Palestinian cinema is a daunting task. While the occupiers of Palestine have enjoyed mega-million-dollar endowments to establish various forms of cultural institutions in "Israel," thus seeking to fabricate a nonexistent legitimacy for their colonial settlement, including a major cinematheque and a corresponding archive and a very lucrative annual film festival, every conceivable dimension of Palestinian cultural life is in a state of shambles, the bits and pieces of their national heritage scattered all over the map and at times heroically salvaged by devoted Palestinians such as Bashar Ibrahim. The task of archiving Palestinian films has technical problems as well. As Kamran Rastegar, who prepared and annotated the selected filmography at the end of this book, explains, one has to address the issue of what exactly accounts for the inclusion of a film in this category. Certainly filmmakers who are Palestinian by birth and breeding, national origin, and parental descent are included in this filmography. However, there are also films made by other Arab filmmakers for Palestinian cultural institutions which equally belong to this category. In his prefatory remarks to this volume, the late Said addresses the larger issue of placing Palestinian cinema in the context of Arab cinema. By no means is the filmography that Kamran Rastegar has prepared exhaustive: it is a task much in need of further careful archival research and systematic documentation. For now, Kamran Rastegar's filmography, combining his own original research with information in existing Arabic filmographies, will be a reliable guide for further research.

Kamran Rastegar has also prepared a suggested bibliography that can facilitate further reading and research into aspects of Palestinian cinema. The bibliography is largely limited to English and French sources, with a number of important sources in Arabic as a few prominent exceptions. There is an increasing body of writing on Palestinian cinema on the Internet. The site we have created, http://palestine.mei.columbia.edu/dreams-of-a-nation, provides such a database on Palestinian cinema, with links to many related sites.

This volume is a labor of love by a group of scholars and activists, a token of our collective admiration for one of the greatest cinematic traditions around, and a preliminary step toward a much wider appreciation of Palestinian cinema. But above all I offer it as a sign of hope, a modest gift, and an olive branch to all the rightful inhabitants of historical Palestine— Jews, Christians, Muslims, agnostics, or otherwise—in the hope that they will all one day live in peace, prosperity, and an all-encompassing forgiveness of a brutish history, in anticipation of a brighter future, when justice underlies peace, and when equality sustains freedom, and when "Arabs" and "Israelis" come out of their compromising quotation marks and embrace their common and liberating humanity.

Six

ON EXILIC INTELLECTUALS

The publication of Edward Said's Representations of the Intellectual *(1994), based on his 1993 Reith Lectures, was a major moment in my re-thinking the category in general but in the context of "the exilic intellectual" in particular. In this book Said suggests the figure of the intellectual as an exile, either in literal or in figurative terms, whose singular responsibility is "to speak truth to power" even at the risk of considerable cost. I have had two encounters with this seminal book: here, where I carry his theorizing of the intellectual to the edges of the ironic mode of the figure, and later when I identify a dangerous shadow in the light of Said's insights, namely when the exilic condition actually generates comprador intellectuals who will sell their souls to the highest bidder. My conception of a public intellectual had been very much formed in my late teens in 1960s Iran when Jalal Al-e-Ah-mad (1923–69) was the towering figure of our political consciousness. Al-e-Ahmad was the figure of the intellectual at home, Said was the selfsame moral voice in exile. Between the two of them I was now placing my own reading of the intellectual. The essay I reproduce here is based on the one and only "review" of a Said book I ever wrote. For much of my academic life and intellectual output I have been in fruitful conversations with him, in one way or another, but this is the only review in the generic sense of the term I*

89

published on one of his seminal books. An earlier version of this essay was published in the journal Critique *(Fall 1994, pp. 85–96). I subsequently included it as a chapter in my* Post-Orientalism: Knowledge and Power in Time of Terror *(2008). Later in this book, in chapter 8, I will share the second time I had reasons to revisit Said's theorization of the figure of the exilic intellectual.*

> *It is part of morality not to be at home in one's home.*
> —Theodor W. Adorno

> *[I am] the outlander, not only regionally, but down bone deep and for good . . . my Texas grandfather has something to do with that.*
> —C. Wright Mills

Edward Said's *Representations of the Intellectual* must be considered a landmark in radically reawakening the crucial consciousness of that critical community of counter-interpreters we have habitually called "The Intellectuals."[1]

It appears that the problem of intellectuals in the United States is reformulated periodically as a crucial barometer of issues and concerns centered around, but much beyond, the immediate conception of this social category. It was in *Democracy in America* that Tocqueville opened his second, theoretically more significant, volume with the startling pronouncement that "I think that in no country in the civilized world is less attention paid to philosophy than in the United States. The Americans have no philosophical school of their own, and they care but little for all the schools into which Europe is divided, the very names of which are scarcely known to them."[2]

To be sure, a century and a half after this observation, and in an age when major European philosophers like Derrida, Foucault, Gadamer, Habermas, Vattimo, and Eco have had a long-standing intellectual engagement in this country, Tocqueville's observation does not appear to be the case anymore. Nevertheless, Tocqueville seems to have detected something crucial in the American intellectual disposition, both in terms of attention to matters of theory and to the social and political implications of that attention. Thus, immediately after this paragraph, he proceeds to detect a sort of "practical philosophy" among Americans almost despite themselves. But one of the most striking of Tocqueville's observations in this respect, which I think still carries a strong element of truth in it, is his assertion that "the Americans do not read the works of Descartes, because their social condition deters them from speculative studies. . . ."[3] Attention to what Tocqueville calls "social condition" will necessarily lead us to some principal material forces that can be either conducive or detrimental to theoretical and speculative concerns which must be considered as the *conditio sine qua non* of the rise and sustained legitimacy of an intellectual group with its contingent collective consciousness.

Since Tocqueville's observations early in the nineteenth century, quite a number of other theorists have periodically raised the question of the responsibility of the intellectuals in society. In 1921, in the wake of a massive migration of American literati to Europe, for example, Harold Stearns raised the rhetorical question, "Where Are Our Intellectuals?" In 1927, Julien Benda's *La trahison des clercs* appeared as a crucial text with an enduring effect on both the European and American conceptions of the fate of the intellectuals and their social responsibilities. More often than not, it is in response to some crucial social event, a moderate or radical change in what Tocqueville called the American "social condition," that the issue of the social responsibility of the intellectuals seems to reemerge. Partially in response to the horrifying implications of McCarthyism, for example, in 1956, H. Stuart Hughes heralded a generation of reflection on the nature and function of the intellectuals. In 1969, again, with obvious attention to events in the decade, Philip Rieff put together a number of, by now classic, statements on the position of the intellectuals. Rieff's edited volume, *On Intellectuals,*[4] included some seminal pieces by Edward Shils, Ralf Dahrendorf,

J. P. Nettl, Isaiah Berlin, and Rieff himself (whose essay is titled "The Case of Dr. Oppenheimer"). In many respects, these, among many other texts, are indices of those very "social conditions" that Tocqueville identified as the primary framework of all (dis)engagements with intellectual issues. At the height of the Reagan era, for example, we saw the publication of Paul Johnson's *Intellectuals*, which was in fact a thinly disguised anti-intellectual tirade.[5]

The most recent concern with the plight of intellectuals in the United States commenced with the insightful volume by Russell Jacoby, *The Last Intellectuals*, in which he launched a scathing attack against the gentrification and suburbanization of the urban (or what he called "public") intellectuals by virtue of which academic careerism fatally aborted the formation of any community of critical counter-interpreters.[6] Jacoby demonstrated how the generation of Irving Howe, Daniel Bell, and John Kenneth Galbraith had failed to produce their intellectual epigones, and thus left the public domain vacant of any autonomous critical judgment. In a collection of essays that Bruce Robbins assembled in 1990, *Intellectuals: Aesthetics, Politics, Academics*, Jacoby's book was taken to task and a number of leading critical theorists began to re-historicize the position of the intellectuals in this country.[7] Among the contributors to this volume was Said, who in an interview with Bruce Robbins outlined the historical roots of an almost total neglect of the Palestinian cause by American intellectuals.

The crucial problem that both Jacoby's text and Robbins's edited volume underlined was that of the professionalization of the intellectual. The radical pacification of the urban intellectuals by the university was the crucial factor that both Jacoby's diagnosis and Robbins's edited response brought to the fore. The changing social condition of professionalization (and such ancillary problems as suburbanization, which Jacoby equally emphasized) was thus identified as the leading cause of the decline and fall of the intellectuals as a community of counterinterpreters.

Said's book on intellectuals came at the end of a long history of institutional concern with the fate and function of the intellectuals, particularly at the concluding dead end of Jacoby's diagnosis, which Robbins's collection had sought to balance. Although Said's lectures were delivered in London as the 1993 Reith Lectures, the brunt of his argument is in fact directed domestically to the United States, which was not only home to his moral and intellectual concerns, but in fact with the demise of the Soviet Union and the obvious dangers of a single, domineering, world superpower, the question of American intellectuals' social responsibility has assumed an added momentum. Whereas Robbins's edited volume had rather successfully rehistoricized the position of the intellectuals, the institutional dilemma of professionalization had remained paramount. The contributors to Robbins's volume were in fact more engaged in an advocative and emancipatory act of inaugurating a new role for the intellectuals rather than providing institutional bases for a way out of Jacoby's highly accurate diagnosis.

Said's text, however, begins to provide a crucial, and institutionally viable, way out of the Jacobian paradox. To be sure, Said's argument, as I shall note shortly, is equally innovating, advocative, and emancipatory, rather than clinical and diagnostic in its assessments. Moreover, I believe he had, in effect, detected a crucial way out of the Jacobian cul-de-sac, which under the changing conditions of the US imperial polity, to paraphrase Tocqueville's assessment, may indeed lead to a renaissance in the social function of intellectuals.

The first thing that Said does is to expand the spectrum of compromising forces that endanger the autonomous judgment of the intellectual. Here we observe that much more than professionalism is present and active in compromising the role of a potential intellectual class. As Said sees them, the intellectuals, as such, are principally compromised by a number of compelling centers of fatal attractions: nations and nationalism (in parts of chapter 2), traditions and traditionalism (in other parts of chapter 2), professions and professionalism (chapter 4), powers and their institutions (chapter 5), and ultimately gods and their latter-day prophets (chapter 6). Said believes that the single most effective way out of the traps of these compromising forces is the condition of exile and marginality, which he theorizes effectively to a level of almost institutional decentrality in an otherwise hegemonic culture. Said's argument here takes to logical conclusions the moral and theoretical implications of what in the 1930s was called "the University in Exile" and was comprised of hundreds of European intellectuals who fled to this country from the Nazi atrocities and thanks to the visionary brilliance of Alvin Johnson were brought to the New School for Social Research.[8]

Said's theorization of the condition of exile, both literally and metaphorically, is of crucial significance here. It is critical to note how Said arranges the progression of his argument and the logistics of his narrative strategies. When one reads the book one notices how he has planted the crucial chapter on intellectuals as real and metaphorical exiles right in the middle of the text, the third of the six chapters/lectures, like a subversive bomb, or a blooming flower, planted/embraced in between the preceding two chapters which unpack the compromising forces of nations and traditions, and the last three chapters on professions, powers, and gods. While logically this chapter should have followed all the other chapters, rhetorically it comes in the middle, where it explodes/blooms like a grenade/tulip to subvert/outgrow all those compromising forces and thus give forceful birth to the expatriate intellectual, in both the real (as in fact exemplified by Said himself) and the metaphoric (as represented by Noam Chomsky, for example) senses of the term.

This is the principal proposition of Said, which because of its significance I am going to quote in some detail:

> While it is an actual condition, exile is also for my purposes a metaphorical condition. By that I mean that my diagnosis of the intellectual in exile derives from the social and political history of dislocation and migration . . . but is not limited to it. Even intellectuals who are lifelong members of a society can, in a manner of speaking, be divided into insiders and outsiders: those on the one hand who belong fully to the society as it is, who flourish in it without an overwhelming sense of dissonance or dissent, those who can be called yea-sayers, and on the other hand, the nay-sayers, the individuals at odd with their society and therefore outsiders and exiles so far as privileges, power, and

honors are concerned. The pattern that sets the course for the intellectual as outsider is best exemplified by the condition of exile, the state of never being fully adjusted, always feeling outside the chatty, familiar world inhabited by the natives, so to speak, tending to avoid and even dislike the trappings of accommodation and national well-being. Exile for the intellectual in this metaphysical sense is restlessness, movement, constantly being unsettled, and unsettling others. You cannot go back to some earlier and perhaps more stable condition of being at home; and, alas, you can never fully arrive, be at one with your new home or situation.[9]

This is much more than a mere self-theorization on the part of Said, or even if it is, it is based on a much larger social reality. What Said has detected is a constitutional change in precisely that "social condition" that Tocqueville had identified as the material condition for Americans not being philosophically minded early in the nineteenth century. Without naming it so, Tocqueville had what Weber would later identify as the Protestant ethic in mind when he diagnosed the conditions of an anti-intellectual trait in American life. As the catholicity of learning, and the caring that follows from it, became a trademark of the Jesuits, the Calvinist theology was translated into an ascetic practicality constitutionally at odds with "wasteful speculation." The predominance of the Protestant ethic in the United States thus became conducive to the rise of the spirit of capitalism, as Weber first theorized the relationship. Equally, it led, in both moral and intellectual senses, to that intellectual iron cage of which Weber wrote with a prophetic clarity: "Specialists without spirit, sensualists without heart; this nullity imagines that it has attained a level of civilization never before achieved."[10] Said does not pay any attention to the centrality of this Protestant ethic in the institutional professionalization of the intellectuals. Jacoby briefly notices it but does not develop it into the major grids of his argument. Yet, rather instinctively and without much theorizing about it, Jacoby narrows in on the "Jewish intellectual" as a prototype. The Jewish intellectuals did not, for obvious reasons, share the Protestant ethic of asceticism and practicality, and thus the so-called "Bohemian culture" was instrumen-

tal in the production of an autonomous critical judgment, always oper-
ating on the periphery of some hegemonic center.

What principally threatens Said's way out of Jacoby's cul-de-sac
is precisely this pervasive culture of asceticism and practicality deeply entrenched in the Protestant ethic now propagated deeply into the
American ethos. What is lacking in the United States is a paradoxically
productive culture of idleness, a culture of counterprofessional, coun-
terinstitutional, and critically questioning imagination. It is only such
an idle imagination that can afford serious engagement with the vital
issues of the time. That bizarre category we call "the academic intellectual" is constitutionally compromised by something much more immediate than the debilitating anxieties of a tenure-track predicament,
that is, by a set of regular and routine responsibilities. To be responsible
in a much wider domain of public interest, an intellectual will have to
be an irresponsible person in the most positive sense of the term. For
the gradual formation of a community of counterinterpreters, a culture
of "idleness" is necessary. Constitutionally opposing the formation of
such a culture of (only inadvertently productive) idleness is the Protestant ethics with its doctrinal denial of "leisure," in a revised reading of
Veblen's theory.

In the context of this engulfing anti-intellectual culture, equally modifying Said's theoretical proposition is the other end of ascetic
practicality, which is the Stardom Syndrome in the US academic scene.
The principal prerequisite for the generation and legitimate operation of an intellectual is the social formation of an intellectual class, or
more accurately a community of counterinterpreters. Said and Noam
Chomsky, as two star intellectuals, are not the representatives of a free-
thinking social enterprise, an active community of counterinterpreters.
They are, among a handful of other urban intellectuals, paid professors
at highly prestigious universities, and then in their public presentations
framed as some sort of professorial stars. If Jacoby's highly accurate criticism of the professionalization of the intellectual is to be overcome, if
the pervasive asceticism of the Protestant ethic of practicality is to be

balanced, and if Said's theorization of the exilic condition is indeed to correspond to a constitutional change in what Tocqueville identified as the American "social conditions," this Stardom Syndrome too must be substituted by a community of critical thinking from which, of course, certain chief spokespersons can and do emerge.

The problem with the Stardom Syndrome is that ideas and their formative social forces become so organically misidentified with the characters representing them that they systematically lose their intellectual anchorage in the public domain. Said's critique of Orientalism, as a chief example, is so thoroughly identified with him that in the domain of civic discourse it has scarce any connection to the discipline of the sociology of knowledge that by about a century predates the publication of Said's masterwork.[11] The principal proposition of *Orientalism*—the structural link between the Orientalist manner of knowledge production and colonialism—can indeed be linked not only to a major branch of the sociology of knowledge that through Max Scheler and Karl Mannheim is rooted in the works of Karl Marx, Émile Durkheim, and Max Weber, but can in fact completely bypass Michel Foucault and trace its origin to Quentin Skinner's philosophical hermeneutics on political theory and the link that he proposes between social meaning and social action.[12] A similar argument can be made linking the argument of Said's *Orientalism* to an even more critical school of intellectual history, now best represented perhaps in the work of Dominick LaCapra.[13] The intellectual fragmentation and the political disembodiment of ideas, coupled with a radical removal of public intellectuals from their moral and normative imaginary, are chiefly responsible for their dismemberment from a sustained body of critical judgment that predates and postdates their public appearance.

Threatening the active formation of that critical community of counterinterpreters is not just the Stardom Syndrome but also the self-perpetuating culture of professionalism that is most detectable among undergraduate students. This crucial community which should ideally constitute both the audience and the main pool of potential intellectuals is increasingly turning into a frightened mass of prematurely career-conscious teenagers with all their innate and natural sense of justice and fairness, as indeed their very biological urge to wonder about the world, completely muzzled by concerns about their professional careers. The result is that there is barely any intellectual joy, wonder, and free exercise of the critical faculties left among undergraduates. Either an intellectually crippling obsession with getting "trained" for their career in engineering, business, law, or medical professions, or acutely joyless symptoms of a life without moral and intellectual vision, now characterizes undergraduate education in the US academy. Seriously curtailed on our university campuses is a free-floating atmosphere of creative and critical imagination that can grasp and direct the moral and political imperatives of a whole generation. Allan Bloom's *The Closing of the American Mind* was the last anti-intellectual manifesto that still sought to save the canons of the "Western civilization" for the hegemonic arsenal of what he wished to be the American imperialist imagination.[14] These so-called "canons" can be as much the icons of dead certainties and nostalgic imperialism à la Bloom as they can be the crucial catalysts of a regeneration of a moral and political imagination at the very heart of a renewed definition of the intellectual. It really does not matter whether one reads Plato or Ibn Khaldun in the curriculum of a core of required courses. It does matter for what purpose one reads them: for the canonical celebration of a fiction called "Western civilization" or for the rejuvenation of a moral and political imagination that can take a full account of life as it is.

Perhaps the most revolutionary aspect of Said's theorizing of the exilic intellectual is the decontextualization of critical judgment whereby no sociology of knowledge can actually explain the intellectual away. "[By] virtue of living a life" Said constructs the image of an exilic intellectual from the fragments of the character of Bazarov in Turgenev's *Fathers and Sons* and the Adorno of *Minima Moralia*, "according to different norms, the intellectual does not have a story, but only a sort of debilitating effect; he sets off seismic shocks, he jolts people, but he can neither be explained away by his background nor his friends."[15] The figure of Adorno as an intellectual in exile, however, remains a problematic one. Because while Said celebrates Adorno alongside Sartre for the direct and catalytically radical effects they have had, he equally notes his deliberate obscurantism as a strategy: "It [Adorno's writing style] represents the intellectual's consciousness as unable to be at rest anywhere, constantly on guard against the blandishments of success, which for the perversely inclined Adorno, means trying consciously not to be understood easily and immediately."[16] Said is here caught between his deep appreciation for Adorno, whom he celebrates as an exemplary exilic intellectual, and his own committed concern with the public accessibility of the intellectual, which first and foremost means the command of a direct and simplified prose. Said is, of course, conscious of this paradox and spares not a moment to side with the positive reading of exile and a denouncement of any gloomy predisposition that can lead to narrative obscurantism as a mode of residual existence in exile. After a close reading of Adorno's assertion that "In the end, the writer is not allowed to live in his writing," Said observes that "This is typically gloomy and unyielding. . . . What Adorno doesn't speak about are indeed the pleasures of exile, those different arrangements of living and eccentric angles of vision that it can sometimes afford, which enliven the intellectual's vocation, without perhaps alleviating every last anxiety or feeling of bitter solitude."[17]

This positive and enabling reading of exile is precisely what distinguishes Said from Adorno, and if indeed it corresponds to some constitutionally enduring changes in the American social conditions, namely to the active and engaged presence of intellectual exiles on the close periphery of the hegemonic center, then it can lead to historical changes in the role of the intellectuals. In taking issue with Jacoby's assessment of the decline of the social significance of the public intellectual, Said's principal argument for the continued political centrality of the intellectual as exile becomes evident: "what Jacoby does not talk about is that intellectual work in the twentieth century has been centrally concerned not just with public debate and elevated polemic of the sort advocated by Julien Benda and exemplified perhaps by Bertrand Russell and a few Bohemian New York intellectuals, but also with criticism and disenchantment, with the exposure of false prophets and debunking of ancient traditions and hallowed names."[18]

But the problem with the social function of the intellectuals is not that it must be predicated on a vocational "office" called "The Intellectuals." A critical community of counterinterpreters always emerges out of the collective concerns of a number of individuals who can and do transcend their class and professional interests. Jacoby's diagnosis about the declining critical apparatus of the intellectuals is thus perfectly accurate not because there is something constitutionally defective about the status of intellectuals in the United States. The reason, rather, is that historically these very people (Jacoby himself, as Gore Vidal so aptly commented upon the publication of *The Last Intellectuals*, Edward Said, Noam Chomsky, Gore Vidal, and so on) have actually managed to speak and be heard beyond their professional concerns and interests and on issues of vital moral and political significance.

With the exception of Gore Vidal, practically all other names in that list are highly successful academics, way beyond being scared of their upcoming ad hoc committees deciding their academic, professional, and, of course, personal futures. But this is not the case with the overwhelming majority of academics, particularly those who in one way or another consider themselves in exile. The junior members of the faculty in particular are by and large scared witless to get themselves through the tenure process which can take anything from six to ten years before they reach the infamous and treacherous "up-or-out" cliffhanger. By the time the tenure process is over, bending over backward to accommodate power and being compromising and appeasing become almost second nature to the junior faculty. The problem is particularly acute for expatriate members of the university, the very center of Said's theorization of their potential status as urban intellectuals. There are not many Alvin Johnsons around anymore, a visionary intellectual who, as the director of the New School for Social Research in the 1930s, provided a safe and enabling haven for hundreds of European intellectuals escaping the atrocities of the Third Reich. Today, expatriate intellectuals, cut off from their native support networks, are at the double mercy of both the university and the society at large, the first target of all the barely concealed anxieties of demonization of "The Other" which the likes of Samuel Huntington and Francis Fukuyama have sustained in the United States.

This is not to suggest that the expatriate (potential) intellectuals themselves are not chiefly responsible for the generation of a culture of self-pity and misery, a jeremiad of pathological nostalgia for a homeland that never was nor will be. That prevalent predicament, constitutional to that branch of cultural studies that caters to the so-called diasporic cultures, is so deeply pathetic and jaundiced that nothing more than a subculture of ghetto mentality and self-deprivation can emerge from it. Perhaps the most exhilarating aspect of Said's very cast of mind and narrative is his humane and humanizing urbanity, his liberating, inaugurating, and emancipatory rhetoric, the deeply moving catholicity of his critical imagination. It is precisely in the cast and character of that critical imagination that we ought to detect the exemplary model of a new generation of expatriate intellectuals who are more amphibian than exilic, more central than peripheral, more actively critical than passively self-negating. "The intellectual in exile," in Said's precise perception, "is necessarily ironic, skeptical, even playful—but not cynical."[19] It is to that emancipatory wisdom that we owe our moment of liberation:

> For the intellectual an exilic displacement means being liberated from the usual career, in which "doing well" and following in time-honored footsteps are the main milestones. Exile means that you are always going to be marginal, and that what you do as an intellectual has to be made up because you cannot follow a prescribed path. If you can experience that fate not as deprivation and as something to be bewailed, but as a sort of freedom, a process of discovery in which you do things according to your own pattern, as various interests seize your attention, and as the particular goal you set yourself dictates: that is a unique pleasure.[20]

There is, however, a profound element of sectarian ghettoization that seriously challenges the possibilities of Said's cosmopolitan liberation of the so-called third world intellectual. As early as Gramsci's *Prison Note-books* (his *Quaderni del Carcere*, which he wrote between 1929 and 1935), we have been warned of this danger. Here is what Gramsci observed:

> One can note, in the case of the United States, the absence to a considerable degree of traditional intellectuals, and consequently a different equilibrium among the intellectuals in general. . . . The necessity of an equilibrium is determined, not by the need to fuse together the organic intellectuals with the traditional, but the need to fuse together in a single national crucible with a unitary culture the different forms of culture imported by immigrants of differing national origins. The lack of a vast sedimentation of traditional intellectuals such as one finds in countries of ancient civilizations explains, at least in part, both the existence of only two major political parties, which could in fact easily be reduced to one only . . . and at the opposite extreme the enormous proliferation of religious sects.[21]

That condition is still present. Against it, Said's resuscitation of an active exilic intellectual, precisely in his moving last chapter, provides what E. M. Cioran once observed as the best condition for an intellectual: anationality. The exilic condition, as Said defines it, supersedes ethnic and religious sectarianism only through a flexing of historical memories through an essentially ironic mode of being. Resistance to theory, which is at the root of resistance to the intellectuals as the counterinterpreters of a culture, is, as Paul de Man once observed, resistance to the rhetorical and tropological, to which one might add "ironic," dimensions of language, and through language, of being. That ironic mode of being is constitutional to the working act of the intellectual, irony in the senses stretched from the countermetaphysics of Søren Kierkegaard to the engaged pragmatism of Richard Rorty. It is in that ironic mode that the intellectual can take to task much more than the relations of power in a political culture and reach down for what Rorty, paraphrasing Heidegger, has called the "Plato-Kant canon." In fact, the intellectual is nothing but the social manifestation of what Rorty has typified, if that is the right word to use in this case, as "the ironist theorist."[22] "The ironist theorist," Rorty has suggested, "distrusts the metaphysician's metaphor of a vertical view downward. He substitutes the historicist metaphor of looking back on the past along a horizontal axis."[23] The horizontality of that historicist irony is precisely what spells out the countertheorizing urge of the intellectual. "The last thing the ironist theorist wants or needs is a theory of ironism":[24] it is precisely in that apparent paradox that the social function of the intellectual may be assayed. The intellectual, too, can only be real if not idealized, can only be historically relevant if undertheorized, institutionally consequential only if not institutionalized. "This means," for intellectuals as self-creating ironists in Rorty's terms, "that their criterion for resolving doubts, their criterion of private perfection, is autonomy rather than affiliation to a power other than themselves."[25] In that autonomy—free from nationalism, traditionalism, professionalism, and neo-prophetic millenarianism—Said stipulates the criteria and conditions of the intellectual.

It is to that ironic mode of being, the exile as the corrective force in a country to which he or she only marginally belongs, that Said repeatedly leads our attention. In that attention rests the possibility of a community of counterinterpreters, permanently in an ironic mode, that belong only to the degree that they depart, morally strengthen only to the degree that they politically challenge. As counterinterpreters, intellectuals are, in the very elegant and true words of Gianni Vattimo, chiefly responsible for weakening the terror of metaphysical categories. The politics of "Truth" is only one such category.

Seven

Paradise Delayed

With Hany Abu-Assad in Palestine

This is the second travelogue I wrote and published after my journey to Palestine. It first appeared as "Paradise Delayed: With Hany Abu-Assad in Palestine," and was published in Third Text 24, no. 1, January 2010: 11–23. While the first travelogue (see chapter 4) was mainly about Jerusalem and Ramallah, this one is about Nablus. I was driven from Jerusalem to Nablus, as you will soon read, by Hany Abu-Assad's assistant while he was location scouting for his widely praised Paradise Now (2005). The travelogue, as a result, has a decidedly filmic dimension to its narrative. This journey was in February 2004, just a few months after Edward Said's passing, and there is a mourning tone to my prose that has become more evident with the passage of time. It was both strange and disorienting to be in Palestine and to write about its major cities when Said was no longer here to read what I had written. In a bizarre and uncanny way, I was writing these travelogues for him to read, knowing full well he no longer could. Mortality here meant very little. He was looking over my shoulder as I was writing, as I feel he is at this very moment, as I write this very sentence.

At about 7:00 a.m. on Saturday, February 28, 2004, I was sitting in the lobby of the Christmas Hotel in East Jerusalem drinking coffee and waiting. I was in Jerusalem to help launch a Palestinian film festival, "Dreams of a Nation," which Annemarie Jacir (a Palestinian filmmaker) and I had organized in collaboration with Yabous, a Palestinian performing arts center that had agreed to host our festival. During the opening night of the festival, which we had to hold at a makeshift theater at the YMCA in East Jerusalem—for there was no alternative—Hany Abu-Assad had suddenly showed up, much to my delight and surprise.

I had met Hany for the first time in January 2003 in New York when we launched the first version of our Palestinian film festival in the course of which we screened two of his films, *Rana's Wedding* (2002) and *Ford Transit* (2002). When he learned that I was Iranian, he told me he was very much an admirer of the doyen of Iranian cinema Amir Naderi, particularly his *The Runner* (1985). While Hany was in New York I thought he should meet Amir, so I invited them over for dinner and had a ball seeing the old master bask in the admiration of his young admirer. Their cinemas, though, are entirely different. Amir Naderi thrives on the solitude of his deeply tumultuous characters. Hany Abu-Assad's cinema is one of visual emancipation from an arrested aesthetics. My love and admiration for it has to do with his uncanny ability for cross-metaphorization, the best example of which is perhaps when he uses Dr. Dre's gangsta rap as soundtrack for a young Palestinian cab driver negotiating to preserve his dignity through an Israeli checkpoint in occupied Palestine in his Ford Transit.

"Mr. Dabashi, there is a telephone call for you." I was lost in my thoughts. My coffee was long since finished and I was staring at the bottom of the small cup. It was Hany on the phone calling from Nablus. "Hammouda is waiting for you at the door. Where are you?" I hurried out of the lobby.

At the wheel of a small car was Hammouda—a young Palestinian I later learned was the line producer of Hany's new film. Hany was in

Nablus having just finished location scouting for his new film, *Paradise Now*, about two suicide bombers. He had changed the original setting of the film from Gaza to Nablus because the unrelentingly volatile and combative zone of Gaza had made it impossible to shoot anything there but bullets and rockets.

"Hi, Hamid, I am Hammouda." Hammouda had a quick manner and a Spartan look about him. He talked fast but in long, carefully crafted sentences. I sat in the passenger seat and fastened my seatbelt. Within minutes he was weaving through the labyrinthine highways around the Haram al-Sharif or Noble Sanctuary, leaving Jerusalem north toward Nablus. We talked about our Palestinian film festival and Hany's new film as he drove on unflustered. His alert intelligence reminded me of one of my former students, Farhad, who for a while drove a cab in Chicago. Farhad too could engage in a heated debate with me about politics, culture, or southern Iranian cuisine while driving his cab around the nooks and crannies of Chicago. There is a quiet certitude to people like Farhad and Hammouda when they are at the wheel.

"How do you know Hany? He is very fond of you."

"We met in New York," I said to Hammouda.

"He tells me you never write about an artist whom you don't know personally." "Yes," I said, as Hammouda slowed down a bit sensing an approaching *machsom* (checkpoint in Hebrew).

Palestinians don't call Israeli checkpoints by their Arabic name, *hajiz*, but by their Hebrew name, machsom. There is a bizarre sense of claustrophobia about occupied Palestine, even if you are driving through the desert. The active memory of one machsom has not completely faded in your mind when another one appears. The result is an interpolation of real and remembered machsom piling on top of each other and crowding your hope of the open horizons of Palestine. There is no escaping the Israeli occupation in Palestine—not even in your mind. Reality in fact plays tricks on you—you see things you do not believe and, before you know it, you start believing in things you have not seen. Is that what is meant by faith—that it is the belief in things unseen? "Now faith is the substance of things hoped for, the evidence of things not seen" (Hebrews 11:1).

Hammouda knew Hebrew. But more than that, he was Israeli-smart (in a Palestinian kind of a way). While other cars waited in line at checkpoints for what seemed like an eternity, Hammouda zipped through the fast lane, mumbled something in Hebrew to the soldiers manning them, and managed his way around their questions and barriers, somber faces and extended guns. I could never tell (for I don't know Hebrew) from his tone whether he was arguing with them, chatting, cajoling, or exchanging jokes. He never seemed to commence a conversation. He always seemed to resume one—"As I was saying, you bastards have occupied my homeland and now I have to secure your permission to go from one of my own cities to another," I thought he might be saying, or else, "Excuse me, sir, I have to go to Nablus where Hany Abu-Assad is about to shoot a film about two suicide bombers, do you mind lifting that barrier there?" Impossible to tell—I could not deduce the nature of his exchanges with these soldiers.

Hammouda drove on. He continued to argue, cajole, talk fast, and speed smoothly along hilly highways dotted with heavily armed Israeli checkpoints, while keeping up a running conversation with me about a project I had in mind of establishing a center for cinema studies at Birzeit University.

"We must stop by at this apartment building and pick up a passenger."

"Fine by me," I said. Who is it, I wondered.

"He is a man who owns a hotel in Nablus and from whom we have rented a floor for our crew. I have to take him with us through the Huwwara checkpoint."

"No problem," I said. "Where is Huwwara checkpoint?"

"It's near Balata Refugee Camp, just before we enter Nablus."

We picked up the passenger Hammouda needed to pick up. We exited the highway and entered a residential area. Hammouda stopped in front of an apartment building where a man was waiting for us. A middle-aged, lanky, wide-faced, and world-weary businessman, I now forget his name. He later gave me his business card, but I lost it when my bag was searched as I was leaving Palestine from Ben Gurion checkpoint. Hammouda introduced me and the businessman to each other and started off toward Nablus. I sat in the front seat, where I already was, and the businessman in the back seat. I tilted toward Hammouda and the back seat so the three of us now had a semicircular range for our conversations. The businessman had a network of business interests in the United States and the United Arab Emirates. He was an exceedingly pleasant, wise, patient, and generous man—full of his own stories. He had just adopted, he told me when he discovered I was interested in Palestinian cinema, the fiery young girl in Mohamed Bakri's *Jenin, Jenin* (2003)—allocated a monthly allowance for her education and livelihood. After a while, sitting with my back against the door, I got a bit dizzy and nauseous and had to turn round and face the road—too many twists and turns and bumpy roads to Huwwara machsom.

Close to the military checkpoint, Hammouda parked his car somewhere near the canopy under which stood the Israeli soldiers. He asked the businessman and me to sit in the car, took our passports, turned off the car engine, and walked briskly toward the Israeli officers. We sat there, the businessman and I, in the parked car as Hammouda approached the officers. We soon lost sight of him and just sat there waiting—having now opened our doors for fresh air. There are moments when you just lose sight of where you are when traveling through checkpoints. Things lose their meanings—humans, road barriers, military uniforms, guns, tired faces of both the occupiers and the occupied. It becomes like a theater of the absurd. Beckett run amok: people barely look at each other as they go through their assigned motions, except when the occupiers look at the faces of the occupied to see if they match the picture on their identity cards. Looking at the scene of a machsom from a distance, you feel you are looking at a home video. There is a surreal aspect to that moment of encounter between these people. They look more like tropes than humans. There is a sense of overwhelming visuality about the scene they enact, always a spectacle.

They act as if they are on a stage and they are not very good actors—they are very conscious of their acting.

Ya akhu ash sharmuta is the most common phrase one hears uttered by Palestinians when nearing an Israeli machsom. It is an uncomplimentary allusion to the officer's sister. Palestinians defy their occupiers in a variety of ways. Their actual face-to-face encounter with Israeli soldiers is in many ways mute, bureaucratic, and even business-like. There is, to be sure, a sense of "what the fuck are you doing in my homeland" in the air. But in that same air, Palestinians make queues, take out their identity cards, patiently march through the barricades, submit their papers, wait unwearyingly as the Israeli officers compare their pictures with their faces, occasionally ask them a few questions, and then let them pass.

I had a sense that Palestinians had learned to pass through these machsoms the way one accepts certain idle time sitting on a toilet seat. You have no choice in the matter. It is a call of nature, so you do what you have to do and you start daydreaming or maybe you pick a book or a magazine and thumb through it. You are not really reading anything, for your bodily movements are preoccupied (as it were) with something Mother Nature has forcefully imposed on you. But you might as well use the dead time distracting yourself from the banality of boredom with the refuse that has to go through your system and cleanse your body (and soul). So do Palestinians appear when they are waiting and passing through these machsoms. The Israeli officers, for their part, have a bizarre matter-of-factness about them. They are exceedingly friendly and jovial with each other, constantly talking, laughing, and merrymaking—like a bunch of kids playing Cowboys and Indians in their own backyard. The rest of their time is spent looking bored and indifferent; yet somehow troubled and nervous in their "God-given land." To watch them is to witness a tragicomic drama that, were it not so bloody horrid, would make you laugh. What are these people doing here? Why don't they just pack up and go home? Everybody go home now, the game is over—Russians to Russia, Americans to America, and leave Palestine to Palestinians. Zi-

onism, when you are in its dreamland, looks like a practical joke that cru-
el history played on two bereaved peoples.

Hammouda finally returned to us with neither a smile on his face
nor our passports in his hands. He got into the car, mumbled a "sorry for the wait," turned the ignition key, and in about five seconds we
were on our way toward Nablus. Everything was OK. He had seen us
through the checkpoint. How I have no clue. But his face gave a whole
new meaning to how to play poker. I now discovered something else
in Hammouda's face. He was never completely where he was. He was
always about ten moves (in twenty directions) ahead of and away from
where his body was trapped. His body was quite tiny and agile, his
moves swift and to the point, with an economy of purpose syncopating
the brevity of his expressions. He did not talk much—but he talked
indexically. It took me almost a day spending time with him for him to
teach me the referents of his indexical expressions. "He was the summa-
ry of himself," I remembered Ahmad Shamlu's line in one of his poems.

Between the time that we left the Huwwara checkpoint and the
time that Hammouda pointed to my right and said, "That's Balata," and
the time he stopped at the entrance of a modest hotel and said, "*tafadd-
alu!*"—all I remember now is just a split second. Geography shrinks
faster than time contracts in occupied Palestine. I saw nothing of Balata—what I knew of Balata blinded me. Some 30,000 human beings
crammed into a godforsaken refugee camp of less than one square mile,
inside their own country. Naturally a major hotbed of both intifadas,
Balata was the target of incessant Israeli raids—men, women, and children killed like fish in a barrel.

Nablus was crowded and dusty, mysterious and magnificent.
Tucked away and veiled, it is completely different from Jerusalem's ex-
hibitionist arrogance. Jerusalem is loud and clear, knowing full well she
has the heart of history by the balls (and that is not a mixed metaphor).
Nablus, on the other hand, whispers. I caught a glimpse on my way
in from the corner of my eyes. Hammouda's moves had become even
swifter than before. Buildings, streets, and dusty roads were passing him

by like the props of a Kiarostami road shot. Nablus was gray with a tinge of brown, a suggestion of blue in its sky. Nablus was jammed—peoples and buildings and cars and markets and gunmen with automatic rifles carried vertically, pointing to the heavens.

It was about 10:00 a.m. when we entered the hotel and took the stairs to some upper floor where Hany was waiting for me at the top of the stairs. In his jeans and a T-shirt, he looked more like a renegade teenager than someone about to launch the most ambitious project of his career so far. He smiled and greeted me. I did the same and followed him for a tour of the floor. One room was a kind of administrative headquarters with computers, a fax machine, and phones, staffed by mostly German and Dutch crew. Another was full of pictures of his location scouting, camera tests of actors, storyboards, files, and such. He introduced me to his crew—many Europeans, a few Palestinians. Then he took me to a room where he was working on the details of his script with an assistant, picked up a fresh copy of the script, and took me to an adjacent empty room with a solitary desk and chair.

"You sit here and read my script. Are you hungry?"

"Yes," I said. "I am hungry, I don't know why, but I am hungry." I had breakfast at my hotel (Christmas Hotel) in Jerusalem. But it now seemed like an eternity ago. Hany left and I sat at the desk and started reading the script, a pen at hand and marking as I progressed through the pages. About half an hour later Hammouda showed up with a tray half the size of the huge desk on which I was reading the script. The tray was full—za'atar (a condiment made from dried herbs, sesame seeds, salt, and other spices) from Nablus and olive oil from Jerusalem, fresh bread, cucumber and tomato, and enough omelet to feed an entire platoon of Fatah fighters.

I read through the script on into the afternoon, when I tired—the hummus and tabbouleh began to work their way to my eyelids. Two strong Arabic coffees, fully sugared as they say, perked me up. I was almost halfway through when Hany stuck his head into my room.

"Let's go for a ride."

"Where?" I asked.

"I want to show you the locations we have scouted." It was now almost 2:00 p.m. I had been reading his script, scribbling in its margins, and munching on my feast for almost four hours.

With Hammouda driving, Hany took me on a quick tour of the city and then up toward a hilltop overlooking the most magnificent city I have ever seen in my life. As Hammouda ascended the winding hilly road, a panoramic long shot gradually began to take shape. The early afternoon light was now caressing the ancient city. Hammouda stopped by the roadside and we all left the car. The first things Hany showed me were the spots where the Israeli army had bombed and scarred the beautiful face of Nablus. Even from that distance you could see the brutality of the bombing. It was as if it deliberately targeted ancient sites to obliterate them and the memories they constituted. Hany told me how Palestinian archaeologists and architects were painstakingly at work to preserve and protect these sites and desperately trying to prevent further damage to them.

Nablus is not just any old city. When in the first Christian century the Roman emperor Vespasian called it Flavia Neapolis, it already had a history that went back to the time of the Assyrians in the eighth century BC. Its every brick and wall sat on layers of time immemorial. The Israeli army in Nablus was like a wild bull in a shop full of fragile china. Visibly scarred, it had been subjected to repeated bombardment of its most beautiful and ancient buildings and sites, most recently in August 2002. Hany's voice was entirely flat, though his habitual smile was no longer there.

We all sat there, the three of us, for a few minutes, on the sharp slope of that hill overlooking the city. There are these silences when you listen to Palestinians marking the scars on their national body. They seem to run out of words and even emotions. There is no anger in the air—nor, though, resignation, just a mere matter-of-factness that leaves life open-ended. "There will be a shot here," Hany suddenly had his smile back, "where Said and Khaled will sit and smoke narghile and watch Nablus."

After a few minutes we got up and descended the winding road deep into the Old City and the congested hustle-bustle of Nablus began embracing us closely and warmly. Battered, bone-broken, bashful, Nablus seemed a bit hesitant at first in the intruding presence of a new pilgrim, mindful that he might find it damaged. In the most sacrosanct moments of my life I remember my late mother, who in her prayerful habits used to kiss the barrier of sacred Shi'i shrines we visited in my childhood—embracing into the bosom of her piety every bruised moment of its charred memories of martyred saints that graced her faith. Nablus was beautiful, and Nablus was rising in the will of its inhabitants defying their fate. Crowded, loud, busy, boisterous, Nablus here had yielded to the worldliness of everydayness. Her confidence gradually restored by a silent respect for its hidden pride, Nablus began revealing her wounds—bombed mansions—the grace and gentleness of which you could still imagine. The Israelis had ripped huge holes inside magnificent buildings and bombed ancient walls out of sight as if they did not exist. Building after building came forward and showed me their wounds: "Look here, see this, can you believe that, and let me show you this one." Aging grace still shone through Nablus's damaged bones. But the site of the city square was broken under the traces of Israeli tanks.

Hammouda parked the car, and Hany guided me through the city center, showing me various places they had scouted for their shoots, among them an old soap factory that he later used for the central sequence in *Paradise Now* when Khaled and Said are being ritually prepared for their mission. He also wanted me to see an old mansion in the middle of which the Israeli army had planted a bomb and made a massive hole. From there, Hany led the way through a labyrinthine passage and we found ourselves in the middle of the Nablus bazaar. We walked casually for a while.

"Do you want to buy anything?" Hany asked.

"Yes. Za'atar." We went into a shop full of magnanimous bags of spices. Palestinians take their za'atar, the sweet soul of their defiant earth, seriously and eat it quite ceremoniously. After I bought some za'atar and we left the shop, we exited the bazaar and headed back to the car. I needed to be in Ramallah for dinner that night with a few Birzeit colleagues and it was getting late. Hany and I said goodbye, his tall figure stooping against the background of an old building. Hammouda drove me to Huwwara checkpoint. He saw me through the machsom and handed me over to Ihsan, whom he had arranged to be there to drive me back to Ramallah. Ihsan could not drive to Nablus because he is from Jerusalem and his identity card and car registration papers prevent him from doing so. When Ihsan saw me approaching him from the checkpoint with my bag of za'atar in hand, a wide smile quietly delighted his face.

"You like za'atar?" I nodded. "I will bring you some fresh za'atar from my village. It is from the ground on which the Hebrew University in Jerusalem is built."

On my way back from Nablus to Ramallah, Ihsan drove me through a New Jersey Turnpike lookalike, with one Israeli settlement after another marching on both sides of the highway, crowding the landscape and marking the horizon on the top of surrounding hills that define the natural boundaries of the valley. Highway signs in Hebrew and English identified the exit and entrance roads to the top of those hills and to the Israeli settlements. The hills on which these monstrosities sat came together in small valleys and brooks—the sites of beautifully laid out Palestinian villages, marked either by the steeple of a church or the minaret of a mosque. These Palestinian villages were studded with budding olive groves and blossoming pinkish flowers even so late in winter. Not a single exit from that New Jersey Turnpike led to any one of these villages, and even their own dirt roads—their blood lines to each other and the highway—were cut off by Caterpillar bulldozers, precluding the inhabitants of these villages from linking to the rest of the world with anything other than mules or horses. I sat in the passenger seat of Ihsan's car, listening to his painful accounts of our surroundings, ashamed of my own humanity. But how proud and how confident looked those steeples and those minarets overlooking the sad solidity of those villages!

Ihsan dropped me off in downtown Ramallah, near the central square and its lions (one lion has a wristwatch on one of its paws), near

the restaurant where I was to meet my Birzeit colleagues for dinner. After the dinner I was off to the Sakakini Center, where we had a screening that night, to meet up with Annemarie to make sure that our festival
was going well. At the door of the Sakakini Center I ran into a young
Palestinian filmmaker I had just met a few days earlier.

"What are you doing here?" he asked with a look of kind incredu-
lity on his face.

"Where?" I asked. "Here in Palestine?"

He was smiling as he reached into his pocket and took out his key
ring. I looked at him. He took his keys off the key ring and asked me
again, this time playfully. "What are you doing here?"

"Nothing," I said. His eyes brightened, his smile becoming laughter. He handed me his key ring, along with a small statuette that was
hanging from it. I took it and looked at it. It was a statuette of Handala.*

"That's for you," he said. "Your Oscar!"

---

* Handala is the most famous of Palestinian cartoonist Naji al-Ali's characters. He
is depicted as a ten-year-old boy, and appeared for the first time in Al-Siyasa in
Kuwait in 1969. The figure turned his back to the viewer from the year 1973 and
clasped his hands behind his back. The artist explained that the ten-year-old represented his age when forced to leave Palestine and would not grow up until he could
return to his homeland; his turned back and clasped hands symbolized the character's rejection of "outside solutions." Handala wears ragged clothes and is bare-
foot, symbolizing his allegiance to the poor. In later cartoons, he sometimes appears
throwing stones or writing graffiti.

POSTSCRIPT

Upon my return to New York early in March I finished my notes and comments on Hany's script and emailed them to him. By early July, he had finished shooting and moved to Amsterdam to begin editing. He wanted to show me an early cut in Amsterdam later that summer but I could not go; nor could I go to Berlin, from where I received an email from Hany early in February 2005, telling me that it would be premiered in the competition at the Berlinale—on February 14 at 4:30 p.m., he added—hoping that I could go there to see it with him. I was quite anxious to see the final cut. In New York I was now in the middle of a maddening political storm at Columbia, where a number of my colleagues and I were under attack from a pack of Zionists—coordinating their assaults from Boston, New York, Philadelphia, and Tel Aviv. In mid-March I received an email from Hany telling me *Paradise Now* had received three prizes in Berlin: Best European Film, the Audience Award, and the Amnesty International Award. He also wrote that Warner Independent had bought it for the United States, Canada, and the United Kingdom markets and that they were planning to distribute it early in September. He made arrangements with the US distributor for me to see it in a private screening. Late in March I finally saw *Paradise Now* in a small private theater near Bryant Park in New York.

Paradise Now opened in New York and the rest of United States the following autumn and, as in the rest of the world, was heaped with an avalanche of praise and prizes including a Golden Globe and a nomination for an Academy Award, both for Best Foreign-Language Film. Many Palestinian friends and colleagues liked the film and were deeply moved by it. Others were not and took exception to any cinematic attempt at tackling this issue. For me, however, reaction to the film seemed to take an entirely different course as references to it by "cinema studies" and "visual anthropology" people began to accumulate.

Hany Abu-Assad's *Paradise Now* is one of a number of films with which I was involved from the very beginning—Mohsen Makhmalbaf's *The Silence* (1998), Ridley Scott's *Kingdom of Heaven* (2005), Amir

Naderi's *Sound Barrier* (2005), Shirin Neshat's *Women Without Men* (2009), and all of Ramin Bahrani's films so far, including his forthcoming *Ship of Fools*, are some that stand out. When I first met Hany in New York in January 2003 and arranged for him and Amir Naderi to meet for dinner at my place, he told me that the opening sequence of his next film begins with the last sequence of Amir Naderi's *The Runner*, as homage to a filmmaker he so deeply admired. His script developed in many directions after that initial thought, and he ultimately cut the scene of Said and Khaled playing soccer when they were young (a reference to the last sequence of *The Runner* where the kids run for the fire).

Reading the initial remarks made by film studies and anthropology academics about the film, I felt there was something terribly amiss—if not about these disciplines, then about the moment at which they begin to look at a work of art. To be sure, my aversion to these sorts of academic writing about art in general and about cinema in particular predates the making of *Paradise Now*. But something about this film in particular made my reaction to them more pronounced. For me, this reaction, negative or even if positive—it made no difference—was prompted by the distance between those who look at a work of art in the context of the pain and suffering that occasion it and the vision and the hope that uplift it, and those who rob that same work of art of these aspects and look at it as a vacated object of filmic or anthropological curiosity, stripping it of its politics and overburdening it with ethnographic abuse. Whether ordinary folk liked *Paradise Now* or disliked it, they did so with an abiding connection with the pain at the heart of it. Not so the cinema studies and anthropological crowd. For them, it seemed, the film had been transposed to an ethereal plane—at once vacated of its humanity and then invested with "ethnographic" informatics that depleted its aesthetic force. Watching them at work convinced me that this thing they call cinema studies is the death of cinema; that anthropology becomes the grotesque funeral of any art it touches. I have never felt so alienated, so estranged, so at odds with academic exercises in writing "about" cinema as I was after *Paradise Now*. Cinema Studies sucks the life out of any film it watches, then hands its corpse to anthropology for a gruesome autopsy.

Cinema to me, like any other form of art, is the sublimation of the pain and pleasure of life into moments of superior sublimity—and neither anthropology nor cinema studies seems to have a blasted clue about what that sublimity is, or how it is generated or sustained. They deal with dead bodies of otherwise living works of art they have murdered with their thick and clumsy analytical tools (anthropology), or else with their fine and delicate utensils (cinema studies). The approach taken by anthropology is defined by putting to use a Steinway piano as a hayrack to feed a horse, or the canvas on which Picasso's *Guernica* is painted to write a prosaic chronicle of the Spanish civil war. It is afflicted with an aesthetic Daltonism that blinds it to what it is they are chopping off in order to offer the most inane conclusions. Anthropology is the death of art, to reverse the metaphor, and cinema studies lays on its elaborate funeral.

Worse fates than this combined calamity can and do afflict works of visual, performing, or literary art—when, for instance, such art is overwhelmed by the abusive prose of political science, gender and women's studies, Middle Eastern (or any other area) studies, or, even worse, Arab–Israeli conflict resolution. Applying garden variety, deadening theoretical cookie cutters, these disciplines strip art of the pain and pleasure that gave it birth.

A work of art is like a beautiful and fleeting butterfly that uplifts this pain and pleasure to aesthetic realms of normative and formal emancipation and agency. It can only teach you the mystery of its life and the liberty of its grace if you learn the humility and patience of sitting still and watching its playful frivolity. If you chase after that butterfly, first and foremost you make a ridiculous spectacle of your foolishness, as you stumble and tumble in vain. And if you finally manage to capture it, pin it down, and begin to slice and analyze it, you have already unwittingly killed that beautiful creature entirely unbeknownst to yourself and your brutal, banal, and dull instruments. No work of art worth the name was ever created to provide excuses for tenure-track professors or their silly indulgence in sillier theories. The only way to sing the song that a butterfly dances is to dance with it, detect its hidden rhythm, and in its graceful neighborhood let it teach you how to dance with it. If you are lucky and your prose has hit the right tone, then you may succeed in bringing a wider community of spectators to dance with you—and with the butterfly.

Take *Paradise Now*. Is it possible to understand the desperation that drives a people to blow themselves up and all that is around them without being witness to the daily humiliation and the suffering that Palestinians endure under the brutal occupation of their homeland and the criminal injustice they must endure on a daily basis? No. The simple answer is a plain no. But is the film reducible to those daily brutalities that inform and sustain the pain that drives people to desperate measures? The answer is an equally if not a more emphatic no. An indifferent analysis cannot reach the creative core of a mimetic act that approximates reality.

When Ihsan was driving me to Ramallah from Nablus, and as we were passing by those ghastly looking settlements interspersing beautiful Palestinian villages, he told me how Palestinian farmers had to travel on their donkeys for miles to find a way around Israeli soldiers and toward a highway where they could sell their produce. Ihsan told me a Palestinian farmer riding on his donkey was caught by Israeli soldiers and, in addition to the regular indignities and harassments he had to endure, was forced to mount and copulate with his donkey. The news was passing through Palestinian communities with a fierce but quiet anger I can never forget. When a Palestinian goes to see *Paradise Now*, or when Hany Abu-Assad makes it, the daily indignities of their people are never far from their active memory: in the battlefields of history, where fragile human beings must fight for a measure of their dignity, art can be a weapon of the weak by virtue of being creatively defiant against the mendacity of the politically powerful but spiritually impoverished.

And yet, like every work of art, *Paradise Now* is an event that crafts the aesthetic terms it entails and celebrates ex nihilo. There is no theoretical straitjacket, one-size-fits-all, here. Art has no history, certainly no anthropology, and one cannot deduce or legislate a manifesto for human rights, women's rights, or any other right or wrong from or for it.

Is politics indifferent to cinema—or to the aesthetics it predicates? As I write this postscript in May 2009, at the Cannes Film Festival the Palme d'Or has just been awarded to Austrian director Michael Haneke for *The White Ribbon* (2009), yet another film about the roots of Nazi violence in Germany. Haneke's film was in competition with yet another film about Nazism, Quentin Tarantino's *Inglourious Basterds* (2009). According to reports, Haneke had said that his film should not be interpreted as being just about Nazism. "You can apply it," he said, "to any form of fanaticism, whether Islamic or left-wing fascism. It comes in all forms." Where did that come from—making yet another film about Nazism and describing it as a metaphor for Islamic fanaticism (Ahmadinejad—right?) or "left-wing fascism" (Chávez, perhaps?). Are these the only fanaticisms that Haneke could think to name? What about Jewish fanaticism, Hindu fanaticism, Christian fanaticism—European fanatical racism against Muslims, maybe? How about the link between European Islamophobia, principally based in Austria, where Haneke lives, and *White Ribbon*? One must of course categorically disregard the fact that the award was given to Haneke by a jury that was headed by the French actress Isabelle Huppert, who in 2001 won a Best Actress prize at Cannes for her part in *La Pianiste* (2001), a film by the same Austrian director Michael Haneke. And the fact that Elia Suleiman's *The Time That Remains* (2009), about the Palestinian Nakba, was also in competition this year—and received nothing. I am quite confident, sight unseen, that Haneke's film must be quite extraordinary and absolutely brilliant. But how do you exactly measure? I have been part of international juries and I ask from personal experience—one filmmaker's brilliant use of Nazism as a metaphor for Islamism as fanaticism over and against another's who might have hinted at the criminal thievery of Zionist fanaticism against Palestinians?

I have long held that national cinemas are predicated on national traumas, and without the pain and promises embedded in a national trauma, no nation, as a nation, can produce an art form that speaks of and to its defining moments. From that premise, I have concluded that the defining moment of Palestinian cinema is a traumatic realism that informs all its particular manifestations—from Mustafa Abu-Ali's *No to the Option of Surrender* (1968) to Hany Abu-Assad's *Paradise Now* (2005). The mimetic crisis at the heart of Palestinian cinema, that no mode of cinematic representation can meet and match the enormity of the catastrophe (Nakba) it must address, demands an entirely different manner of looking at the centrality of an aesthetic reason that must act as substitute for the public space that a nation under occupation cannot claim. No generic application of film theories, as we have received them, can correspond to that reality. As nations narrate their politics of defiance, so must their art be allowed to articulate the aesthetics of that very act of liberation. For want of that mode of worldly and effective theorization, great works of art are wasted on vacuous speculations that add nothing to them, but take everything away.

Eight

ON COMPRADOR INTELLECTUALS

The whole project of my book Brown Skin, White Masks *(2011) from which I reproduce its chapter 2 here, began by two prior pieces I had written, my critique of the role of "The Native Informers in the Making of American Empire," and my initial reactions to Edward Said's notion of the exilic intellectuals. While I had shared his positive reading of such exilic conditions, I never thought of myself as an "exilic intellectual," and thus, in the figure of the native informer like Fouad Ajami and Azar Nafisi, I could see the dangers of a homeless intellectual becoming a native informer and a gun for hire. In this chapter I map out in details the blind spots hidden in Said's insight, in which I had detected the terror of an intellectual who is not committed to one or any other nation.*

> We must at present do our best to form a class who may be
> interpreters between us and the millions whom we govern; a class
> of persons, Indian in blood and color, but English in taste, in
> opinions, in morals, and in intellect.
> —Thomas B. Macaulay, "Minute on Education" (1835)

> An Eastern race well versed in Western culture and profoundly in
> sympathy with Western ideals will be established in the Orient.

Furthermore, a Jewish state will inevitably fall under the control of American Jews who will work out, along Jewish lines, American ideals and American civilization.

—William Yale, US State Department (1919)

In those days he was called a "house nigger." And that's what we call him today, because we've still got some house niggers running around here.

—Malcolm X (1963)

Just as, hidden in the self-loathing colonized mind that Fanon diagnosed seethed the future native informer, so did the defiant exilic intellectual whom Edward Said saw as the locus of dissent at the heart of the empire conceal the figure of comprador intellectual. In his 1993 Reith Lectures, published the next year as *Representations of the Intellectual*, Said proposed this exilic intellectual as the savior of an otherwise lost cause. In his 1987 diagnostic essay *The Last Intellectuals*, Russell Jacoby had written the obituary of the public intellectual in the United States.[1] Said, in response, detected a critical character that had escaped Jacoby's notice at the margins of the American metropolis:

> While it is an actual condition, exile is also for my purposes a metaphorical condition . . . Even intellectuals who are lifelong members of a society can, in a manner of speaking, be divided into insiders and outsiders: those on the one hand who belong fully to the society as it is, who flourish in it without an overwhelming sense of dissonance or dissent, those who can be called yea-sayers; and on the other hand, the nay-sayers, the individuals at odds with their society and therefore outsiders and exiles so far as privileges, power, and honors are concerned.[2]

Said's exilic intellectual (clearly a self-projection) is never at home anywhere, always opposing the arguments that serve power. His concept contains references to a range of intellectuals as diverse as Theodor Adorno, Eqbal Ahmad, Noam Chomsky, and, of course, Said himself, all solitary souls rebelling against the power that seeks to silence or assimilate them.

This exilic condition does not refer to an actual separation from a homeland (Adorno from Germany, Ahmad from Pakistan, Said from Palestine) but to a critical angle on power and a defiant character ill at ease with any communal claim on his or her loyalty. Chomsky is thus an exile in his own homeland. The prototype is a sort of amphibian character who has left the colonial site of his upbringing for the presumed center of capital ("presumed" because capital no longer has a center) to dismantle its ideological edifice and subvert its claim to political legitimacy. As a Fifth Column, or a Trojan Horse, the exilic intellectual assumes the guise of a migrant laborer, a passenger in transit, a homeless vagabond, fooling the customs by smuggling subversive ideas through gates, pretending to innocence while carrying a backpack full of explosive ideas.

From Exilic to Comprador Intellectuals

In the shadow of Said's exilic intellectual, however, has always lurked a parasite called the comprador intellectual. In his reflections on the various manners of Africa, Kwame Anthony Appiah locates this character in a "relatively small, Western-style, Western-trained group of writers and thinkers, who mediate the trade in cultural commodities of world capitalism at the periphery."[3] Despite its usefulness, that limited definition of comprador intellectual is much in need of reconsideration. For Appiah, the idea is very much contingent on a nebulous category called "the West," and it operates between a binary center-and-periphery that is no longer valid.

The Portuguese word *comprador* dates from 1840 and refers to a Chinese agent engaged by a European business interest in China to oversee its native employees and to act as an intermediary in its business affairs. Later, it was extended to refer to any native servant in the service of a colonial commercial interest—someone "employed by Europeans, in India and the East," according to the Oxford English Dictionary, "to purchase necessaries and keep the household accounts: a house-steward." The concept carries an obvious ideological subtext that becomes crucially functional in mobilizing public sentiment in support of colonial and imperial projects. The comprador intellectual is a cultural broker, a commissioned operator, a "ten-percenter" paid to facilitate cultural domination and political pacification. He has some familiarity with the dominating culture, which he serves out of self-interest (not conviction), he speaks its language (with an accent), and by virtue of the proximity he seeks to power becomes abusive of his own compatriots.

But Appiah's characterization falls short of the nature and disposition of the category. Far sharper is Malcolm X's designation of the functional equivalent of the comprador intellectual in his "Message to the Grass Roots," delivered in Detroit on November 10, 1963:

> There were two kinds of slaves. There was the house Negro and the field Negro. The house Negroes—they lived in the house with master, they dressed pretty good, they ate good 'cause they ate his food—what he left. They lived in the attic or the basement, but still they lived near the master; and they loved their master more than the master loved himself. They would give their life to save the master's house quicker than the master would. The house Negro, if the master said, "We got a good house here," the house Negro would say, "Yeah, we got a good house here." Whenever the master said "we," he said "we." That's how you can tell a house Negro.[4]

Malcolm X has moved the figure of the comprador intellectual from the periphery—the field—into the normative universe of the master. His figure is more dialectical than Appiah's, for he moves back and forth between the field and the house—informing and/or misinforming the master about the nature and disposition of those in the field. The master takes the house slave for the authentic thing, while the house slave himself believes he is serving the master best by informing him about the field slaves—when in fact they are both delusional, caught in a dialectic of reciprocity in which they are abusing each other without knowing it. This is Malcolm X's superior insight.

In the context of French domination in North Africa, Albert Memmi offered an equally accurate diagnosis of the malady in his *Colonizer and the Colonized* (1957):

> The situation of the Jewish population—eternally hesitant candidates refusing assimilation—can be viewed in a similar light. Their constant and very justifiable ambition is to escape from their colonized condition, an additional burden in an already oppressive status. To that end, they endeavor to resemble the colonizer in the frank hope that they may cease to consider them different from him. Hence their efforts to forget the past, to change collective habits, and their enthusiastic adoption of Western language, culture and customs. But if the colonizer does not always openly discourage these candidates to develop that resemblance he never permits them to attain it either. Thus they live in painful and constant ambiguity. Rejected by the colonizer they share in part the physical conditions of the colonized and have a communion of interest with him; on the other hand, they reject the values of the colonized as belonging to a decayed world from which they eventually hope to escape. The recently assimilated place themselves in considerable superior position to the average colonizer. They push a colonial mentality to excess, display proud disdain for the colonized and continually show off their rank, which often belies a vulgar brutality and avidity. Still too impressed by their privileges, they savor them and defend with fear and harshness; and when colonization is imperiled, they provide it with its most dynamic defenders, its shock troops, and sometimes instigators.[5]

Memmi's analysis is not limited to the Jewish population; he has diagnosed the overwhelming power of white supremacist hegemony. Rabindranath Tagore's description, in his famous novel *Gora* (1910), of the English-identified Bengali comprador intellectuals halfway around the globe from North Africa perfectly matches Memmi's. The comprador intellectual is a by-product of colonialism, not a character trait of any given culture.

Said's exilic intellectual defies the power relation operative in his domain, whereas Appiah's comprador intellectual is subservient to it. The one has migrated to the heart of darkness, where the empire manages its domestic and foreign affairs; the other has stayed behind and provides his services on the colonial site. But if we place Malcolm X's analysis between Said's and Appiah's, we come to a far more accurate conception of both the exilic and the comprador intellectuals, because each is involved in a dialectical traffic between the center and the periphery (thus collapsing both into one world). Malcolm X has a dynamic conception of political manipulation, social mobility, and the economic underpinnings of power:

> If the master's house caught on fire, the house Negro would fight harder to put the blaze out than the master would. If the master got sick, the house Negro would say, "What's the matter, boss, we sick?" We sick! He identified himself with his master more than his master identified with himself. And if you came to the house Negro and said, "Let's run away, let's escape, let's separate," the house Negro would look at you and say, "Man, you crazy. What you mean, separate? Where is there a better house than this? Where can I wear better clothes than this? Where can I eat better food than this?"[6]

Malcolm X's house negro and Said's exilic intellectual are two sides of the same analytical coin, one serving the white master and the other revolting against him.

Just as Said's exilic intellectual may be in actual or metaphoric exile, the comprador intellectual can actually be in the field or metaphorically there, or alternatively, he can move into the house. Whichever way, he is always located on the side of power. The advantage of Said and Malcolm X's combination of insights is that, in an increasingly amorphous and boundary-less world, it no longer requires us to divide intellectuals along a fictitious center–periphery axis. The actual location of the comprador intellectual on that axis has become increasingly tenuous. In a 1997 essay on the same phenomenon as it relates to the Palestinian predicament, Joseph Massad maintains that the events of 1967 facilitated the emergence of a new breed of comprador intellectuals. "The Arab defeat in the 1967 war announced the retreat of a period of secular revolutionary thinking, with the Camp David Accord of 1978 and 1979 dealing it a final coup de grace,

giving way to a new crop of thinkers: Islamists and realist-pragmatists."[7]
The latter are Massad's Palestinian comprador intellectuals:

> This transformation wherein Palestinian intellectuals who previously
> opposed the occupation, PLO concessions, and US hegemony, but
> now support, wittingly or unwittingly, all three, is not a unique trans-
> formation. It would seem that like their Soviet counterparts who
> rushed to trade in their communism for realist pragmatism upon the
> fall of the Soviet state, or their Latin American counterparts who,
> like Fernando Henrique Cardoso, traded in their dependency the-
> ory approach for positions of power ... Palestinian intellectuals, at-
> tuned to the exigencies of political power and the benefits that could
> accrue to them from it, traded in their national liberation goals for
> pro-Western pragmatism.[8]

Massad's comprador intellectuals could be in or out of Palestine,
within the 1948 or 1967 borders or out in the diaspora. Where they
reside does not really matter; they no longer have a fixed location on
what Appiah calls "the periphery," and thus the whole axis of center–
periphery reveals itself as misplaced and active.

THE COMPRADOR INTELLECTUAL MOVES IN

Comprador intellectuals have always been close to the mobilized center of
power—which in this rapidly globalizing world might be just about anywhere but is increasingly at the center of empire. In a 2003 essay, "The
Native Informant,"[9] Adam Shatz has done a service by placing a prominent example of the comprador intellectual at the heart of the mobilized
Imperium: Fouad Ajami, who lives and works in Washington, DC. Ajami
advises high-ranking US officials and regularly works as a media pundit
when American imperialism flexes its muscles around the Muslim world.
Ajami does not perform his compradorial services from Southern Lebanon; he has moved so deeply into the normative imagination of the imperial power that he does not quite hear the macabre humor when he says,
"We Americans ought to understand how the mind of these Arabs works!"

This question has in recent years assumed an intriguing turn with a writer who publishes sensational tirades against Islam and Muslims under the pseudonym Ibn Warraq. That readers have no clue as to who or where they really are (Ibn is Arabic for "the son of," but a pseudonym need not be truthful) beautifully demonstrates how tenuous the physical location of the comprador intellectual can be; what is important is the move to the symbolic center of power. In a series of highly provocative titles (including "Why I Am Not a Muslim," "The Quest for the Historical Muhammad"), this character has launched flamboyant attacks on the verities of the Islamic religion, the prophet, and the sacred Islamic text. His compradorial courtship of anti-Muslim sentiment is exceptionally valuable to the "clash of civilizations" proposition.

Precisely because he is dislocated, he demands attention. In book after book, Ibn Warraq takes a perverse pleasure in recounting the most offensive assertions about Islam that European Orientalists (Dante, Hobbes, Voltaire, Hume, Gibbon, Carlyle) have uttered over the years. He suffers from a severe case of Rushdie syndrome, trying to "up the ante" in his ever more perverse assaults on his own ancestral faith. That a book like *Why I Am Not a Muslim* resurrects a long-dead manifestation of Orientalism is not really much of a problem.[10] The political economy that once necessitated Orientalism as a system of colonial knowledge production has long since generated a new propaganda machinery, under whose modus operandi Ibn Warraq's obscenities have to be understood.

The case of Azar Nafisi bears on this same question of location. Her memoir, *Reading Lolita in Tehran*, recounts how she has saved the souls of seven students in Tehran (and with them, symbolically, the rest of Iran) by inviting them into her home to teach them Vladimir Nabokov's novel and "other masterpieces of Western literature." She did live in Tehran. She subsequently moved to the United States, and she now lives in the vicinity of the American capital and teaches as an adjunct at the Paul H. Nitze School of Advanced International Studies at Johns Hopkins University in Baltimore. (At the time she was writing her memoir, she was reporting directly to its dean, Paul Wolfowitz.) The location Nafisi claims by virtue of her bestselling book is, in fact, fictitious: it purports to be Tehran, but the book was actually written in Washington, DC.

We can no longer automatically place comprador intellectuals at the periphery of any center, nor indeed at the center of any periphery; they are everywhere, because they are nowhere in particular, and they are nowhere in particular because they simply try to keep close to the mobilized center of power. "How do you define your own status in this country?" one interviewer asked Azar Nafisi—"exile, emigre, a citizen of the world?" She answered, "I would like to think of my own status as what you called 'citizen of the world' or a 'citizen of a portable world,'" which in this situation, one could argue, suggests a homeless mind, a "carpetbagger," a very doctrinaire sort of intellectual.[11]

Given the rapid deterioration of the smokescreen historically separating the domestic and foreign abuses of labor by capital that goes by the code name "globalization," we can no longer sustain a distance between a presumed center and a projected periphery in the amorphous operation of capital. As a result, the comprador intellectual needs to be categorically reconsidered as a type— thematically extended, functionally globalized, and physically relocated to any place the emerging empire seeks to sustain the operation of capital. The type has become more bourgeois in style and training, no longer simply mediating the trade of cultural commodities but in fact manufacturing them in such a way as to facilitate the operation of globalized capital and its corresponding empire-building projects.

Rethinking the Compradorial

If, based on these examples—which can be extended with many others (including V. S. Naipaul, Salman Rushdie, Dinesh D'Souza)—we shift the emphasis from the physical location to the place that the comprador intellectual imaginatively resides, then the entire category assumes a significance beyond the classical definition of colored individuals in ideological servitude to white masters. Through the opening up of horizons, we can radically recast these intellectuals according to the newly globalized service they now provide to power.

As a case in point, consider the *New York Times*'s Thomas Friedman, who is fond of signing his name to his columns from one troubled part of the world after another. In his ideological services to the American empire he is all but identical to Fouad Ajami, Dinesh D'Souza, Azar Nafisi—they all think alike and speak the same language, and they often endorse one another. The category can become perfectly color-blind, because capital and its changing ideologies are ultimately color-blind.

The word *comprador* comes from the Spanish and Portuguese *comprar*, "to buy," and thus entails the specific function of facilitating the flow of capital through trade. Its original meaning, "a native servant employed by Europeans in the East," refers to a specific period in the history of capital when it divided the world between white masters and colored natives along an East–West axis no longer valid in a world of globalized capitalism and 24-hour trading. The world today is more than ever divided between the overwhelming majority who are abused by capital and the very few who are its beneficiaries. The defining function of the comprador intellectuals is to shore up that relation of commerce to power. Birthplace, nationality, religion, creed, and color are all irrelevant. Capital will use whatever and whoever is convenient for each particular time, place, and situation.

At the same time, we may note that the emergence of this comprador character in the shadow of Said's exilic intellectual coincides with a particularly anti-intellectual episode in contemporary American history. As intellectuals such as Ajami, Nafisi, Ibn Warraq, and Rushdie are set loose during George W. Bush's "War on Terror" to discredit their own culture, they leave a void in the public space for a far more radical eradication of the defiant public intellectual—a task most recently performed by (among others) Mark Lilla, who, in a series of essays originally published in the *New York Review of Books* and the *Times Literary*

Supplement and subsequently collected between hard covers as *The Reckless Mind*, launched an attack against dissenting voices raised in objection to the imperial terrors perpetrated by the United States against the world at large. Close attention to Lilla's anti-intellectual diatribes will help clarify the comprador intellectual's transit beyond color and creed into the normative paradigms of the belligerent empire.[12]

Lilla goes through a gamut of European intellectuals, from Martin Heidegger and Karl Schmidt to Walter Benjamin and Alexandre Kojève and on down to Michel Foucault and Jacques Derrida, who have in his judgment committed some political atrocity or other; the *reckless* of his title has condoned fascism, communism, or "countless national liberation movements" (for Lilla they are all one and the same) and has portrayed "Western liberal democracies" in diabolical terms.[13] In his systematically anti-intellectual defense of the vacuous cause of a twentieth-century "Western liberal democracy" that he never subjects to critical inquiry, not once does Lilla utter a word about the global atrocities of classical European colonialism or of present-day imperial American warmongering. For him it is a given that only reckless intellectuals and demagogues would take issue with "Western liberal democracies" or with what he calls, in jest, "the tyranny of capital, of imperialism, of bourgeois conformity." In Lilla's eyes, "the facts were rarely in dispute; they were apparent to anyone who read the newspapers and had a sense of moral proportion." Those facts would, of course, appear in newspaper stories written by embedded journalists. That "sense of moral proportion" apparently does not apply to the torture chambers in Bagram Air Base and Abu Ghraib, or to the elaborate arguments in their defense that Alan Dershowitz and Michael Ignatieff have taken straight from the "Western liberal democracies."

What is most astonishing about Lilla's attack on European public intellectuals is that it coincides with one of the most vicious periods of American imperial hubris, of violence perpetrated against weak and colored peoples in violation of international laws. This anti-intellectualism (so definitive of American cultural history that it was recognized by as early an observer as Alexis de Tocqueville), denouncing any public figure who dares to speak out against US military thuggery around the world, is essential to the function of comprador intellectuals and native informers at the service of the predatory empire. Lilla suffers from a transcontinental ahistoricism that leaps easily from ancient Greece to contemporary Iraq. He traverses the distance between Plato and Saddam Hussein without the slightest hesitation or concern—and with a single-minded determination to discredit any public intellectual who has ever taken a public stand against any atrocity committed by the "Western liberal democracies."

After a volume's worth of gossip about Martin Heidegger and Hannah Arendt's love affair, Walter Benjamin's extramarital indiscretions, Michel Foucault's homosexuality, and other equally irrelevant aspects of these prominent intellectuals' private lives, Lilla turns to Plato and Dionysius in order to issue a verdict against a few minor dinosaurs, completely ignoring—and thus exonerating—the major source of violence in the world, the military might of the United States. His attacks have an uncanny similarity to the smear campaigns now endemic to presidential electioneering. Do we really care about Foucault's sexual preferences or Sartre's indiscretions? Is Arendt disqualified from speaking about Auschwitz because as a student she had an affair with her professor? Do these entirely private aspects of these public intellectuals' lives discredit their principled stands against criminal atrocities around the globe? Of course not.

Equally puzzling is Lilla's equation of Heidegger's Nazi affiliation with Foucault's anti-fascism. But we may solve the puzzle when we realize that via such ahistorical and illogical links Lilla discredits any political concern on the part of public intellectuals. In the course of equating National Socialism with every other national liberation movement, he remains under the delusion that he is not taking a political position himself—that he is not placing his laptop squarely at the service of a predatory empire. "Dionysius is our contemporary," he writes, and in Saddam Hussein and Ayatollah Khomeini he finds reincarnations of that terrible tyrant.[14] In a moment of naked indiscretion, he declares, "the harems and food-tasters of ancient times are indeed gone but their places have been taken by propaganda ministers and revolutionary guards, drug barons and Swiss bankers. The tyrant has survived. The problem of Dionysius is as old as creation."[15] Texas ranchers without a "harem and food-tasters" to shame them, with CNN and Fox News functioning like "propaganda outlets," and a mercenary army to act as their "revolutionary guards" do not cross Lilla's mind.

What, then, are the subjects of a predatory empire to do when faced with the criminal monstrosities of a George W. Bush or an Ariel Sharon—or, for that matter, of a Saddam Hussein, an Ayatollah Khomeini, an Osama bin Laden? Are they to remain silent, to implicitly endorse Bush's "liberation" of Afghanistan and Iraq as a way of spreading "Western liberal democracy"? Would that exempt one, in Lilla's view, from the transgressions of a reckless mind? What about those caught in the snare of tyrants—should they not utter a word? And what, exactly, is Lilla doing himself? Is his own text denouncing public intellectuals a work of pure, politics-free philosophical speculation?

Had Heidegger had an affair with Arendt but no affiliation with the Nazis, or vice versa, would he have passed Lilla's test as a responsible philosopher? How could one equate Carl Schmitt's visceral anti-Semitism and Walter Benjamin's despair at the terror looming over European Jews, which could not but have included a passing attraction to messianic politics? And what did Benjamin's love affair with the Latvian intellectual Asja Lacis have to do with his turn to Marxism? What did Alexandre Kojève's intellectual grandfathering of a triumphalist theorist like Francis Fukuyama have to do with Michel Foucault's politics, or Foucault's homosexuality with his position on power? When Lilla comes to Jacques Derrida, having failed to find any "dirt" on him, he simply expresses utter contempt for French philosophers as public intellectuals. His greatest disdain, however, is for the US academic left, which in his estimation has misunderstood the paragons of the European engaged philosophy and concocted a postmodernism for which he does not hide his contempt.

The moral of Lilla's story is that "whoever takes it upon himself to write an honest intellectual history of twentieth-century Europe will need a strong stomach."[16] Lilla suffers gastroenterological distress be-cause European intellectuals have sacrificed the cause of pure philoso-phy to impure political engagement. He expresses his judgment via a binary opposition between Sartre (the Indian of his personal political Western) and Raymond Aron (the cowboy):

> In his influential Plaidoyer pour les intellectuels, texts of lectures given in 1965, Sartre portrayed the intellectual as a left-wing Jeanne d'Arc who stands for what is essentially human against the inhuman forces of economic and political "power," and also against those re-actionary cultural forces, including traitorous fellow writers, whose work "objectively" supports the modern tyrant.
>
> For his nemesis Raymond Aron, it was precisely this sim-ple-minded opposition of "humanity" to "power" that demonstrated the incapacity of French intellectuals since the Dreyfus Affair to un-derstand the real challenges of twentieth century European politics. In Aron's view, it was no accident, indeed it was utterly predictable, that Sartre's romantic ideal of commitment would turn him into a heartless apologist for Stalinism in the decade after World War II. In L'Opium des intellectuels (1955) Aron retold the story of the rise of the modern intellectual but with a decidedly antimythical intent, demonstrating how incompetent and naive the intellectual as a class had been when it came to serious political matters. In his view, the real responsibility of European intellectuals after the war was to bring whatever expertise they had to bear on liberal democratic politics and to maintain a sense of moral proportion in judging the relative injustices of different po-litical systems—in short, to be independent spectators with a modest sense of their roles as citizens and opinion-makers. Sartre and his fol-lowers accepted no such responsibilities.
>
> Aron was right: in France it was the romantic, "committed" in-tellectuals who served the cause of tyranny in the twentieth century.[17]

Thus, if Aron intervenes in politics on the conservative side he is not irresponsible; but if Sartre does the same on the opposite side, he is utterly irresponsible. The same is true of Lilla's own politics. His telling us that we have to keep our mouths shut as George W. Bush wreaks havoc on the world is not irresponsibly political; but if we cry that our emperor's pants are on fire, we harbor reckless minds.

But why should Bush or Tony Blair be exempted from the same sort of critical inquiry we apply to Joseph Stalin and Saddam Hussein? An Iraqi journalist named Muntadhar al-Zaidi threw his shoes at George W. Bush in Iraq as a protest against a war criminal, with the words "This is for the widows and orphans and all those killed in Iraq." Is he, too, a "reckless mind"—and how would Lilla deal with him? How can an intellectual be so impervious to crimes against humanity? Is it because the perpetrators are white and the victims are colored and situated halfway around the globe?

The anti-intellectual catastrophe that Lilla exemplifies is not limited to right-wing professors and think-tankers. As Lilla rampages against any political engagement by public intellectuals, the very few of them who venture to lift voices of reason and sanity are left at the mercy of the empire's propaganda machinery. Today, even among the most perceptive voices in the United States, we discover that Islam and all its sacred, historical, and institutional referents have mutated into a metaphoric universe of terror and fanaticism. Thus Lewis H. Lapham, in his otherwise plangent critique of David Frum and Richard Perle's book *An End to Evil: How to Win the War on Terror* (which he rightly places among "the hundred-odd books made to the design specifications of a Pentagon press release"), falls into the trap of accepting the mutation of Islam from a world religion into an allegorical simulacrum of terror, backwardness, gibberish, and stupidity. He ridicules Frum and Perle for having borrowed their inspiration from "the verses of the Koran," for issuing "fatwas" like Osama bin Laden, and for summoning "all loyal and true Americans to the glory of jihad." He mocks them as "Mullah Frum," "Mufti Perle," and "the two Washington ayatollahs," and he says, "Provide them with a beard, a turban, and a copy of the Koran, and I expect that they wouldn't have much trouble stoning to death a woman discovered in adultery with a cameraman from CBS News."[18]

If Lapham needs an appropriate metaphor to use for violence and unreason, can he not think of any other one than the Qur'an? Why can he not pause for a moment to think through the implications of his wording when he blasts Frum and Perle's book? He says:

> As with all forms of propaganda, the prose style doesn't warrant extensive quotation, but I don't do the authors a disservice by reducing their message to a series of divine commandments. Like Muhammad bringing the word of Allah to the widow Khadija and the well Zem-Zem, they aspire to a tone of voice appropriate to a book of Revelation.[19]

If Lapham needs an allegory to help with indoctrination in hatred and terror, why are Islam and Quranic language the first things that come to his mind?

> The result of their collaboration is an ugly harangue that if translated into Arabic and reconfigured with a few changes of word and emphasis (the objects of fear and loathing identified as America and Israel in place of Saudi Arabia and the United Nations) might serve as a lesson taught to a class of eager jihadis at a madrasa in Kandahar.[20]

Far worse than the gibberish of a nonentity like Ibn Warraq is the lack of hesitation by one of the most acutely critical minds in the United States today in collapsing the entire sacred universe of a world religion—from its holy book to its prophet to its honorific titles—into a metaphor for stupidity, terrorism, banality, and fanaticism. One would have hoped for something finer in public discourse. But the propaganda machinery that generates and sustains its imperial imagery is so overwhelming that even critical thinkers like Lapham are not immune to it. Even those holding vigil against disastrous alliances with the ideologues of the New American Century have accepted a narrative constitution of evil, code-named Islam, that has dyed the very fabric of our public discourse with a self-fulfilling prophecy of doom and disaster.

THE TREASON OF INTELLECTUALS

This was the ideological atmosphere in which the figures of the comprador intellectual and the native informer suddenly emerged in force.

The horror of the torture that occurred while Bush was driving the American military machinery also came to light in this atmosphere—and some key and crucial questions remained unanswered about this. According to a US Army report issued in August 2004 (known as the Fay Report), for example, at least twenty-seven military intelligence personnel were guilty of torturing Iraqi prisoners at Abu Ghraib, near Baghdad. Senior commanders at the prison knew about the abuses but failed to act. (General Paul J. Kern, speaking on behalf of the committee that wrote the report, noted that the worst abuse occurred when dog handlers used their animals to try to make teenage detainees defecate out of fear.) The report found systematic torture of inmates "ranging from inhumane to sadistic." Meanwhile, as the *New York Times* reported, "classified parts of the report say Lt. Gen. Ricardo S. Sanchez approved the use in Iraq of some severe interrogation practices."[21]

Most of the public discussion that ensued focused on the responsibility of Secretary of Defense Donald Rumsfeld and officers at the Pentagon for the atrocities. And they were, of course, principally responsible. But a more thorough consideration must include the intellectual atmosphere of the moment. Public statements by a number of leading American legal and human-rights scholars and public intellectuals called, in fact, for legalizing torture. This idea gathered currency after the events of 9/11 and the revelation that the United States had created an extraterritorial and extrajuridical concentration camp in the Guantanamo Bay detention facilities—where those designated "suspected terrorists" by the US government could be held indefinitely without charges or access to legal advice and, as "enemy combatants" denied even POW status, exempted from the mandates of the Geneva Conventions.

Shortly after the events of 9/11, Alan Dershowitz, the Felix Frankfurter Professor of Law at Harvard University, began campaigning for the legalization of torture—in newspaper articles, on television shows, and ultimately in a book. He argued for the viability of legalized torture in a *Los Angeles Times* article entitled, "Is There a Torturous Road to Justice?"[22] A year later, under another colorful title, "When All Else Fails, Why Not

Torture?" he made the same case in *American Legion* magazine.[23] Shortly
thereafter he made it again in a *60 Minutes* interview with Mike Wallace.
He used the example of the "ticking bomb" to argue for torture as a legitimate way to prevent massive death tolls, and he added that because torture
already existed it might as well be legalized: "If anybody has any doubt that
our CIA, over time, has taught people to torture, has encouraged torture,
has probably itself tortured in extreme cases, I have a bridge to sell you in
Brooklyn."[24] In a subsequent interview with CNN's Wolf Blitzer, conducted before the revelations of Abu Ghraib, Dershowitz offered more specifics as to the forms of torture he would countenance: "I would talk about
nonlethal torture, say, a sterilized needle underneath the nail, which would
violate the Geneva Accords, but you know, countries all over the world
violate the Geneva Accords."[25] In time he collected his thoughts into a
definitive argument in his 2002 book *Why Terrorism Works*. (See chapter
four: "Should the Ticking Bomb Terrorist Be Tortured? A Case Study in
How a Democracy Should Make Tragic Choices."[26])

One might dismiss Dershowitz as a propagandist for the Jewish
apartheid state, a committed Zionist, and argue that he is merely taking advantage of a frightened nation to score quick political points
that support his worldview. One might also argue that he is not really
approaching this from an academic point of view, but rather from a
legal-technocratic angle. For a genuine intellectual discussion of torture we can turn to Michael Ignatieff—essayist, novelist, broadcaster,
biographer of Isaiah Berlin, recipient of numerous literary prizes, former director of the Carr Center for Human Rights Policy at Harvard
University, and current leader of the Liberal Party in Canada: a major
North American intellectual, widely read, deeply cultivated, and mar-
velously eloquent.

On the surface, Ignatieff seems to reject Dershowitz's call for legalized torture. But it takes him quite a few erudite pages in his book
on the subject, *The Lesser Evil: Political Ethics in an Age of Terror*, to say
so—and these learned pages demand a very careful reading. Ignatieff
says he believes that legalization of torture "is well-intentioned," but

he is concerned that "as an exercise in the lesser evil it seems"—*seems!* —"likely to lead to the greater." He then adds emphatically, "Legalization of physical force in interrogation will hasten the process by which it becomes routine."[27] This is not exactly a rousing denunciation of torture, but it is nevertheless a qualified rejection of Dershowitz. If one were asked on the basis of this book whether Ignatieff is for or against legalizing torture, the answer would thus have to be in the negative, and in fact he states in the conclusion that "torture should remain anathema to a liberal democracy and should never be regulated, countenanced, or covertly accepted in a war on terror."[28]

But here, precisely, is the difference between a dangerous thesis lurking under learned and caring language and the bluster of a propagandist. Between Ignatieff's and Dershowitz's arguments, the lesser transgressor in the court of morals is Dershowitz's—his is only a distraction. Ignatieff's argument is infinitely worse. Without the slightest hesitation he calmly lays out all the legal, moral, ethical, and political ramifications of torture under certain extraordinary circumstances, weighing options, striking a balance here and a counterbalance there, and altogether appearing very judicious in his goal of saving a maximum number of lives under rather nasty circumstances—but, in effect, pursuing an agenda that lends justification to torture under certain circumstances.

The single acceptable response to the question of whether we should torture is no. Any other or lesser answer carries with it heinous implications that demand to be exposed—for here the intellectual has opted to serve the normative imaginary and stated objectives of his empire to the point of no return.

"There is no doubt about the moral facts," Ignatieff writes; "the question is whether democratic survival or national security could override the overwhelming claim that these facts usually make upon the allegiance of a liberal democracy."[29] It is a question he does not quite answer, but by raising it he has (cleverly) put it on the table— and thus suggested that one possible answer is yes, "democratic survival" and "national security" do override the moral prohibitions on torture. And with this move he has set in motion a discursive strategy of consistently providing excellent reasons for torture and then dismissing them with a sudden, single, perfunctory line. A crucial justification for torture followed by a shallow and empty rebuttal—thus he exploits all the fears and anxieties that the Bush administration sustained in the aftermath of 9/11.

Ignatieff thus operates on two simple and simultaneous narrative tracks: (1) providing the intellectual groundwork that eloquently and persuasively articulates why torture might sometimes be deemed necessary and (2) providing a cursory, vague defense of inalienable human rights. Consider the following example. First he posits the necessity of torture ("they" in the first line refers to "the terrorists"):

> The knowledge they possess may pose a mortal danger, if not to the survival of democratic society itself, then at least to [a] large number of its citizens. Because this is so, many democracies nominally committed against torture have felt themselves compelled to torture in the name of necessity and national security.[30]

Then he proceeds to offer examples: France in Algeria, Israel in "the Occupied Territories" (as he calls Palestine), and the United States in Iraq. But first he dismisses the allegations of torture in Iraq (he wrote the book before the Abu Ghraib revelations) by noting that we do not have enough evidence; then he adds,

> Given the uncertainties about the facts, it would seem essential for Congress to insist on the right to tour detention facilities, to hold interviews with detainees in camera, and to disclose the information they get in closed session, so as to keep interrogation technique under democratic scrutiny.[31]

Compare the angry fist raised by "mortal danger," "survival of democratic society," "a large number of its citizens," and "national security" (all straight out of the post-9/11 propaganda machinery) with the pallid "it would seem essential for congress to insist on the right to tour detention facilities," "in camera," and "closed session." On one side we have a massive mobilization of Bush administration buzzwords, on the other a limp attempt at reasonableness.

In a related move, Ignatieff first posits a logical inconsistency: "how can one object to the torture of persons to ensure valuable information for reasons of state, and not object to killing them? Both could simply be regarded as acceptable lesser evils, forced on unwilling liberal democracies by the exigencies of their own survival."[32] And, once again the voice of fair-minded liberalism, he rejects his own suggestion—"the first takes a life; the second abuses one."[33] But in the process he has again planted an insidious seed and deepened the binary relation he consistently posits between "liberal democracies" (we, the civilized) and "terrorists" (they, the savages). In effect, he is telling readers: We are killing them anyway, so why can we not torture them, which not only is not as bad, they have forced us into it. (This is a well known rationalization of rapists: "She asked for it.")

"To save innocent civilians from imminent attack"[34] is the central leitmotif of Ignatieff's discussion. By "innocent civilians" he means Americans and Israelis. He fails to mention Iraqis, Afghans, Palestinians, Algerians, Arabs, and Muslims in general, and by extension any community that by resisting colonial occupation becomes "terrorist." Consider these sentences:

> It might be argued that such dignity commitments [not to torture other people] are a luxury when a state is fighting for its life. But the Israeli case shows that a democratic state engaged in a war with terror can still maintain these commitments.[35]

Now, do not set foot on the immediate land mine and fall prey to anger at the identification of an apartheid, racist, supremacist, ethnocratic, fanatical, colonial settlement as "a democratic state"—that is a distraction. Concentrate instead on the even more insidious subtext of the proposition, which is (not so) hidden in the phrase "fighting for its life." Notice what that phrase does. It places a belligerent nation (either the imperial United States or the colonial Israel) in a state of emergency under which it is forced to do things that under ordinary circumstances it would not wish to. So, if it tortures, assassinates, dispossesses, demolishes homes and livelihoods, forces populations into the indignity of exile and appropriates their land, it does so not out of its quintessential character but out of an incidental necessity—an accident rather than an essence, as medieval philosophers used to put it. This humanist proposition puts the theorist in the superior position of making excruciating moral choices on behalf of two democratic states and thus ipso facto dehumanizes the object of its analysis—the Palestinian, the Iraqi, the Afghan, the Arab, the Muslim—every colored person who fails to grasp "the civilizing mission of the white man."

Ignatieff makes his case furtively, with a "there had been cases, in Israeli history, where physical methods of interrogation had actually saved lives"[36] here, an "if an interrogator violated the rules and engaged in torture, however, the [Israeli] court was prepared to accept necessity as a plea in mitigation, not as a justification or an excuse"[37] there. Euphemisms such as "physical methods of interrogation" gradually take the place of "torture." By now, Ignatieff's readers may be ready to accept his stipulation that the question is not simply torture but rather that "the problem lies in identifying the justifying exceptions and defining what forms of duress stop short of absolute degradation of an interrogation subject"—that is, how much, when, and where to twist arms, break bones, or pile prisoners naked on top of one another for a picture. Even now we must be careful not to be derailed by this obscenity, because the real atrocity lies in the phrase "an interrogation subject": the prisoner has ceased to be a person with a name, a family, convictions, politics, humanity. He or she is nothing but "an interrogation subject" ready to be tortured at Abu Ghraib or some nameless Israeli site.

But Ignatieff does not stop at dehumanizing the tortured; he must also reassert the primary humanity of the torturer. "A further problem with physical torture," he stipulates "is that it inflicts damage on those who perpetrate it as well as those who are forced to endure it." More specifically, "Torture exposes agents of a democratic state to ultimate moral hazard."[38] The point is that since the torturers belong to the humanity of the "democratic states," they can ultimately pose a threat to "the health of their own societies." While one could argue that torture also damages the torturer, it is perverse, to say the least, to imply any equivalence between the damage inflicted on the torturer and the tortured. He gives too much significance to any hazard there might be to the health and humanity of his fellow citizens in the United States and Israel.

One may deduce (or hope) that the phrase "as well as those who are forced to endure it" at least acknowledges the humanity of the tortured. But such is not the case. The principal problem with torture is not the violation of the victim's humanity but, Ignatieff writes, that "those who are subjected to physical torture, when not actually broken psychologically, usually conceive undying hatred for their torturer."[39] Now we have a problem on our hands—but Ignatieff, as usual, has a handy solution. "One way around this problem, obviously, is to dispose of the tortured, in order to prevent their returning as a threat."[40] How more meticulously premeditated could a criminal act be? To be sure, Ignatieff then insists that the "democratic state" should have nothing to do with such a final solution, because "once torture becomes a state practice, it entrains further consequences that can poison the moral reputation and political legitimacy of a state."[41] But he puts the proposition on the table anyway, while attributing it to such "non-democratic" states as Chile and Argentina in past decades. He fails to mention that CIA agents—"agents of a democratic state," as he calls them—were directly involved in the atrocities in Chile and Argentina (and any number of other strategic countries around the world, including Iran).

It is not enough for Ignatieff to dehumanize the victims of torture (at the very moment when American guards were perpetrating their crimes against humanity at Abu Ghraib). It is not even enough for him to cast them as criminals to begin with who become even more murderous after being tortured. He must go further. Since he finds a "moral hazard" in the act of torture "for everyone involved,"[42] he proposes that "it is worth listening to the testimony of one of torture's victims."[43] At this point in a book about the systematic dehumanization of populations who say no to the imperial hubris of a criminal attempt at empire building, you might reasonably expect to hear the voice of one of them: an Afghan, a Palestinian, an Iraqi—an Arab, a Muslim. Yet again you would be wrong in such an assumption.

The only example that Ignatieff can come up with is "Jean Amery, a Belgian resistant" who was "arrested in Brussels in 1943 for distributing tracts in German urging soldiers of the German occupation to desert. He was tortured by the SS in a Belgian jail in 1943, before being shipped off to Auschwitz."[44] Not an Arab, not a Muslim, not one of the current victims of torture that Ignatieff has dehumanized with George W. Bush and his cabal by labeling them "terrorists." To have a Palestinian tell what it means to be tortured by Israelis in Tel Aviv, or an Iraqi by Americans in Abu Ghraib, or an Afghan by Americans in Kandahar would risk giving them back an iota of their humanity. The small dignity he might restore to thousands of tortured Palestinians, Iraqis, and Afghans at the threshold of the twenty-first century he awards to a Belgian in 1943. The European becomes the voice of the tortured body. Now, if you allow yourself to become angry at and get distracted by Ignatieff's use of the loaded name "Auschwitz" to drum up the memory of the Nazi atrocities and thus lend legitimacy to the Zionist colonial settlement in Palestine, you may miss the far more serious crime he has perpetrated by robbing millions of people around the world of their humanity.

Having systematically dehumanized the whole of humanity, minus those with the honor of living in such liberal democracies as the United States and Israel, Ignatieff identifies Iraq, Burma, and North Korea (his slight variation on George Bush's Iraq-Iran-North Korea "Axis of Evil") as representative of the rest: "For these societies, the practice of torture is definitional of their very identity as forms of state power. This idea helps us to see why torture should remain anathema to a liberal democracy and should never be regulated, countenanced, or covertly accepted in a war on terror."[45] Having just laid out, in detail, exactly the opposite of this bravura conclusion on torture by demonstrating how liberal democracies—"alas"—have to perpetrate it, the finale brings his argument to the level of a manifest destiny and the civilizing mission mandated as the white man's burden. "Definitional" to these societies—that is,. the portion of humanity not blessed to live in Israel and the United States—is the practice of torture, which is what the United States and Israel must face, and this, Ignatieff believes, is no new challenge to the white man. "Terrorism does not present us with a distinctively new temptation. This is what our institutions were designed for, back in the seventeenth century: to regulate evil means and control evil people."[46] The Arabs and Muslims resisting colonial domination of their homeland today thus find themselves placed next to millions of native Americans and African slaves as "evil people" with the "evil means" to disrupt the white man's civilizing mission and destroy his plantations.

As we have seen, if you are careful, it is possible to avoid all the booby traps that Michael Ignatieff has planted, catch him at his game, and force him to expose his hand. Now, let us plant a few booby traps of our own for him.

Suppose that on the evening of July 1, 1946, the British authorities had captured a certain Menachem Begin (the future Prime Minister of Israel), whom they had solid reason to believe was the leader of a terrorist organization called Irgun, and who was about to blow up the King David Hotel in Jerusalem and kill scores of innocent civilians. Suppose that on the evening of April 9, 1948, the Palestinian residents of Deir Yassin had captured a certain Yitzhak Shamir (another future Prime Minister of Israel) and were led to believe he was in possession of vital information about a pending massacre of the residents of their village. Suppose, alternatively, that in December 1947 Palestinians had captured both Begin and Shamir with solid information about pending attacks on Palestinian civilians in villages near Haifa and in Safad, Tabariyya, al-Tireh, Saasa, Kfar Husseiniyya, Sarafand, Kalounya, Beyt Sourik, Aylaboun, al-Shajara, and Nasser al-Dine that would place the lives of thousands of Palestinian men, women, and children in imminent danger. Suppose that in February 1942 the Turkish authorities had just captured Zionist

terrorists who were about to blow up the ship Stroma carrying 770 il-
legal Jewish emigrants. Suppose that, in 1948, the Iraqi authorities had
captured members of Zionist terrorist organizations who were about to
implement the operations they called Ali Baba and Magic Carpet to blow
up Jewish residential areas in Baghdad in order to force the Iraqi Jews
to move to Israel. Just to play the devil's advocate, suppose also that in
autumn 1956 the Palestinian residents of Kfar Kassem and Khan Younis
had captured a member of the Hagana terrorist organization that they
had been led to believe was about to wipe out Palestinian civilians. Suppose that in the early morning hours of October 14, 1953, the Palestinian
residents of the village of Qibya had captured a certain Ariel Sharon (another future Prime Minister of Israel) and were almost sure he was about
to lead his squad on a mission to blow up their houses and murder their
families. Suppose that one fine April day in 1973 Lebanese authorities
captured a suspicious-looking woman and her companion, took them
to a police station in Ras Beirut, and discovered that she was actually a
man in disguise—a certain Ehud Barak (another future Prime Minister
of Israel)—and that he was about to assassinate a number of Palestinian
leaders. The list can go on ad nauseum.

But just for good measure, imagine finally that on the evening of
September 16, 1982, members of the PLO had yet again captured Ariel Sharon and knew that he was about to unleash the savage Lebanese
Phalangists on the two camps of Sabra and Shatila in Beirut, where they
would slaughter hundreds of Palestinian refugees. Now then: under
these circumstances, would Michael Ignatieff consider the possibility
of torturing Menachem Begin, Yitzhak Shamir, Ehud Barak, and Ariel
Sharon and all their terrorist accomplices in what he calls "the liberal
democracy" of the Jewish state of Israel in order to extract information
from them about these particular ticking bombs?

If the renowned terrorists of yesterday are the recent and current
leaders of a "liberal democracy," then what is the difference between
them and the man who once said, "After all, who today speaks of the
extermination of the Armenians?"

Venal, Vagabond, Rootless, and Mercenary

To understand the political climate and the social conditions in which the comprador intellectuals in general and the native informers in particular fermented and emerged in the United States of the neoconservative era, it is imperative not to be limited by the notion of exilic intellectuals as Said understood it, which is effectively a sword and can cut both ways—for every Said there are at least ten Fouad Ajamis. Nor is it sufficient to map out the panoply of rogue American leadership, from George W. Bush on down. We must add a militant cell of neoconservative Zionists (now active, now sleeping)—Irving Kristol, William Kristol, Norman Podhoretz, and their ilk—to the picture, along with such prominent theoreticians as Francis Fukuyama and Samuel Huntington and their kindred spirits Mark Lilla, Alan Dershowitz, and Michael Ignatieff. All this gives us a clearer conception of the calamity that has conditioned the rise of the malady we call native informers, and it all points to a more fundamental malady in the American social condition—historically known as the politics of mass society—that makes it chronically susceptible to intellectual charlatanism.

In his study of the relationship of various social classes to mass societies, *The Politics of Mass Society*, William Kornhauser examined the function of what he called "unattached intellectuals" in facilitating a frenzied atmosphere of fear and domination that is conducive to atomization of individuals—citizens of a republic cut off from the "web of group affiliation,"[47] as the German sociologist Georg Simmel put it, and thus susceptible to populist and fascist movements. Separated from their organic links to their class, community, and nation, these unattached intellectuals "create millennial appeals in response to their own sense of the loss of social function and relatedness in the mass society."[48] Over them hovers an atmosphere of anomie, isolation, disconnectedness, anxiety, and rootlessness. "Free-lance intellectuals," Kornhauser observes, "appear to be more disposed toward mass movements than intellectuals in corporate bodies (especially universities)."[49] He then summarizes:

Five reasons may be advanced for the hypothesis that free-lance intellectuals are more receptive to political extremism than are other types
of intellectuals. First, the free-lance intellectual . . . has been dependent
on an anonymous and unpredictable market. He has had to start his
enterprise anew every generation, and as a result is in an anxiety-arous-
ing position similar to that of the first-generation small businessman.
Much more rooted and culturally integrated are those intellectuals
who enter into old and stable organizations, such as universities. Second, free-lance intellectuals tend to have fewer institutional responsibilities than intellectuals in professional organizations, and therefore
are less likely to be committed to central institutions. Third, rewards
are much less certain to be forthcoming for the free-lance intellectual,
the form of reward less predictable, and the permanence of the recognition more tenuous . . . Fourth, free-lance intellectuals . . . tend to
be more dependent on their audience, over which they have relatively
little control, and to feel greater social distance from it, in contrast to,
for example, the professor in relation to his students. Fifth, free-lance
intellectuals suffer more when there is an over-supply of intellectuals.
In general, a condition of chronic overcrowding of the professions en-
genders large numbers of discontented and alienated intellectuals of
all kinds. This was the situation in Germany following World War I.[50]

It is remarkable to see how applicable Kornhauser's observations,
made in 1950s Germany in the aftermath of the Nazi era, are to the
United States in the neoconservative era. A common thread links Lewis, Ajami, Nafisi, Hirsi Ali, Rushdie, Ibn Warraq, and scores of others
like them as comprador intellectuals. They are all (1) immigrant, (2) either scholars or academics, and (3) intellectuals with close connections
to the US centers of power, and the military establishment in particular.

Equally important in understanding comprador intellectuals are
the insights of Theodor Geiger, who as early as 1949 (and also on the
basis of his observations in Nazi Germany), declared:

Those less qualified aspirants for practical-academic positions, especially those who have not even succeeded in passing their exams,
will attempt to make their way as "free intelligentsia." Journalism was
(and in part still is) a preferred refuge for such types . . . To fill the

demands of a practical-academic profession, a specified and mea-
surable amount of knowledge is required. The entrance into the free
intelligentsia is not subject to such a control. There are no exams or
minimum qualifications.[51]

Kornhauser's insights now need updating to encompass our more
advanced stage of a globally atomized planet over which a predatory
capitalism wishes to preside. Moreover, we cannot share his rather too
sanguine optimism about the tenured professoriate's innate resistance
to the danger of incorporation into the class of rootless or what he calls
"unattached" intellectuals. Though both he and Geiger are correct in
their observation that scholars who have not succeeded in establishing reputable academic credentials are much more likely to become
mercenary intellectuals at the whim of the politics and commerce of
the free-market economy, he disregards a danger of a different sort that
threatens the tenured professoriate. This latter category is obviously
more susceptible to the internal politics of universities, not to mention the external politics of grants and fellowships from both private
and governmental sources.[52] While their institutional affiliations, the
review processes integral to universities, and their tenure all help to
protect them against the political and commercial whims of the free
market, the very same forces are likely to produce minds that, if they do
not exactly serve power, systematically accommodate it.

For this reason, the question of academic freedom is something of
a red herring. The more fundamental question is intellectual freedom,
which is a public concern not limited to the private sphere of the university. Those very few academic intellectuals who venture out of their
classrooms and speak openly and courageously on public issues are, in
fact, the exceptions that prove the rule that academic privatization has
made them not so much complacent as indifferent to power—because
by the time they receive their tenure, bending backward to accommodate power has become second nature to them.

The home-grown comprador intellectuals and the native informers imported from the furthest corners of the empire, white or white-

washed, have joined forces with capital, very much like the mercenary armies that the empire recruits to fight its wars; it is no accident that both Ajami and Nafisi have worked for Paul Wolfowitz or that Vali Reza Nasr and Ray Takeyh have taught at US military colleges. The task of the globalized comprador intellectual is quite clear. The empire needs to destroy all communities and cultures that may be the potential sites of resistance to what Max Weber called "predatory capitalism" and its corresponding planetary (homogenized) culture. The labor is divided between immigrant intellectuals (Ajami, Nafisi, Rushdie, Lewis) and comprador intellectuals native to the empire. But this division of labor disappears in the larger context of an economic and cultural globalization contingent on an amorphous, decentered capitalism and the disappearance of communal, national, and regional cultures, convictions, and principles. The imperial machinery has put them all to work and made them homeless thinkers, the intellectual arm of Blackwater USA.

The current conception of the "terrorist" tends to be a stateless, homeless, cultureless, violent entity set to destroy the "civilized" world—that is, the United States and Israel. And that is precisely the image of the comprador intellectual, and above all the native informer, that has emerged to combat this "terrorist"—equally stateless, homeless, characterless, and cultureless, a "citizen of a portable world."

EMPIRES DO NOT LAST

If empires were permanent, everyone would be speaking Persian now, and I would be writing in my mother tongue. I write, instead, in the mother tongue of somebody else whose ancestors had guns more powerful than Cyrus the Great could ever have imagined. Thus (fortunately), I had to learn another imperial language.

In the remnants of the Persian imperial imagination, however, we have a medieval text, *Chahar Maqaleh-ye Aruzi*, in which a chapter is devoted to poets and their necessity to the smooth operation of a kingdom—or an empire.[53] They sing the praises of the emperor in beautiful and memorable words, which are memorized by the courtiers and through them handed along to the rest of the world. It is not so much that people are ignorant of the emperor's atrocities as that they have fallen prey to the beauty of the poet's lies.

There is a popular twist to this notion in a story told about a court poet who was exceptionally talentless in invention but who had a prodigious gift for memorization. He had to hear a poem only once to know it by heart. His wife had an almost equally amazing memory, but she had to hear the poem twice. Their son had inherited his parents' gift, but he had to hear a poem thrice to remember it. And the household's nearly-as-talented servant had to hear it four times. The entrepreneurial consequence of these four prodigious memories was that whenever a poet came to the court to recite a new poem for the king, the court poet would call him a liar and a plagiarist, and to prove that even the lengthiest poem was his own he would proceed to recite it from beginning to end. Then he would add, "Your Majesty, my wife knows it, too"—and, having now heard it twice, she would recite it, too. Then would follow the son and the servant.

For years, the story goes, no poet in the land could win glory at this notorious court because his poem would be stolen on the spot by this bandit family. Finally, one day a wily poet appeared and declared that he had a new poem for the king. The court gathered, and the new arrival began reciting his poem. Two lines into it he stopped, turned to the court poet, and said, "If this poem is yours, then finish it." Thus was the court poet's charlatanism exposed.

The moral of the story is that even if you can fool everyone once and you can probably fool an emperor all the time, you cannot, in Abraham Lincoln's words, fool all of the people all of the time. The difference between Said's exilic intellectual and the comprador intellectual who has treacherously lurked in the shadow of that very defiant voice is the difference between those two proverbial poets. While they both recite at the court of the emperor, one of them serves his master by consistently repeating a lie, while the other subverts and disrupts that lie by commencing a poem that his rival can neither conceive nor complete. I will leave it to Michael Ignatieff to find out how this particular parable will end. Then he can tell Alan Dershowitz.

Nine

THE DISCRETE CHARM
OF EUROPEAN INTELLECTUALS

I had yet another occasion to visit the issue of intellectuals in 2009 when the Green Movement in Iran began and Slavoj Žižek wrote an essay on the matter. Here again I was thinking of Edward Said and the difference between him and Žižek and the manner in which they wrote and reflected on world affairs. The essay first appeared in International Journal of Žižek Studiese *3, no. 4 (2009). I include it here as an indication of how thinking with, through, and beyond Said enables us to sustain a critical course of reflection on vital issues of our time, rooted in his unsurpassed critical consciousness and yet branching out into uncharted territories.*

> *One morning, as Gregor Samsa was waking up from anxious dreams, he discovered that in his bed he had been changed into a monstrous verminous bug.*
> —**Kafka,** *The Metamorphosis* (1915)

The idea of Slavoj Žižek waking up one morning from anxious dreams and discovering that in his bed he had been metamorphosed into a Shi'i Muslim and catapulted into the rambunctious capital of an Islamic Republic is quite wickedly intriguing. Whoever put him up to that idea? "What's happened to me," he would wonder like the good old Gregor Samsa, as his bewildered gaze would turn to the window and notice the dreary weather—the raindrops falling audibly down on the metal window ledge in Evin Prison in Tehran, making him quite melancholic for his comfortable apartment in his native Ljubljana. I can well imagine Žižek in those prison pajamas, sitting next to an array of Iranian reformists, wishing he were only there in name and spirit, like Max Weber, Jürgen Habermas, or even Richard Rorty. But here he was, in person, in Tehran, jailed and charged with having plotted a velvet revolution to topple the Islamic Republic. With your permission though I will only imagine Professor Žižek in Evin Prison and not in Kahrizak, for given what the custodians of the Islamic Republic have been doing to their inmates in that particular detention center it would be quite disconcerting, if not outright disrespectful, to imagine the leading European intellectual under those circumstances.

After Michel Foucault terribly misread the Iranian Revolution of 1979, wrote a few quite curious articles for *Corriere della Sera,* and kept his admirers and detractors busy and confounded for over some thirty odd years, we have had no prominent European philosopher collecting his courage, mustering his wits, and crossing that proverbial psychological barrier to say something sensible about those Muslim Orientals the way Žižek did recently about the postelectoral violence in Tehran. This was a good thing to have happened under circumstances when American neoliberals and neoconservatives had joined forces, patting Iranians on the back for their knowledge of Nabokov and Habermas alike—all in the condescending and custodial tone of "now, ain't that cute, they are reading *Lolita* and *Legitimation Crisis* in Tehran." In no uncertain terms, bless his soul, and at a time when what in North America and Western Europe passes for "the Left" was quite baffled as to how to respond to the mid-June uprising in Iran, Žižek came out and brushed them all aside and defended our cause, all in a clear and confident prose. We— the native sons and daughters, as Richard Wright would say about us colored folks from Chicago's South Side to Iran's southern provinces— were quite happy to welcome the dandy, groovy, and cool philosopher in our midst.

This was no "orange" revolution Georgia-style, Žižek told Europeans; nor was it a neoliberal-democratic secular uprising. He countered those who thought "Ahmadinejad really won: [that] he is the voice of the majority, while the support of Mousavi comes from the middle classes and their gilded youth."[1] He dismissed those "who dismiss Mousavi as a member of the cleric establishment with merely cosmetic differences from Ahmadinejad," and above all he denounced "the saddest of them all [who] are the Leftist supporters of Ahmadinejad: what is really at stake for them is Iranian independence. Ahmadinejad won because he stood up for the country's independence, exposed elite corruption and used oil wealth to boost the incomes of the poor majority—this is, so we are told, the true Ahmadinejad beneath the Western-media image of a Holocaust-denying fanatic." He missed a couple of crucial characters who also championed Ahmadinejad's cause—failed academics and career opportunists who seized upon their chance to cash in on the beleaguered "President's" need for someone with half-decent English to rush to CNN to defend his cause, or else deeply alienated second generation Iranians growing up in suburban North America and rushing to Tehran and Isfahan to discover their roots in Ahmadinejad's deep pocket and take a stance against "Western decadence" and its "liberal democracy." It was and it remains quite a pathetic scene. But we thought Žižek was quite eloquent in sorting things out and setting the record straight.

We all read all those wise, timely, and true words and admired the big old funny philosopher and thought he deserved all those accolades coming his way, including a whole *International Journal of Žižek Studies*, no less, and being dubbed "the Elvis of Philosophy." How could he be so smart and know all these things? Europe may not be literally the creation of the Third World after all, as Fanon suspected, and "Western civilization" does indeed sound like a good idea, as Gandhi conjectured.

The analytic becomes a bit blearier, however, when Žižek comes to his own assessment of what's happening in Iran. "The green colors adopted by the Mousavi supporters and the cries of 'Allahu Akbar!' that resonated from the roofs of Tehran in the evening darkness," he surmised, "suggested that the protesters saw themselves as returning to the roots of the 1979 Khomeini revolution, and canceling out the corruption that followed it." What happened, how, and by what authority? How did Žižek make that conclusion? Just from the color green? Wow! That is some serious *Farbenlehre*! How can we, mere mortals, make that transcontinental assumption, that thirty years after the Islamized revolution of 1977–79, this new generation wishes to go back and relive that experience—and saying so on the basis of two floating signifiers of a color (green) and a chant (*Allahu akbar*)? No, sir! It makes no sense. So the question is: who was the native informer who thus misinformed the European philosopher? For that is precisely how Foucault was mishandled by his handlers when he was chaperoned to Tehran in 1979— some Islamist activists got hold of him and kept feeding him food to theorize.

Žižek provides more evidence: "This was evident in the way the crowds behaved: the emphatic unity of the people, their creative self-organization and improvised forms of protest, the unique mixture of spontaneity and discipline. Picture the march: thousands of men and women demonstrating in complete silence. This was a genuine popular uprising on the part of the deceived partisans of the Khomeini revolution." This is all partially apt and impartially accurate. But how does it amount to these demonstrators wishing to go back thirty years ago and no longer being "the deceived partisans of the Khomeini revolution"? Logic? It does not add up. What we were witnessing was a genuine, grassroots, social uprising (in part spontaneous, in part *the logical growth* and in fact the forbidden fruits of a crescendo of events that began thirty years ago and thus by definition cannot be a going back to thirty years ago)—but whence and how the assumption of a retrograde, nostalgic return to the fetal position of the nascent revolution? Shouldn't in fact "the improvised forms of protest" (a very apt description) alert the philosopher that we have had, perhaps, a massive generational shift, an epistemic shift even (occasioned by the narrative exhaustion of ideological legacies, exacerbated by the internet, computer literacy, and cyberspace social networking) after which there is no illegal/illogical U-turn?

I am, to be sure, completely on the same page with Žižek when he rightly says, "We should contrast the events in Iran with the US intervention in Iraq: an assertion of popular will on the one hand, a foreign imposition of democracy on the other"; or when he asserts that "the events in Iran can also be read as a comment on the platitudes of Obama's Cairo speech, which focused on the dialogue between religions: no, we don't need a dialogue between religions (or civilizations), we need a bond of political solidarity between those who struggle for justice in Muslim countries and those who participate in the same struggle elsewhere." I so wish Žižek had written Obama's Cairo speech, instead of Rahm Emanuel (or whoever else helped him write it). But none of this provides evidence that those who were demonstrating wanted to relive their parents' lives thirty years ago. No, sir! If anything, they were (all the indications suggested that they were) sick and tired of that revolutionary zeal and political animus, and were in fact holding their parents responsible for the calamity they had found themselves in, hanging over their heads the banality of the idea of an Islamic republic, or even worse a *Velayat-e Faqih* (the juridical authority of Grand Ayatollah). So still the mystery persists—how in the world did Žižek conclude that these masses of demonstrators were seeking a return to thirty years ago? The man is a philosopher, must have studied logic—so where is the 2+2 that equals this particular 4?

I am also (almost entirely) with Žižek when he rightly says that "Ahmadinejad is not the hero of the Islamist poor, but a corrupt Islamofascist populist, a kind of Iranian Berlusconi whose mixture of clownish posturing and ruthless power politics is causing unease even among the ayatollahs," though I wish he had reconsidered that "Islamofascist" bit— for it exposes his Eastern European angst of out-Western-Europeanizing Western European anxieties more than it reveals anything about Iran. Iran is not fascism, though fascism has always threatened Iran. Islam is an abstraction, as much capable or abhorrent of fascism as Judaism and Christianity—and I have not heard of any talk about "Judeofascism" six-ty years after the Zionist armed robbery of Palestine, or "Hindufascism," for that matter, after any of the Hindu slaughters of Muslims in India. Be that as it may, Žižek has me on his side when he says, "His [Ahmadine-jad's] demagogic distribution of crumbs to the poor shouldn't deceive us: he has the backing not only of the organs of police repression and a very Westernized PR apparatus. He is also supported by a powerful new class of Iranians who have become rich thanks to the regime's cor-ruption—the Revolutionary Guard is not a working-class militia, but a mega-corporation, the most powerful center of wealth in the coun-try." *Chapeau*—as some Francophone Lebanese say on such occasions! But, yet again that nagging "but," the assumption that if you are poor you are gullible and for Ahmadinejad, or you don't see through his incompe-tence and chicaneries, that you have no dream, no democratic aspiration for your homeland, is positively disconcerting to come from an other-wise progressive European philosopher. I know of quite a number of rich second-generation Iranians, grown up in suburban North America, who are totally taken by the Darvishi demeanor and lumpenism of the demagogue infinitely more than any poor person from southern Tehran would. But, hey, what can you do—but move on?

Žižek, again, loses me completely when he declares that:

> We have to draw a clear distinction between the two main candidates opposed to Ahmadinejad, Mehdi Karroubi and Mousavi. Karroubi is, effectively, a reformist, a proponent of an Iranian version of identity politics, promising favors to particular groups of every kind. Mousa-vi is something entirely different: he stands for the resuscitation of the popular dream that sustained the Khomeini revolution. . . . Now

is the time to remember the effervescence that followed the revolution, the explosion of political and social creativity, organizational experiments and debates among students and ordinary people. That this explosion had to be stifled demonstrates that the revolution was an authentic political event, an opening that unleashed altogether new forces of social transformation: a moment in which "everything seemed possible." What followed was a gradual closing-down of possibilities as the Islamic establishment took political control. To put it in Freudian terms, today's protest movement is the "return of the repressed" of the Khomeini revolution.[2]

"Closing down of possibilities" might be a fine euphemistic way of saying how Khomeini & Co. brutally suppressed alternative voices that wanted to have a say in the aftermath of the revolution—but the revolution itself, what occasioned these possibilities, was no meteor coming at Iran from the heavens. It was in the making for some two hundred years—and it was polyvocal from the outset. Khomeini aborted a full delivery of a healthy and robust republic and delivered a mismatched twin called "Islamic Republic," topped by an authoritarian doctrine called Velayat-e Faqih. What is happening today in Iran, as a result, is the full-bodied, material, symbolic, discursive, and institutional historicity of the multifaceted Iranian cosmopolitanism (that just remembering it makes you cringe with anger against these neoliberal Americans who think they have discovered an earth-shattering phenomenon that Iranians read Habermas!) finally bursting out of the tight and unbecoming medieval jurisprudence that was violently clothed around it.

Unless we begin where we must begin, upstream from the violent over-Islamization of the 1979 revolution in the course of the American hostage crisis of 1979–80 and the Iran-Iraq War of 1980–88, a fact that Žižek's precursor, Foucault, terribly failed to see, we are bound to fall into Žižek's trap of cyclical historiography, which in our case amounts to a vicious circle, spinning after our own tail, chasing after yet another charismatic father figure we want to follow to kill by way of our version of what Freud called "deferred obedience," which in our case is actually "deferred defiance." That cyclical historiography also prevents you from seeing the nature of *leadership* in this movement and misleads you to come up with flawed assessments of people like Mousavi, Karroubi, or Khatami. Both Karroubi and Mousavi, and before them Khatami, are the product of this movement; this movement is not the product of their visions and leadership. If we begin with any kind of typological contradistinction between Karroubi and Mousavi in reading this movement, we will end up on a goose chase, or worse (better metaphor) yet, chasing like a puppy after our own tail, trying to figure out this movement. This movement invented a Mousavi, crafted a Karroubi, and envisioned a Khatami out of its deepest visions for a different future, which means killing its future father figures at the very beginning by splitting them into at least three alternates, and thus celebrating its own boastful bastardy—once and for all for Sohrab to outwit Rostam and set his mother Tahmineh and the rest of us free.

Let's not get too carried away with Persian mythology, lest we lose the European philosopher, and return to his familiar turf and simply suggest that instead of a Freudian "return of the repressed" in this particular case, we are better off with a Jungian "collective unconscious."

There is something about the Green Movement that prompts Žižek toward the Freudian "return of the repressed," except it is not repressed, for what we have is a perfectly alert and conscious attempt at the retrieval of the violently denied cosmopolitan political culture of a people that was militantly "repressed" (not in the Freudian psychoanalytic sense but in the Khomeinian political terms of sending club-wielding thugs to close down your newspaper and beat up your editorial staff so you would shut up and be quiet and not utter a word against the violent over-Islamization of a multifaceted revolution). But Žižek's preference for Mousavi over Karroubi, and the way he talks about him, gives me a nagging suspicion that his native informer must have been a pro-Mousavi activist who set the European philosopher off on the same wrong track that Foucault was on by his overzealous Islamist activists. Now, as someone who actually voted for Mousavi, I have nothing against that particular presidential candidate, but not to the point of collapsing the analytic of the phenomenon we are now facing into yet another cult of personality, to which we Orientals (so we seem to our European Orientalists) are particularly prone.

It is upon this Freudian slip, as it were, that Žižek then falls down like that very cat he invokes early in his essay, and just like that cat, he does not immediately notice it: "What all this means is that there is a genuinely liberatory potential in Islam: we don't have to go back to the tenth century to find a 'good' Islam, we have it right here, in front of us." Here, Žižek in fact picks up precisely where Foucault left off—concurring with the militant over-Islamization of a worldly and polyvocal political culture, and then seeing an emancipatory force emanating from it. While Foucault saw this as the very "soul" of a soulless world that Marx had prophesied, Žižek sees it as a warning to "the West" that unless they see Ahmadinejad for the charlatan that he is, Berlusconi and even worse is what it is in the offing for his fellow Europeans. The result, yet again, is all the same: Iran, Islam, as the rest of the world, is just a laboratory for testing the maladies that are threatening "the West." One might even trace this particular proclivity back to Max Weber himself, who begins his diagnosis of capitalist modernity with a reading of the Protestant ethics and "Western nationalism" and ends up in an Iron Cage that can only be broken down by chronic charismatic outburst. Fortunately for him, Weber was not alive to see Hitler and the Holocaust coming his particular German/European way, though he (and even before him Tocqueville) certainly saw them coming. In the European context, and in the aftermath of the horrors of the Holocaust, at least Adorno and Horkheimer saw to it that the dangerous instrumentalization of reason, written into the dialectics of the Enlightenment, was fully exposed for Europe. But the same old nostalgia for charismatic outbursts (and thus Žižek's jaw-dropping "[but] Mousavi is something entirely different") seems to have transmuted into European philosophical fascination with bearded or bespectacled third-world revolutionary prophets—at the heavy cost (for us) of helping distort our cosmopolitan worldliness, to which our religions are certainly integral but by no means definitive.

The problem with the European Left is that they care a little bit about just about everything, and yet there is nothing in particular about which they care deeply. This is very similar to what my old teacher Philip Rieff used to call "the Monroe Doctrine"—not the famous President James Monroe doctrine of warning Europeans to keep their hands off the Americas, but the little known Marilyn Monroe doctrine, named after the famous actress for having once said, "I believe in everything" and then pausing for a moment before saucily adding, "a little bit." The difference between European and colonial intellectuals is summed up in the difference between Sartre and Fanon, or between Foucault and Said. Sartre and Foucault cared widely about the entirety of the colonial and colonizing world, while Fanon and Said cared deeply about Algeria and Palestine, and from these two sites of contestation they extrapolated their politics and ethics of responsibility toward the rest of the world. Žižek is precisely in the same tradition and trajectory as Sartre and Foucault—caring widely but not deeply enough, for (and here is the philosophical foregrounding of their political proclivity for vacuous abstractions) they know widely and variedly but never deeply and particularly. What passes for the Left in the United States is even worse. Since they have seen me (as one example among many) preoccupied with Iran, they think I have compromised my stand vis-à-vis American imperialism or its Israeli colonial outpost—for they too care in abstraction and act in generalities. I am preoccupied with Iran in 2009 precisely in the same way I have been with Iraq since 2003, and with Afghanistan since 2001 (when the best of these Americans thought Afghanistan was a "just war") and precisely the same way I have been with Palestine all my adult life: the site of specific crimes against humanity opens up your frame to see the rest of the world.

There is something charming about the European intellectuals when bored with nothing happening in Europe and turning their theorizing gaze beyond the banks of the Danube River. That antiquarian charm hangs over the memory of the Europe of our youth when we colored folks sought to sustain the hope with which we have been born and bred. Kafka concludes his *Metamorphosis* with a happy ending to Gregor Samsa's demise, when Mr. and Mrs. Samsa notice how much their young daughter Grete has grown up and become a "good looking, shapely" girl. Thinking to themselves that "the time was now at hand to seek out a good honest man for her. And it was something of a confirmation of their new dreams and good intentions when at the end of their journey their daughter stood up first and stretched her young body." The same is with the tall and handsome body of Žižek's fine essay on Iran, an indication that the European philosopher is finally ready to get up and move and wed his piercing intelligence to a singular cause, stop the promiscuous philandering with generalities, and learn the honesty of a monogamous commitment to one moral site. Who was it who said, "O Plato! I can see horse, but not horseness"? Bless his soul! There used to be something worldly and exciting about European indulgence in generalities they call "Philosophy," which now seems only so irresistibly charming the way one might feel about an old armchair sitting idly by at a marché folklorique in an old European town off the shores of Lac Leman. Yea—I do sometimes miss them!

No—come to think of it I wish never to see Professor Žižek in any of those unseemly prison pajamas at Evin in Tehran. It would be so unbecoming of our old Oriental ways to put a prominent philosopher on display like that. Let's wait for a few years—hopefully this Green Movement will become a *vanishing mediator* and we will all be able to give him a warm welcome at Tehran University.

Ten

THE NAME THAT ENABLES

REMEMBERING EDWARD SAID

I wrote this essay on September 25, 2013, on the occasion of the tenth anniversary of Edward Said's passing. It first appeared on Al Jazeera *as one of my regular columns and was subsequently cited in multiple other sites. By then a decade had passed since Edward left us. History was beginning to set in. We were able to find our whereabouts in the neighborhood of his memories. He had become a memory.*

> *Stop all the clocks . . . let the mourners come.*
>
> **—W. H. Auden**

The common leitmotif of writing on the milestone anniversary of a friend's passing is a strong element of nostalgia—how wonderful things were when he was alive and how sad that he is no more. This element of nostalgia becomes even stronger when the fallen friend is a towering intellectual figure whose voice and vision were definitive to an age that now seems almost irreversibly altered. When the

167

site of that dramatic alteration is the home and habitat of that colleague, with Palestine as its epicenter and the larger Arab and Muslim world all gathering momentum around it, the act of remembrance becomes positively allegorical.

This September, we mark the tenth anniversary of Said's passing at a time when the entire Arab world is in turmoil and Palestine is being stolen even more savagely by the hour. As a community of his friends, comrades, and colleagues, we actively remember his voice, his vision, and his steadfast determination to lead our causes around the globe. But how is it exactly that he still shows the way a decade after his silence?

The fact is that when today I think of Said and the more than a decade that I was fortunate to know him personally as a friend and a colleague here at Columbia, my paramount feeling is not a sense of loss—but a sense of suspension. Some people, it seems to me, never die for those whose moral and political imagination is organically rooted in their living memory. For me at least, the temporal timber of our politics has frozen ever since that fateful morning of September 24, 2003, when Joseph Massad called me to say Edward had taken his last breath. I had just received the news of my own younger brother Aziz having passed away—so the sense of loss of a brother, of two brothers, a younger and an older brother, is frozen in time for me, framed as it were on a mantelpiece that defines the focal point of where I can call home.

I have written a few pieces specifically on Said's passing, my immediate thoughts and feelings when he passed away, and then my travelogue to Palestine, from which trip I brought back a fistful of dust from a sanctified cemetery of the Prophet's companions in Jerusalem near the Dome of the Rock to take to Brummana in Lebanon and place it on Edward's last resting place, and then another piece that his widow Mariam Said had asked me to write for a small circulation volume when we were having a memorial for him at Columbia in March 2004.

But none of those pieces have been able to put anything resembling a full stop at the end of my moral, imaginative, political, and scholarly engagements with Said. They are far less about who Said was than what he enabled me to become. I now read them more like various punctuation marks in my evolving conversations with his enduring memory. After Phillip Rieff and George Makdisi, the two towering intellectual figures whose gracing shadows bend over every sentence I write, Said is sitting next to my laptop, as always dashingly well-dressed, inquisitive, playful, and determined all at the same time, wondering what I am cooking.

CITING SAID

Much has happened since Said's passing—and on too many occasions we have all thought what would he have said if he were with us today—particularly when the Arab revolutions started. What would he have said of the carnage in Syria, of the coup in Egypt, of the NATO bombing of Libya, of the revolution in Tunis—and above all of the continued barefaced armed robbery of Palestine?

Though he is no longer here to share his thoughts, he has done enough to enable us to think with him. Certain towering intellectuals become integral to the very alphabet of our moral and political imagination. They no longer need to be here physically for you to know what they might have thought or said or written. They live in those who read and think them through—and thus they become indexical, proverbial, to our thinking.

Said lived so fully, so consciously, so critically through the thick and thin of our times that he is definitive to our critical thinking, just like Marx, or Freud, or Fanon, or Du Bois, or Malcolm X are. They are the sound with which we sing, the sight with which we see, the aroma with which we smell things, definitive to the intuition of our transcendence.

On many occasions I would run into Said on our campus while I had a conversation with him in my mind, and as soon as I saw him I just continued with that mental conversation out loud. And he seemed to do the same—he would just abruptly say something, as if we had a conversation started long before we saw each other on campus. That sense of suspended and continued conversation is still very much alive and running—perhaps it is a state of denial, perhaps the fact that thinkers like Said are epistemic to our thinking, a time-lapsed dosage of themselves that keep unpacking themselves.

I don't think I can mourn Said as long as I live, if mourning is a ritual of reconciliation with a loss, for I don't believe my kind of conversations with him are ever over. I still live in the same block where he and his family lived for decades. I still run into his widow Mariam once in a while almost exactly on the same spots I used to run into him.

I still read his books and essays with his voice in my ear, and am still moved by the joy and anger of his principles on the bone marrow of my own politics. I have traveled quite a distance from where Said was in terms of his literary and historical theories, for I had also started from different vantage points from where he did. But I think him in my own thoughts, feel him in my own sentiments, and echo him in my own politics. I feel at home with him almost exactly the same way he was at home anywhere, slightly out of place, having come to similar (but not identical) conclusions as he did, but from different embarkations and looking at adjacent shores. He was an enabler, not a guru. He did not replicate himself. His friends became more of themselves by his virtue.

Towering intellects like Said or Fanon or Césaire enable you in your own voice, and making sure you never repeat but extend them, expostulate their logic, domestic their politics to their own rhetoric, navigate unchartered territories with their compass but not their itinerary. To me, it is impossible to be a Saidian or a Fanonite, for they were so particular in their universalities that could not but trigger your own particularities awaiting their own intuition of transcendence.

A New Intellectual Organicity

With the death of Said, we immigrant intellectuals ceased to be immigrant and became native to a new organicity. We are the fulfilments of his battles. He theorized himself to be out of place so timely and so punctiliously, so that after him we are no longer out of place, at home wherever we can hang our hats and say no to power.

After Said there are no native, no national, no international, no first world, no second, no first or third world intellectuals. Battlefields of ideas are site specific and global. You cannot wage any battle at any local level without simultaneously registering it globally. If you are not global, you are not local, and if you are not local, you are not global.

The most boring and irrelevant intellectuals are those who think the United States, Iran, India, or North Pole are the center of the universe. The universe has no center, no periphery. We are all free-floating. Said was very site specific about Palestine—and thereby he made the Palestinian predicament a metaphysical allegory, and he grounded it in the physical agony and heroism of his people.

It is meaningless after Said to speak of "exilic intellectuals," precisely because he so thoroughly theorized the category for his own age. There is no home from which to be exiled. The capital and the empire that wishes but fails to micromanage it are everywhere. There is no exit from this world, and home and exile are illusions that late capital and the conditions of empire have dismantled.

The new intellectual organicity that Said enabled requires that you roll up your sleeves and get down and dirty, so that in the midst of chaos you can seek solace; of darkness, light; of despair, hope.

MISSING SAID

There are times that I do not even miss Said for, in an enduring sense, he has never left us. You think your phone will ring and it is he calling to chat about one thing or another, or that you will run into him on campus, or that his name will appear in your inbox. I don't miss him because I think I am still not quite done talking, arguing, agreeing, disagreeing, confiding in him. He is always there—there in the midst of a haze of happiness and despair that agitates and endears all his writings.

And then there are times, especially in the heart of the very early morning darkness when I habitually get up and start reading and writing only a few buildings away from where he used to live and do the same, that I suddenly sense the weight of his absence, the hollowed presence of his absence, the aura and audibility of his voice, the inquisitive frivolity of his gaze, his always speaking with you directly, pointedly, specifically, and yet from the rested assurances of distantly assured seashores he had seen. It is the accidentality of those encounters, just as I turn the corner of 116th and Broadway that I suddenly see him coming—"you and your postmodernity," he would tease me, and as I was about to protest, "don't you worry, I invented the vocabulary!"

He loved to add an entirely superfluous *shadda* to the middle of my last name and pronounce it not just with two but it seems five or six extra Bs. "He is not even an Arab," he would say tongue in cheek, when praising me to his friends and family. Countless memories, voicemails, emails, casual encounters, planned collaborations, formal academic occasions connect my life at Columbia to Said, and I live them all in my mind and play with them happily in my soul every single day of my life, for as long as I live, for as long as I am able to think, to remember, recollect, rethink him in my own thought.

I have a mental picture of Said that is increasingly fading in my mind, and the more it gets faded the more actively I remember it. It was April 28, 2003. We were all in Swarthmore College in Pennsylvania to celebrate the poetry of Mahmoud Darwish, who had just received the Lannan Cultural Freedom Prize. At the end of the ceremony, Said, Massad, and I went to pay a visit to our friend and colleague Magda al-Nowaihi who was on her deathbed and would soon die of cancer. Magda was lying on her bed, a shimmering shadow of herself, but her paradisiac smile still mapping her beautiful face. I cannot recall a word that was said by anyone around that bed—only a mental picture, frozen, freezing, a fresco carved on the deepest wall of my memories, and upon it the three faces of Magda, Edward, and Joseph now shine more brightly.

"Perhaps," Levinas once wrote, "the names of persons whose *saying* signifies a face—proper names, in the middle of all these common names and commonplaces—can resist the dissolution of meaning and help us to speak." It is in that sense that the name, the persona, and the memory we call "Edward Said" is definitive to the sense and purpose of the moment when I sign my name over or under this homage and call myself by a proper name.

Eleven

ORIENTALISM TODAY

A CONVERSATION

In 2017 I was invited to Geneva by Mohammad-Mahmoud Ould Mohame-dou, a professor of international history at the Graduate Institute, Geneva, Switzerland. The following conversation took place in Geneva in the course of that conference with Professor Mohamedou. It was taped on video. I am grateful to my assistant Laila Hisham Fouad for transcribing it. The central significance of Edward Said's Orientalism *(1978) was of course now proverbial in multiple disciplines. In my own scholarly work I had repeatedly returned to it in various ways. My* Post-Orientalism: Knowledge and Power in Time of Terror *(2008) is the most sustained engagement with that seminal text. This conversation, however, posed questions by a younger generation of scholars who were reading it afresh and asking more urgent question about a text to which my generation was perhaps too close.*

Mahmoud Mohamedou: Professor Hamid Dabashi, many thanks for taking the time to speak with us today on the question of Orientalism.

Hamid Dabashi: My pleasure!

MM: It's been almost forty years ago now that Edward Said published this central and paradigm-shifting work. Often we speak of works that change our ways of understanding knowledge or regions, and it seems that this has really made a mark in many ways, not only in the region of the Middle East and more generally the Islamic world, but it has very much influenced postcolonial studies more broadly in other places.

HD: True.

MM: So what can we take fundamentally in terms of the importance, historically, of the work that Said published at the time . . .

HD: I think you mentioned the key word, it is epistemic-shifting. Up until the publication of Said's *Orientalism*, we didn't know how do we know what we know. What he managed to do—he made us conscious of the instrumentality of this, for example, camera, that what your audience, your students will later see from our conversation is through that camera. So Said made us conscious of the instrumentality of modes of knowledge production and interest in knowledge production.

As you know there were people before Said who, like Anwar Abdul-Malek, like Talal Asad—four years before the publication of *Orientalism* he wrote a fantastic essay in an edited volume, *Anthropology and the Colonial Encounter*, and more or less he says the same thing.[1] But Said did it with such literary panache, and power and authority . . . and also remember historically the writing of *Orientalism* happens between the two wars of 1967 and 1973, and he says in an interview that this is the environment in which he wrote the book.

MM: Why is that important?

HD: Because as Said says in an interview, he had noticed as a young professor at Columbia University how the perception of Arabs and the fight with Israel began to change between 1967 and 1973 and so forth, and he became fascinated with this change of perception, which defines the nature of Orientalism that he subsequently did. You know Said was not a historian, he was a literary theorist—a genius literary theorist—a monumental figure in literary theory. So *Orientalism* is from the perspective of literary mimesis, of representation, who gets to represent whom—and by what authority, and how that representation changes.

Back in the 1950s Raymond Schwab had written a book on Orientalism, *La Renaissance Orientale*, but none of them had the impact of Said. Again, partially because by then Foucault had become known, and Said's notion of Orientalism heavily borrows from Foucault's relation of knowledge and power. So there are many reasons that locate Said's *Orientalism* back in 1978 when it was published that resonated with a generation of young scholars. Now I'm not one of those scholars, because when I read *Orientalism* in graduate school at Penn, I had already read, I was deep into the sociology of knowledge, so Max Scheler tells you there's a me before an I. So the proposition that there is a correspondence between colonialism and knowledge production was not a big deal.

But, what became a big deal for a generation slightly younger than me when they began to realize that there is something the matter with the manner of knowledge production, that there is power involved in the modes of knowledge production, there is a process of canonization—who gets to choose what is the canon. So from the epistemology of knowledge to the idiomaticity of knowledge being produced, to the institutions that produce knowledge—all this became an issue, and as a result became the reasons for its success. But another reason is that Said's *Orientalism* enables you—as all great works of the scholarship in theory do—to disagree with him. When a book is able to do that, that book has guaranteed its success.

MM: Indeed it does. And I think it's precisely its richness that it offers this possibility to think, reflect, disagree . . . and work with as an intellectual tool.

HD: Exactly.

MM: Now we tend to forget a little but today because it has been so successful in helping us shift our ways of thinking, but at the time, the reaction to it, in some sectors, was quite violent. Reading now some of the correspondence in the *New York Review of Books* with Bernard Lewis and many others, one can see also that this resistance, and I think this is literally the term one should apply—intellectual resistance or power, politics resistance—has stayed with us as well. What is the reason for that?

HD: First of all, up until recently the same sources and institutions of knowledge production that continue to produce knowledge and establish it as truth, they haven't ceased, they have metamorphosed. And as a result, the terms *Orientalism* and *Orientalist* have become catchwords to point to the relation between knowledge and power. So who finances what for what reasons. Some of those exchanges in fact with Bernard Lewis that followed the publication of *Orientalism* in my opinion were counterproductive for our understanding of Orientalism. Orientalism is basically a critique of epistemology. It is a critique of knowledge production. In Said's exchanges with Bernard Lewis, this became enmeshed with the Arab-Israeli conflict, and Said (as you know) was a very passionate defender of the Palestinian cause—and rightly so—the most significant spokesman of the Palestinian cause abroad. And as a result, it did some, in my opinion, enduring damage for us to deal with. In *Orientalism,* Said doesn't say Orientalists are evil people—it is a critique of a mode of knowledge production. So we have to in a way bypass and bracket aside—you know, given our own politics on Palestine we've become enmeshed in that debate. We have to bracket it, we put it aside . . .

MM: Yes, it's a side issue.

HD: It is a side issue with which we have a position. But going back to *Orientalism*: [We need to] look at the critique of knowledge production, and do what Said didn't do—namely historicize it, because Said was not a historian. Go to the period . . . in one sentence Said says

Aeschylus's *Persian*, Dante's *Divine Comedy*, and [then alludes to] . . . something contemporary. He is at the moment of revelation, he is at the moment that he is telling us something we didn't know, so he is allowed to do all of these conflations. But as the next generations, we need to historicize and realize that in the aftermath of Said's publication of *Orientalism*, and because Orientalism was coterminous with classical colonialism and its modes of knowledge production, during the Cold War, we didn't have that similar kind of knowledge production. Because now, you have departments of Middle Eastern and Near Eastern and Far Eastern studies, or Soviet studies, or Eastern European studies. All of these departments were actually like a belt around the Soviet Union . . .

MM: Area studies generally . . .

HD: Exactly. So there is a transfusion, as I argue in my book *Post-Orientalism*, between Orientalism and area studies.[2] Now, the same sentiments of knowledge and power exist in the period of area studies. But then the question is: what happens after the collapse of the Soviet Union? Well, departments of area studies become irrelevant—epistemically they become irrelevant. What emerges are these think tanks in Washington, DC.

MM: So precisely, to follow that, now your own work in continuing, not so much a tradition, but as I think you precisely said an intellectual invitation to think and rethink. You then come to work with this. Of course you knew Said and you worked with him. But your own work as a thinker on these issues comes in the second generation in which you take the concept, I think to, precisely as you said to historicize it and add to it.

HD: Yes.

MM: But I think it is also made even more interesting because the context itself of the early 2000s and the late 1990s gives us a bit of a neo-imperial moment, which is the stuff for you to work with.

HD: That is because imperialism as you rightly said is a living organism. It is not stable. I always say when the World Trade Center was attacked, "World Trade Center" was a misnomer, for the world trade has no center. It is all over, 24/7. Because capitalism has become amorphous. First of all, imperialism has become amorphous because capital has become amorphous. Capital is amorphous, imperialism is amorphous, and knowledge production is amorphous. You could have think tanks in Doha, Qatar, you can have them in Saudi Arabia, you can have them anywhere. They're part of amorphous, decentered modes of knowledge production to sustain the power that exists, but that power itself is not self-conscious, it's like a wild animal. It is not just sitting in a smoke-filled room, deciding things. It doesn't have a form and as a result wants to invade Afghanistan, it goes to a think tank and asks, "Okay, what is the language, what is the anthropology, how do we do that?" And the advantage of think tanks is, contrary to you and I who are accountable to an academic tradition, if we say something embarrassing, our colleagues, our students etc., they hold us accountable, but not in think tanks. Fouad Ajami says, "Go to Iraq—invade. They will love you, and throw baklava at you, and rosewater . . .

MM: It's part of this new mode of . . .

HD: Exactly, they go—I call it disposable knowledge in my book *Post-Orientalism*. It's not a knowledge that you hold accountable. I mean classical Orientalism; they were masters of languages . . .

MM: Much more rigorous.

HD: Much more rigorous, and they spoke to the history of Orientalism. But not this generation. My point is one should not fetishize the insight of Said. One must learn from it, and then unfold it as we move on. As imperialism changes, modes of knowledge change, agencies of knowledge production change, institutions of knowledge production change. Then you look at this—today, in 2017, if you live in the United States, and I'm sure as you know also in Europe, no longer is Islam a subject of knowledge. They don't want to understand Islam. If you look at the culmination that has come to Steve Bannon, there is a kind of Christian eschatological triumphalism. They want to destroy Islam. Islam is the enemy. That is wholly different from generations that wanted to understand Islam, and they produced a kind of Islam—an understanding of Islam that was compatible with colonialism. But today, in the age of Trump and Steve Bannon, there is no attempt to understand Islam.

MM: Well, many thanks for this.

HD: My pleasure.

Twelve

His Unconquerable Soul

Translating Said into Another Key

The following is the original unpublished essay I wrote as an introduction to the Persian translation of Edward Said's "Last Interview" (2000). In May 2017 I was invited to write this introductory essay by the translator of that iconic interview, Azim Tahmasbi. He subsequently translated my essay into Persian and in October 2018 published it along with his translation of Said's "Last Interview." Reading Said in Persian at this stage of my academic life was a bit of foreign familiarity. Tahmasbi had done an utterly magnificent work rendering Said into Persian. I was happy to see him speak Persian, as it were, and yet I saw him so distanced from his colloquial English. The exercise was an experiment to see how he sounds in other languages in which he was so lovingly received and read—in Arabic, Turkish, Urdu, and so on. We will in fact not come to understand the globality of his reception unless we read him in another language. I was lucky to have had a small role in introducing him to the Persian-speaking world.

Out of the night that covers me,
Black as the pit from pole to pole,
I thank whatever gods may be
For my unconquerable soul.

—**William Ernest Henley (1849–1903)**

T he timing of the interview that today we know as the "Last Interview," taped just one year before the untimely passing of the now-legendary Palestinian public intellectual, literary critic, and postcolonial theorist Edward W. Said, would not dovetail with the ominous title of calling it the "Last Interview" when it was conducted. This interview was not ominous, prophetic, or premonitory. It was not supposed to be his last interview. It turned out that way. Said was mortal, like everyone else, but he thrived on an unconquerable will to life. His commitment to Palestinian national liberation had connected him to a posterity beyond his own mortal life. Without understanding the enduring moral arc of that noble cause, we will not comprehend the contour and demeanor of his prose and diction. Said was born a Palestinian and he was born to have the ennobling cause of Palestine dwell in him. He spoke with the voice of the historic injustice perpetrated on his people in his towering, unflinching voice. What today we know, watch, or read as the "Last Interview" projects that mortality into a posterity that is always here and now, not just there and then.

I write these few lines as an introduction to the Persian translation of what is now known as *Edward Said: The Last Interview* (2002). It is now late in 2017—some fifteen years after that interview. I am now almost as old as Said was when he passed away. My own memories of Said are now fading into a posterity that is the cause and consequences of the sustained cause of the Palestinian people. I was committed to the Palestinian cause long before I knew or met Said, and my solidarity (my dwelling in) with Palestinians has strengthened long after we lost him. I write these lines therefore at a posterity I did not anticipate when I first read

Said's *Orientalism* in 1979, or when I first met him and began our lifetime friendship and comradery a decade later in 1989, where he was a towering intellectual presence and I a mere newcomer. The Persian translation of his "Last Interview" is therefore the instance when he and I finally meet in my mother tongue, though perforce I am writing this introduction in the language he and I spoke to each other, for it to be translated by someone else into my own mother tongue. This projection therefore, this deferment, is where he and I once again meet to converse.

The Palestinian cause is a paradox of light and darkness—the light of a noble struggle that graces the life of anyone who joins it and the darkness of despair that accompanies any such solidarity with a cause facing the banality of the evil that is embedded in the European settler colony in Palestine. "Contrapuntal," as Said would say, is the delayed defiance, embedded in the instance that anyone ever comes close to read him in another language, one linguistic register removed from his habitual eloquence with and in the English language he helped decolonize.

There is therefore a *delayed defiance*, as I always say, a *deferment*, anytime anyone comes close to reading Said in another language. As fate would have it this "Last Interview" has turned out to be a master class with Said—his flawlessly fluid intellect swimming through his lifetime preoccupations: his commitment to Palestine, his larger political frame of reference, his mutinous critical acumen defying academic disciplines as he moved to break new grounds for emerging forms of knowledge.

For people like me who remember those last few years of his life and his struggles with his illness, it is difficult to watch this interview and relive Said's reluctant encounter with his own mortality. When you hear him talk about his inability to read or write or listen to music or play piano, you hear him grudgingly succumb to the fact of his fading life.

Two aspects of this interview have now assumed increased significance for me: (1) the fact that he has effectively abandoned the American site except for very few comrades he had and turned morally and politically to address the Arab world, and (2) the fact that what moved him out of his sick bed was just a flashing of a picture of Ariel Sharon, the Israeli warlord responsible for the slaughter of so many Palestinians.

It is now deeply troubling (the allegory of his endearing innocence) that the mere prospect of an Israeli incursion into Gaza or the US invasion of Iraq would have moved his ailing body toward his writing desk. What would he have said or done if he were alive today, multiple invasions of Gaza after his death, the destruction of Iraq, the rise of the Arab revolutions, and the pernicious support of the Zionist thievery by even more corrupt US presidents like Obama and then Trump? Today it is useless to ask these sorts of questions. He is no longer here to tell us. We can only surmise what he would have said, done, or suffered. The world is spinning down, time is running out, injustices heap upon more insufferable injustices. His "Last Interview" is always our first sight of wonder.

But I also think that these accumulated fragments fail to grasp the significance of the manner in which Said thought and the way we now read him. We read or hear him talk about atrocities now long overshadowed by unfathomable horrors. We look at Afghanistan, Iraq, Libya, Syria, Yemen, or Palestine and we can only shiver with fright of what he would have said.

Such conjectures will not take us anywhere. We must look for the quintessence of his moral outrage. What moved him most, what agitated his soul, from which everything else flew naturally. Said dwelled on Palestine, and Palestine lived in him through a momentous atemporality that is irreducible to one or another episode in the Palestinian or any other peoples' struggles.

> In the fell clutch of circumstance
> I have not winced nor cried aloud.
> Under the bludgeonings of chance
> My head is bloody, but unbowed.

The circumstances of Said's thinking were sublated into another level of critical reflection on Palestine as both truth and narrative. We must listen to this interview or read all his other words in the shade and shadow of his larger and more enduring frame of critical thinking. For there and then we hear him speak to history, not to a person or condi‑ tion. There is an axiomaticity to his words, a condition of critical think‑ ing that point to a deeper grounding of what he said and what he meant. When you hear him frustrated, tired, or short of breath, remember he is dwelling in Palestine as a metaphor, speaking a truth through the moral authority of an allegory.

> *Beyond this place of wrath and tears*
> *Looms but the Horror of the shade,*
> *And yet the menace of the years*
> *Finds, and shall find me, unafraid.*

Said linked the Palestinian fate to the fate of abused people every‑ where—in Asia, Africa, and Latin America. His courage, his imagina‑ tion, had made his political will rise to the occasion of an aesthetic of defiance. He had an uncanny ability to dwell on the here and now and pull whatever he saw and detected into a superior condition of critical thinking. The power of his narrative emerged out of the critical inti‑ macy with a national liberation movement that had become the pure symbolic register of our history. Palestine thus dwelled, Palestine thus dwells, on a porous borderline between fact and fury, between pain and triumph, a fusion of truth and narrative that has haunted Zionism since it began its armed robbery of Palestine.

> *It matters not how strait the gate,*
> *How charged with punishments the scroll,*
> *I am the master of my fate:*
> *I am the captain of my soul*

Said single-handedly altered the very language of how we speak about the globality of the condition we know as *colonialism*. He did so by theoretically universalizing the particularity of Palestine. The Zionists went after him as their top enemy, maligning his name, bombing his office, denying his identity. But he remained steadfast, determined, defiant.

I remember vividly one day early in the morning walking toward my office, which was close to his, and he saw me disgruntled and frazzled. "What's the matter with you," he wondered, particularly bright and frivolous. "They attack you just to intimidate you," I conjectured. "Well don't be intimidated," he said. Disarming and flat was his reasoning, simple and compelling. This is because he spoke from the simple certainty of a truth that had assuredly lifted itself into a metaphor.

In this sense, the "Last Interview" is really his *lasting* interview, the way we think of the moment that contains an eternity, the way the fact of a struggle has successfully sublated itself into the thin air, there not to disappear, but to resonate with every breath of reason we sustain in our sanity.

Said raised the truth of the Palestinian struggle to the metamorphic power of a metaphor from which no human being can come to moral consciousness.

Translating Said into another key is to reach for the metamorphic quintessence of his power and elocution, where the truth of the Palestinian cause reaches out to touch the nobility of any other cause attentive to the originary language of his towering ability to speak truth to power.

Thirteen

EDWARD SAID'S *ORIENTALISM*

FORTY YEARS LATER

I wrote this essay on the occasion of the fortieth anniversary of the publication of Edward Said's Orientalism, *and it first appeared on May 3, 2018, as a column on Al Jazeera. By this time it had become quite clear that Said had become a memory and that his most famous book had become a classic, a book that everyone quotes but no one reads. The task at hand is to see how we could read a classic afresh.*

There is a video tucked away somewhere deep in the attic of the internet—of me fifteen years ago, convening an international conference on Edward Said's book, *Orientalism*, at Columbia University.[1] Said at that time was still with us. In this video, you can see me briefly introduce him (not that he needed any introduction on our campus) before he takes up the stage to share his very last thoughts on his groundbreaking masterpiece.

There is another video from just a few months ago, in September 2017, in which I was interviewed by a young colleague in Geneva

189

offering my latest thoughts on the significance of *Orientalism* today.[2] In between these two events I wrote and published my own book *Post-Orientalism: Knowledge and Power in Time of Terror*.[3] These three dates—2003, 2009, and 2017—are very much typical of the temporal trajectory of critical thinkers of my generation and their enduring debt to Said and his magisterial text that turned an entire discipline of scholarship upside down and enabled a mode of thinking hitherto impossible to fathom in postcolonial thinking around the globe. In *Orientalism*, Said unleashed our tongue and unsheathed the sword of our critical thinking.

Orientalism hit the right note at the most momentous occasion when the postcolonial world at large most needed it—when the condition of coloniality needed a thematic and theoretical decoupling from the framing of capitalist modernity at large.

There is another crucial date I need to record here: October–November 2000, when the Italian Academy for Advanced Studies at Columbia University hosted the eminent founding figure of the school of subaltern studies, the Indian historian Ranajit Guha, to deliver a series of lectures that were subsequently published in the book *History at the Limit of World History*.[4]

On this occasion, my other distinguished Columbia colleague Gayatri Spivak and I organized a two-day conference around Guha's lectures that we called Subaltern Studies at Large. Said was present at this conference and gave a keynote speech at its first plenary session.

The Empire Writes Back

These among many other seminal hallmarks of the two interrelated fields of postcolonial and subaltern studies, as defined by towering critical thinkers like Said, Spivak, and Guha, are indices of a seismic groundswell in transforming modes of knowledge production that have historically framed and provincialized the received Eurocentrism of our understanding of the world around us.

Before these seminal thinkers, the world of colonial modernity was at the receiving end of European scholarship. Their writing enabled generations of scholars to think in terms contrarian to the epistemic foregrounding of Eurocentric social sciences and humanities.

There are a number of crucial texts at the epicenter of this historic reorientation of critical scholarship in social sciences and humanities—chief among them Spivak's powerful essay, "Can the Subaltern Speak?"[5] But no other text has assumed the iconic importance of Said's *Orientalism* for a number of substantive and circumstantial reasons.

Orientalism was the right book at the right time by the right author. Solidly established as the preeminent literary theorist of his generation, Said wrote many books and articles before and after *Orientalism*.

But *Orientalism* hit the right note at the most momentous occasion when the postcolonial world at large most needed it—when the condition of coloniality needed a thematic and theoretical decoupling from the framing of capitalist modernity at large. We on the postcolonial edges of capitalist modernity needed a defining text, a totem pole, a worldly testimony, to bring us all together—and Said was born to write that text and build that edifice.

Like all groundbreaking texts, *Orientalism* has attracted many significant critical encounters—chief among them two seminal essays by Aijaz Ahmad and James Clifford. In my own *Persophilia: Persian Culture on the Global Scene*, I found myself seriously diverging in some crucial ways from Said's positions.[6]

Like all other seminal thoughts, *Orientalism* has a number of important precedents in the work of Anouar Abdel-Malek, Talal Asad, and Bernard S. Cohen. But all such precedents and critical encounters, in fact, come together to stage and signify Said's *Orientalism* even more than if it were denied such encounters.

Even those abusive readings of *Orientalism* that have turned it into a diatribe against "the West" have had their contributions to making the book the defining moment of a discipline. Said's own courageous and pioneering defense of the Palestinian cause was, in fact, paradoxically instrumental in facilitating such abusive readings. As the borderline between useful and abusive readings of *Orientalism* blurred, the text loomed ever larger as a classic thriving on its own mis/interpretations.

REWRITING THE WORLD

Against the background of all such cacophony, *Orientalism* was and remains a cogent critique of colonially conditioned modes of knowledge production. It is a study of the relation between knowledge and power, and as such, deeply rooted in and indebted to the work of Michel Foucault and, before him, Friedrich Nietzsche.

There is an even longer and more substantive critique of the sociology of knowledge that goes back to Karl Marx and Friedrich Engels's *The German Ideology* and comes down to such seminal sociologists as Max Scheler, Karl Mannheim, and George Herbert Mead. Said himself was not fully conscious of this veritable sociological trajectory, for he was primarily a literary critic and his critique of *Orientalism* was primarily a critique of figurative, tropic, and narrative representations.

The enduring lesson and abiding truth of Said's *Orientalism* is in its clinical precision diagnosing the pathological relationship between interested knowledge and the power it serves. As I have argued in detail in my *Post-Orientalism* book, today, the relation between power and knowledge about the Arab and Muslim world, or the world in general, has gone through successive gestations.

The classical age of European Orientalism eventually degenerated into American area studies and further down to the rise of mostly Zionist think tanks in Washington, DC, and elsewhere, writing the interests of the Israeli settler colony into the imperial interests of the United States. Today, Arabs and Islam are no longer subjects of knowledge and understanding, but objects of hatred and loathing.

Today, two notorious Islamophobes with a sustained history of the hatred of Muslims and their faith, Mike Pompeo and John Bolton, are the US secretary of state to US President Donald Trump and his national security adviser, respectively. We are no longer in the field of Orientalism as Said understood and criticized it.

Today in Europe, hatred of Judaism and Jews has successfully transformed itself to the hatred of Islam and Muslims. At its height, classical Orientalism generated a monumental scholar like Ignaz Goldziher, who, at great personal cost to himself, refused to yield to the pernicious power of Zionists trying to recruit his knowledge into their ranks. Today, a Zionist propagandist like Bernard Lewis is the chief ideologue of the neocons' hatred of Muslims and imperial designs on their homelands.

Today, a close and critical reading of Said's seminal masterpiece requires an even more radical dismantling of the European project of colonial modernity and all its ideological trappings. Said paved the way and pointed us in the right direction. The treacherous path ahead requires not just the sparkles of his critical thinking but also the grace of his courage and imagination.

Fourteen

Rosa Luxemburg

The Unsung Hero of Postcolonial Theory

I published this essay on Al Jazeera on May 12, 2018, on the occasion of the 200th anniversary of the birth of Karl Marx, in which I tried to retrieve the intellectual legacy of the Polish-born German Jewish Marxist theorist Rosa Luxemburg for postcolonial theory. In this essay you notice the marked difference between my kind of postcolonial theory and that of Edward Said, taking off from him to be sure but coming much closer to Marxism than he ever did. The point here is to see the varieties of ways in which Said's legacy can be extended into a decidedly Marxist direction, even though he himself was not a Marxist.

The world at large is celebrating the two hundredth anniversary of the birth of Karl Marx (May 5, 1818), the revolutionary political economist who, with a single act of theoretical genius, redefined our enduring understanding of the material foundations of our economic class, social life, political positions, and ideological proclivities in his three-volume magnum opus, *Das Kapital* (1867–1883). His very vocabulary of theorizing the economic foregrounding of social and political (and even religious) forces has now become integral to the social sciences and the humanities—used and abused by friends and foes alike.

In a world ravaged by the wanton cruelty of predatory capitalism—now most notoriously led by the imperial presidency of Donald Trump and his billionaires' cabinet, aided and abetted by their European and regional allies—the enduring wisdom of Marx's theory of capital and its political consequences continue to guide the course of our struggles for global justice.

Marx, however, was incurably Eurocentric in the very cast of his critical thinking. Although he was aware of the expansionist proclivities of a capitalist economy, Marx never fully developed a theory of how colonialism was the modus operandi of this capitalist tendency. Although in the 1850s Marx wrote brilliantly in his essays for *New York Daily Tribune* on various aspects of European colonialism, his Eurocentric blind spot led him to his notorious notion of "Oriental Despotism" and the scandalous argument that colonialism was actually good for India because it "modernized" the subcontinent.

Such theoretical blinders and political blunders barred the extension of his own insights into a more global theory of capital and its political consequences. When it came to his perception of the non-European world, Marx was as much an Orientalist as the rest of his European contemporaries—though he, of course, wished to see the world liberated globally from the terrors of an abusive capitalist system. But when he said, "Workers of the world unite," he basically had European workers in mind. The rest of the world had to be liberated from their feudal ways and "modernized" before reaching the revolutionary consciousness of his European audience.

The necessary and crucial task of extending Marx's groundbreaking ideas to the world at large remained for the next generation of Marxist critical thinkers, the Polish-born German Jewish revolutionary thinker and activist Rosa Luxemburg (1871–1919) in particular.

Bourgeois Nationalism
on the Postcolonial Sites

There is a legitimate Marxist critique of aspects of postcolonial theory as it is received and perceived on North American university campuses and made palatable to soft-spoken liberalism, where the bitter roots of this critical movement in colonial experiences are sweetened for bourgeois palatability. In this version, Césaire, Fanon, Malcolm X, and even Edward Said are robbed of their experience as African, Caribbean, African American, or Palestinian and given a gentle and sociable aura so as not to frighten white people.

But there is another version of postcolonial theory that in fact begins long before Césaire, Fanon, Malcolm X, or Said and is rooted in such radical Marxist thinkers as Rosa Luxemburg who, early in the twentieth century, were busy thinking far more globally about the significance of Marx's thought—even more poignantly than did Marx himself.

As a Jew, a woman, and a socialist revolutionary, Rosa Luxemburg was in a unique position to think about the meaning of Marx's ideas from the vantage point of disenfranchised segments of the world in or out of Europe. As a Jew, she was the internal other of Europe; as a woman, its gendered alterity; and as a socialist revolutionary, its nightmare.

In her groundbreaking book, *The Accumulation of Capital* (1913), Rosa Luxemburg demonstrated how capitalism expands the domain of its predatory operation globally to exploit resources, abuse cheap labor, expand its insatiable need for new markets, and accumulate ever-increasing surplus value.[1] European imperialism, she suggested, was the military machinery to enable and facilitate this globalization of capital.

Without Rosa Luxemburg's correction of Marx's theory of capital, his blindfolded Eurocentrism would have had two fatal deficiencies. He could not account for the European longevity of the capitalist system and he would have been irrelevant to the colonial extension of capitalism. Luxemburg's argument that the endemic crisis of the capitalist system propels it to imperialism and colonialism effectively brought the realm of the colonial into the critical apparatus of Marxist thinking.

RETHINKING MARX "ON THE MARGIN?"

To be sure, in his *Imperialism: The Highest Stage of Capitalism* (1917), published about half a decade later, Vladimir Lenin, too, connected the economic vicissitude of capitalism and the military logic of imperialism together, arguing military expansionism was the mechanism through which European countries delayed the endemic economic crisis in their own countries.[2]

Other major Marxist theorists, such as Karl Kautsky and Nikolai Bukharin, had also paid close attention to the link between capitalism and imperialism. These figures were pioneering theorists dismantling the racist colonialist assumption that colonialism was instrumental in the process of so-called "modernization." It was because of them that "modernization" was exposed for what it has been: a euphemism for colonization.

In an excellent recent book, *Marx at the Margins*, Kevin Anderson has sought to rescue Marx from his European provincialism and offer us, with some degree of success, a different version of Marx.[3] The only problem with such revisionist accounts and other Marxist theorists seeking to expand Marx's insights is that even in their closer attention to global consequences of capitalism they remained Eurocentric in the sense that, even in their "world-system" theories—à la Immanuel Wallerstein—they still believe in a "core-periphery" dichotomy between capital and its colonial consequences.

There is no "core" or "periphery" to the global operation of capital and the military forces that sustain it. The ruling elites in the United States, the European Union, Asia, Africa, and Latin America are as much the beneficiary of the system they violently uphold as those who are disenfranchised by it are dispersed in these very places.

Racism is a mere ideological veneer to the hardcore economic logic of colonialism and imperialism. Predatory capital is color-blind and gender-neutral. It abuses white and colored labor identically and it makes no difference to its maddening logic if you are a Donald Trump or a Saudi prince, an Egyptian general, an Indian entrepreneur, a Russian oligarch, or a Chinese businessman. Those who are abused and maligned by the selfsame system are as much among the poor of the United States and Europe as they are in Asia, Africa, and Latin America. Color and gender codification of power is a mere false consciousness to the economic logic of power and domination.

The migrant laborer, more than 300 million of them, roaming around the globe in search of a half-decent wage, are neither in the center nor in the periphery of any system. They are the most obvious victims of the predatory capitalism made invisible by a false geography of "center and margin" or "core and periphery."

By giving detailed accounts of the British economic atrocities in India and French colonialism in Algeria, Rosa Luxemburg anticipated the more detailed accounts of postcolonial theories by decades. By bringing the presumed margins of self-centering Europe to global consciousness, she enabled the postcolonial theorist a veritable voice at the worldwide gathering of critical Marxist thinking.

Fifteen

Palestine Then and Now

The following interview took place in Doha, Qatar, in December 2018. I was interviewed by Palestinian student Majd Hamad, and Naye Idris, a Lebanese student at Columbia University, transcribed it in May 2019. Its Arabic translation was published by my good friend Samah Idris in Lebanon. Its original English is published here for the first time. What is important for me in this interview is that the questions come from a younger generation of Palestinian students and critical thinkers. They are rightly disgusted with the Palestinian leadership and inquisitive of the future direction of their nation. On occasion of such interviews, I feel I am among the connecting links between the generation of Edward Said that I have experienced and the generation of Majd Hamad and Naye Idris that he did not see.

Majd Hamad: We want to talk about the Palestinian issue today. You recently published an essay in Al Jazeera English about the day of the official relocation of the US embassy to Jerusalem and about the events in Gaza. So, I thought we could start from there. How do you see the events unfolding after months of weekly protests in Gaza?

Hamid Dabashi: I think this particular *yaum al-ard*/Land Day, which as you remember began on March 30, is a global event, we all mark it, but particularly our attention has been on Gaza because on that day *yaum al-ard* became the inaugural moment of *al-'awda al-kabira*/The Great Return—and I think because of that we are marking the name of *'awda* from the location of Gaza, even before a single shot was shot, and a single person was killed or injured . . . it marks yet another momentum in the history of the Palestinian struggle. Before this particular set of marches began, the events in the region and around the globe were casting the Palestinian issue into oblivion. Yet again with one bold and principled move Palestinians took the initiative and brought global attention back to their struggles. Remember a chief project of Israel is to create distraction. Right now, that distraction is the nonexistent Iranian nuclear project, while Israelis themselves sit on a massive nuclear arsenal. They create these distractions so they can steal the rest of Palestine quietly. Well, the events of the Great March of Return shows Palestinians cannot be fooled.

To understand the Great March of Return, we have to understand the nature of Palestinian resistance. Palestinian resistance is multifaceted, it is amorphous; it is not—it has never been—led by a single political party or faction. Yes, you have Fatah, you have Popular Front for the Liberation of Palestine, you have Hamas, you have all these political formations. They are all parts and aspects of resistance and as such they are all manifestations of Palestinian people—different factions, sentiments, politics, and ideologies, of the Palestinian people. Palestinians are a nation, a struggling, defiant nation, and as a result they have multiple modes of expressing their collective will. If you go back, from the earliest moments of the Nakba, even before the Nakba, Palestinians have always surprised history, they don't follow any particular route in part because there is no complete legitimacy to any one of the political representations. Palestine is a living organism of resistance and defiance. A poem of Mahmoud Darwish, a short story by Ghassan Kanafani, a work of art by Mona Hatoum, or a film by Elia Suleiman is as important as any political or social movement.

What we need today is not just speculation about the nature of Palestinian statehood, but far more importantly, in my opinion, theorizing of the Palestinian nation. In grand historical terms I have always said Palestinians are a nation without a state, ruled by a state without a nation. Jews have always lived in Palestine and will always be part of the Palestinian people, as Jews in Iran or Argentina or the United States belong to the national aspirations of those countries. As a result, the body of Palestinian resistance is a living body—it grows, it expands, it matures, it learns, it experiences, and it manifests itself differently. We are here specifically talking about a history since the generation that experienced Nakba—multiple generations of Palestinians coming together, from those who live within Palestine ("the 48-ers"), those who live in the 1967 borders, and those who live in the refugee camps, those who live in diaspora, those who are successful and powerful and rich, those who are ordinary Palestinians. We must have a gestalt view of Palestine and Palestinians.

Because of the organicity of this living phenomenon of Palestinian resistance, there is always, as I said, a surprise to the outside world as to how things may appear; they may appear as, for example, a Great March of Return in Gaza, they may appear in a recent film, it may appear in a poem, it may appear in scholarship, and it may appear as simple as a young Palestinian couple marrying, as I saw, for example, in Sabra and Shatila, and the young couple going there to live inside an UNRWA apartment, and yet recognizing, knowing themselves, as Palestinians, keeping the memory of the return to their homeland alive, and to any other manifestations. The banality of the Zionist propaganda is that they have tried in vain to project Palestinians as a fixed and inanimate target so they can shoot it down. They have not and they will never succeed.

The Gaza phenomenon, going back to your original question, is particularly important because it is sustained. The Israeli reaction to it was vicious, violent, vulgar, and desperate. They do not know how to deal with peaceful protest except by bullets. Historically, because of the nature of Palestinian resistance, because they are a defenseless people . . . contrary to the *hasbara* (propaganda, particularly powerful in the United States) that have consistently characterized Palestinian resistance as violent, whereas the overwhelming majority of Palestinian resistance is not violent, it is actually by ordinary human beings living their lives . . . yes, they have, as it is their right, resisted "by any means necessary," and that is not a phrase that came from Palestine or is exclusively the Palestinians'. "By any means necessary" is the famous phrase of Malcolm X in reference to the right of another repressed people to resist.

The fact is the body of the population of Palestinians living in Gaza moved forward toward their homeland—it is very important never to call this "a border" because there is no border—marched toward their homes from where they were expelled, without arms. There were even signs of Palestinians singing and dancing the dabkeh, along with medical care, and even press covering it, and even if they were recognizably press or medical care they were still shot and killed point-blank.

There are many examples of extraordinary heroism, but to me, perhaps the picture of the amputee, Ibrahim Abu-Thuraya, twice amputated and then point-blank shot and killed by the Israelis, while sitting on his upper torso raising the Palestinian flag, is the single most important iconic picture of this particular phase. I say "iconic" hesitantly because there was recently another picture of a Palestinian young man, half naked, raising a flag and throwing a stone, and that was branded "iconic." I'm hesitant because when we say "iconic" something becomes outside history. Palestinians are not outside history, the resistance of Palestinians is historical and is sustained and is multifaceted, and as a result that phenomenon itself, that body of resistance itself, is represented through the iconic fact of the ongoing movement. We need to keep a careful balance between Palestine as a gushing wound and Palestine as a metaphor.

So, what we saw in the latest episode of Palestinian uprising is the beginning of a new mode of resistance. After the first and the second intifada, people were wondering when would the third intifada happen. Palestinians as always surprised the world, despite the fact of massive change in technology information . . . massive transformation of the media, mass media, and the 24/7 news coverage that has shortened the attention span of people, they have sustained the attention of the world on their particular predicament.

MH: Do you think that Palestinians still have the energy to go out and keep continuing what they are doing?

HD: It is hard to tell, and it is unfair to predict. There is an optimum level of resistance among Palestinians from Gaza, and also solidarity from the West Bank and diaspora, but particularly the pressure is on Gaza where the circumstances are dire and thus they have sustained it. We are now in the middle of December, it began in March ... so it went all through the spring and all through the summer and now has gone all the way through the fall. What I have learned from Palestinian resistance is that there have always been episodes that emerge, sustain themselves, and then they exhaust themselves, and then give birth to another mode of resistance. I don't believe the current uprising from Gaza has exhausted itself, it is still ongoing, also on a daily basis things are happening, the number of casualties and death and maiming, injuring, permanently injuring, that Palestinians have endured is beyond epic. This is a whole different mode of resistance, which we have to watch carefully and learn how it works. I think human history has rarely seen a mode of resistance which is just ordinary people. It's not a military organization, there are also some accusations that Hamas is behind this March of Great Return ... there is no indication that it is initiated by Hamas, or if it is, Hamas did not fall from the sky, Hamas is also part of the Palestinian resistance. How long it will last? I don't know. No one can tell. When it has run its course, like any other aspect of Palestinian resistance, then we take a step back and look at it and see what has been its historical significance. But it's too early now. Since the Balfour Declaration of 1917, the Zionists thought Palestinians would bend backward and pretend they are dead. It is now more than a hundred years later and Palestinians are resisting the armed robbery of their homeland with more resilience than ever before.

MH: Can we see an armed movement; do you think we can see something more armed later on?

HD: First of all, armed resistance has never ended, armed resistance has always been part of Palestinian resistance. Sometimes their armed resistance is an earlier part of Fatah, or in the Popular Front, Democratic Front, Jihad Islami, Hamas, and so on . . . it is marked as such. And sometimes it's just a desperate Palestinian picking up a knife and going up the street because they have had it up to here. But again, as I said, it is very important to look at any mode of armed resistance—to which Palestinians are entitled, like any other people—there is no point in history, in which people under occupation, people whose homeland has been stolen from them, have not resisted by any means necessary. Did Native Americans not have armed resistance, the Vietnamese, the Algerians, the Indians, the Cubans? Now, whether or not this would be the beginning of a new mode of armed resistance, it's hard to tell. What is important for Palestinian resistance is that it is unpredictable . . . it is not following any script. But, you have to look at it from the other side . . . that because of the consistency of the multifaceted Palestinian resistance, the overwhelming majority of it has been peaceful; they have denied the Zionists any excuse, any legitimacy . . . they have nothing, no word, no concept, no ideology, no explanation, no theory, nothing, just futile propaganda, and this is because the consistent pressure of peaceful Palestinian resistance has taken away from Israelis any and all excuses . . . the only thing they have is a gargantuan military and the atom bomb. That's all they have. Both of them entirely useless in the face of the dignity of Palestinian peaceful resistance.

MH: Moving on a bit to Arabs in 1948 [i.e., Palestinian citizens of Israel], you've seen the protests that were going on all along these past years, more than, or in a different mode than before. Where do you think that is going, where do you think Palestinians in Israel are going?

HD: The Palestinians who live within Israel are subject to second class citizenship, they are living with the enemy, they have become "intimate enemies," as Ashis Nandy would say, going to schools, same universities, same place of work as second-class citizens . . . learning the language of their occupiers, learning the language of their tormentors. This language is in and of itself not the enemy. No language is. The Hebrew language is not the enemy. It's the way the Zionists have abused it and turned it into the language of the occupiers which is at issue here. In and of itself, you might even say Hebrew is a Palestinian language, as Anton Shammas proved in his magisterial *Arabesque*, which he wrote originally in his superior Hebrew.

Because of the connection among the multiple aspects of the Palestinians' resistance and self-consciousness (1948, 1967, the camps and the diaspora), because there is this connection among all of them, they have catalytically affected each other. If you see an event happening in Gaza, it has an effect on what is happening inside 1948, and the way that suddenly—for example, overnight, when al-Aqsa Mosque was being attacked, overnight Palestinians poured into Aqsa and began praying, irrespective of whether they were Muslim or Christian. That has nothing to do with anything. It's an indication that there is a collective awareness that affects the 1948, and they are totally conscious and aware of what's happening in 1967, what's happening in Gaza, the rest of Palestinian diaspora . . . one thing that happens has an effect on the other. This is an at once fragmented and collective consciousness. It cannot be co-opted or trapped.

I have experienced this personally. I have had postdoctoral fellows from Tel Aviv University coming to do a postdoc with me. They had finished their PhD inside, and had come to Columbia to do a postdoc with me. I have had long conversations with them and with their families. The 1948ers are completely connected to the rest of Palestine. Namely, the attempt at brainwashing the 1948ers has been completely failing, even now after the passing of this Jewish Nation-State Law... which is not anything new, and of course was always practically the case. Netanyahu and Likud are so vulgar that they put it as part of their Basic Laws. Even now, we are beginning to see the Druze, because the Zionists want systematically to sever Druze Palestinians from the rest of Palestinians. Palestinians are Christian, Palestinians are Muslim, they are Druze, they are Armenian—I mean I just had dinner with an Armenian Palestinian from Jerusalem. Now, of course, Armenian Palestinians have always been aware they were Palestinians, we are talking about the Druze. The Zionists went through all sorts of song and dance to alienate the Druze from who they are. Now they are beginning to recognize that they are Palestinians.

My point here is very simple, the more Zionists try to divide and rule, the more the divided fragments of Palestine and Palestinians rise to the occasion to form a whole that Zionists can neither understand nor control.

MH: Do you think this has to do more with the more Arab identity that has been formed?

HD: Palestinian. Palestinian identity. I'm not much for Arab identity, or Iranian identity, or Turkish identity. Of course, Palestinians are Arabs. One of the modes of resistance to Zionist occupation has been the Palestinian awareness that they belong to the larger Arab world, and I would say to the larger world of revolutionary resistance. The Palestinian cause, however, is not just an Arab cause. You go to Latin America, I've traveled to Mexico City to Argentina ... the amount of solidarity with Palestinians, not just on university campuses or among the intellectuals ... we are talking about the Native Americans, First Nations from Canada to Argentina, because of the legendary fame of Palestinian resistance. You have to understand the Palestinian cause is something much larger than the Arab world, where you also have deeply corrupt Arab leaders and businessmen working actively against the Palestinian cause.

So, yes, Palestinians are part of the larger Arab world, larger Islamic world, larger world of third-world revolutionary resistance, but for me what we need is Palestinification of the Arab cause, not Arabification of the Palestinian cause. Arabs should learn from Palestinians, not Palestinians from Arabs. The Arab world in general—I'm not talking about people, I am talking about governments, the horrors of the governments. Look at Saudi Arabia, United Arab Emirates, Bahrain, Oman, etc. The best of them are accommodating Zionism, they think the only way that they can protect themselves against their own people is to cater to the Americans by appeasing the Zionist cause . . . which is a false assumption. The countries that do this don't know American society.

This professor at Temple University, Marc Lamont Hill, a professor of media studies, who also was a columnist for CNN, who recently went and said Palestine should be liberated from the river to the sea. This is the tip of the iceberg—he's not an exception. If you went to the national convention of the Democratic Party in Philadelphia back in 2016, you would see a palpable solidarity with the Palestinians. Yes, if you look at the platform of the Democratic Party, they refuse (under the influence of the Clinton faction) to utter the word "occupation" when it comes to Palestine. But, if you follow the camera, and the camera did follow the actual rank and file, on the floor of the convention you had a sea of yellow buttons: "Free Palestine," "Solidarity with Palestine." And you saw the same thing at the convention of the Labour Party in the United Kingdom. The cat is out of the bag, the time of deception is over, and this again is thanks to nothing but the resilience of Palestinian people. Yes, we know the towering intellectuals who have been writing, the novelists, the poets, the artists, the filmmakers, they are all great and wonderful and indispensable, but the core of resistance is the first two Arabic words I learned when I was five: *al-sha'ab al-Falastini*. Two words.

MM: We always talk about how it's "the Palestinian people"—*al-sha'ab al-Falastini*—but we never talk about if it's going to be an upcoming

Palestinian leader, because no one knows what's going to happen right now, especially with the West Bank.

HD: Very good point: Palestinian leadership has failed, the best of them. Again, we have to be historically conscious and careful. When Fatah was formed, when Popular Front was formed, these were generations of heroic revolutionaries. So, for my generation to look at a figure like Leila Khaled, who was a hero of my childhood, of my teenage years, it would be disgraceful for me to say that all the Palestinians' leaderships have been a failure. It has not been a failure. Ghassan Kanafani was not a failure. They have done what they could and things went forward. Between the current Palestinian people and their failed leadership, particularly in the course of Oslo and post-Oslo peace accord, and the Zionist deception of Oslo to which Palestinian leadership collapsed—but Palestinian critical thinkers did not. I remember vividly Edward Said was from the beginning against Oslo, as were many other Palestinians.

Between the failed leadership and the body of Palestinian resistance, what we need today is a younger generation of Palestinian thinkers, intellectuals, journalists, artists, and so on to begin to think actively, critically, progressively, proactively, in terms of what I have in my work called a "post-Zionist polity." Zionism has collapsed. Zionism has no pretense even to moral authority or political legitimacy. It is held together by the flimsy scaffolding of corrupt and reactionary US politicians and their anti-Semitic outlook that as soon as they see a Jew they see a dollar sign. Because right now what we are seeing in Israel isn't even Zionism as its founding figures envisioned it. It is something beyond that. With the failure of Zionism and the brute violence that now we witness in the occupation, there are indications that they are thinking of a post-Zionist polity. Here it makes no difference if you are a hardcore Zionist or a liberal Zionist, in fact the worst kind are the liberal Zionists because they provide the grease for the machinery of oppression and occupation. In actively imagining, articulating, and theorizing a post-Zionism polity, Palestinians will have to have a major role. Just calling it "one state solution" is perhaps necessary but not sufficient. In fact, I am less concerned about the "state" part of that proposition than the polity that it will entail.

In this regard, the chief task facing the younger generation of Palestinians, your generation, is the direction of your critical thinking. Now, Boycott, Divestment and Sanctions (BDS) is of course crucial, because it is global and it is transnational, and Israel is desperate and unable to stop it. BDS began by Palestinians, but it is now a transnational phenomenon. But BDS is still in the form of resistance. In my opinion, the point is no longer resistance, the point is triumph. We need to change our attitude. And the point of triumph is to begin to have critical thinking in the form of conferences, special issues of journals, and so on, all directed toward actively imagining a post-Zionist polity. Many post-Zionist Jews have already started thinking in those terms—Palestinians need to join force with them. How would a post-Zionist polity look? Whether the institutions of civil society or the democratic institution at large. Because there is no existing apparatus with the slightest mode of legitimacy right now in Palestine. The Palestinian leadership has failed the Palestinian people. So they are out of the equation. What we need, and what we lack and what needs to be done, any time students, faculty, critical thinkers, journalists get together—either Palestinian or those committed to the Palestinian cause—is to begin to think how would a Palestinian society, a post-Zionist Palestinian society look—a polity in which Jews, Christian, and Muslim Palestinians live together? Palestinians ever since the Nakba, even before the Nakba, have made serious contribution to thinking about what this post-Zionist polity would be. But they also need to look at other revolutionary mobilizations, in Africa, in Latin American, certainly in South Africa, certainly in the Zapatista movement, certainly in the genuine part of the Rojava revolutionary mobilization, not the way that the Americans are abusing it for their own purposes, and Zionists are abusing it for their own purposes. The task is to look around the globe, in Asia, in Africa, in Latin America, to begin to think in terms of a post-Zionist polity that is Palestinian, and is rooted in Palestinian history, and is rooted in Palestinian suffering, but no longer in terms of telling the world how the Palestinians have been wronged. Enough of that.

MH: So, you don't believe Palestinians can stay within the same political borders that they are now?

HD: Yes, they can, but the state that will represent them is less important than the polity that will hold them together. Their post-Zionist polity is rooted in where they are, but where they are is fragmented: the 1948ers have had one sort of experience, slightly different than the 1967ers, slightly different from the camps, slightly different from the diaspora. And all we do at this stage is document oppression, document occupation, document dispossession, document suffering, document sacrifice, which is necessary and important, but it's not sufficient. What is required beyond these documentations is active critical thinking about what sort of society Palestinians want to have, and beginning to add to that prospect such sorts of issues as gender, class, race, components of the civil society in which they will build institutions of democratic survival, based on their historical resistances. This is all in my humble opinion of course. I will always defer to the Palestinian experiences themselves. What I suggest here is what I think is the crucial component lacking when we have gatherings of Palestinian critical thinkers. Without actively and proactively beginning to imagine the day after liberation, the day before the liberation will always look dim and desperate. Once praising Elia Suleiman's cinema, I wrote that once Palestinians are free, they see him waiting for them. This is what I mean—though in more political not in merely aesthetic terms.

MH: The last thing I wanted to talk about more is the Palestinians in the diaspora, if we can call them "the subaltern," those speaking English, like you put it in one of your latest essays. So the Palestinians and their role in the movement in the United States . . . how do you see their role, how has it changed?

HD: First of all, as you know, there are different kinds of Palestinians, not just one kind of Palestinian. Second, for legitimate and correct reasons, the Arabic language is definitive to the identity of Palestinians because it has been a mode of resistance to assimilation, acculturation, and ultimately of destruction of who they are and the manner/matter of their resistance. My good friend Esmail Nashef has a book about what has happened to the Arabic language in the course of its colonization, which paradoxically he first wrote and published in Hebrew, but the Arabic version of it is coming out soon and then the English. It is important to note he has published a Hebrew version of it, so in a way he is re-appropriating Hebrew for Palestinians, because Hebrew is a Palestinian language, as English is a Palestinian language. Hebrew has always been spoken in Palestine, as has Arabic and other languages, long before the first Zionist settler colonialists moved to Palestine. It is important to reverse the colonial attitude. You know how Zionists call Palestinians "Israeli-Arabs"; well those Zionists who are native to Palestine are actually Palestinians Jews, and there have always been Palestinian Jews—the most famous of them was Jesus Christ, right?

This episode of the European Zionist colonialism is just a phase and it will end. Palestine has always been the house of Jews, Christians, Muslims, and God bless them all, atheists and agnostics. They are all there. So, you have to reverse the Zionist designation of the people they have conquered. Right now, as I said, English is also a Palestinian language. I travel from New York City to Mexico to Argentina talking about Palestine—all in English. Ilan Pappé and I were just part of a panel together in Mexico City on Palestine. If you leave Ilan Pappé to his Hebrew and me to my Persian, and our audience to their Spanish, then we would not be able to speak and understand each other—precisely when we are all talking about Palestine. This is what I mean by English has become a Palestinian language—we have decolonized the English language, liberated it from its colonial heritage. Edward Said, Joseph Massad, Rashid Khalidi, Nadia Abu El-Haj, Lila Abu-Lughod, among scores of other scholars and critical thinkers, all write their Palestine (mostly though not exclusively) in English. They may be translated into Arabic but their major scholarly work is done in English. It is very important not to fetishize language. Language is a medium. The overwhelming majority of Palestinians speak Arabic, as they should, but again in Latin America we see deeply committed Palestinians who speak Spanish—what do you want to do? Or English or French. The point is that they know who they are, they are aware of their identity. Language belongs to the people who speak it, not people belonging to the language they speak.

So, to cut to the chase, you always go to the heartland. One of my blessings is that I have prayed with my Palestinian brothers and sisters on one of the holiest sites for us Muslims, and one of the amazing things about Qubbat al-Sakhra, al-Masjid al-Aqsa, is that men and women pray together. As an Iranian accustomed to Iranian mosques, I'd never seen it. In Qubat al-Sakhra, I saw a woman standing and praying right next to men praying, and I stood there praying with them right there, when back in February 2004 I was there. The globality of this vision, and the epicenter of Palestinian resistance, has been and will remain Palestine, but the dimension of this revolutionary mobilization is global, and the more global it is, the more necessary it is for us to put our resources together, support BDS by all means; it's a Palestinian civil society-initiated movement, but it's not sufficient. It's necessary but it's not sufficient. We need to think after BDS is successful and Palestine is restored to its historic multicultural character, represented by one democratic state that is the collective will of all its peoples: Jews, Christians, Muslims, and as I said, the agnostics and atheists too. But the issue should never be solely that state—for all states, by definition, are monopolies of violence. The issue should always be what is upstream from the state, namely, the post-Zionist polity, namely, the national sovereignty of Palestinians as a people that can give or withdraw legitimacy from that.

Sixteen

ALAS, POOR BERNARD LEWIS, A FELLOW OF INFINITE JEST

I wrote this article on Bernard Lewis and his extraordinary capacity for get-
ting everything wrong upon his passing in May 2018. The essay appeared
first on Al Jazeera on May 28, 2018. I wish to conclude this volume that con-
sists of a record of my prolonged conversations with my late colleague and
comrade Edward Said with this piece on his arch nemesis—a historic battle
of good and evil to which I was an eyewitness. I was present in the audience
during the famous encounter between Said and Bernard Lewis during the
Middle East Studies Association conference in Boston in November 1986.
This was a couple of years before I joined Columbia and met Said for the
first time. It is only apt that I conclude this book of memories of Said with a
moment in which he did not know me from Adam.

"Here's a skull now; this skull has lain in the earth three-and-twenty years," the gravedigger tells Hamlet. It turns out the skull is Yorick's, the king's jester.

It is here that Hamlet says his famous lines: "Alas, poor Yorick! I knew him, Horatio, a fellow of infinite jest, of most excellent fancy."

I was instantly reminded of Yorick's skull and Hamlet when I heard Bernard Lewis had died. Then the lines of an Omar Khayyam poem and his unceasing awareness of the mortality of human presence ran through my mind:

> For I remember stopping by the way
> To watch a Potter thumping his wet Clay:
> And with its all-obliterated Tongue
> It murmur'd—"Gently, Brother, gently, pray!"

It is unseemly to recall the horrors of a horrible man upon his passing. But Bernard Lewis was not a regular rogue. He was instrumental in causing enormous suffering and much bloodshed in this world. He was a notorious Islamophobe who spent a long life studying Islam in order to demonize Muslims and mobilize the mighty military of what he called "the West" against them.

Just imagine: What sort of a person would spend a lifetime studying people he loathes? It is quite a bizarre proposition. But there you have it: the late Bernard Lewis did precisely that.

He was the chief ideologue of post-9/11 politics of hate toward Islam and Muslims.

"Dr. Lewis's friendship—and ideological kinship—with the Cold War hawk and Israel-supporting Sen. Henry M. 'Scoop' Jackson (D-Wash.)," we are told, "opened prominent doors in the capital, eventually giving Dr. Lewis favoured status among top White House and Pentagon planners before the 2003 invasion of Iraq."

That is the most recent legacy of Bernard Lewis: the invasion, occupation, and destruction of Iraq.

But Lewis's affiliation with powers of death and destruction went much deeper than that. Afghanistan and Iraq are in ruins today; millions of Arabs and Muslims have been murdered, scarred for life, subjected to the indignity of military occupation and refugee camps; in no small measure because of the systemic maligning of Muslims Lewis advanced in his books and articles, which influenced generations of imperial officers.

For them, Lewis was the source for what Islam is and who the Muslims are. When US President Donald Trump said, "Islam hates us," it was Bernard Lewis speaking. When Trump's first National Security Adviser Michael Flynn said, "Islam is . . . like cancer," it was Bernard Lewis speaking.

I was still a graduate student at the University of Pennsylvania when I first encountered Lewis in person at a Princeton University conference. There was always a distance, a manufactured aloofness between him and the rest of the scholarly community.

He was more at home with heads of state, spy chiefs, military officers, intelligence communities, settler colonialists in Palestine, imperial viceroys in conquered Muslim lands.

He had power and basked in it. We detested power.

He is now showered with praise by the most powerful Zionist Islamophobes in the United States and Israel. We are on the opposite side of the fence—with Palestinians facing Israeli sharpshooters whom he favored, enabled, encouraged, weaponized with a potent ideology of Muslim and Arab hatred.

"HOW ABHORRED IN MY IMAGINATION IT IS"

With the death of Bernard Lewis, the long saga of exchanges between him and Edward Said finally comes to an end. I was a postdoctoral fellow at Harvard and present at their now legendary debate in Boston on November 22, 1986, during the Middle East Studies Association conference.

Long before that, like thousands of other young scholars, I followed their debates on the pages of the *New York Review of Books*. I was, and I remain, squarely on Said's side. But that was not, nor is it now, a merely political position; rather, it was and is a potently moral and intellectual disposition.

The difference between the two men was the difference between the politics of lucrative power and the intellectual courage to revolt.

Lewis was a historian of power and in power and for the power that ruled us all, and he served happily and rewardingly. The more powerful the imperial audacity of a mode of knowledge production, the more Lewis pursued and served it.

Said was precisely on the other side of the fence, in the tradition of the anticolonial struggles of Asia, Africa, and Latin America—which he theorized into our reading of Palestine.

You looked at Lewis, and you saw Lawrence of Arabia incarnate—a British colonial officer with a clumsy command over the natives' language and culture, out in the field to serve the most vicious colonial enterprise of the century. You looked at Said, and you saw him in a direct line from the most revolutionary critical thinkers of all time—alongside Aimé Césaire, Frantz Fanon, V. Y. Mudimbe, Enrique Dussel, and of course Antonio Gramsci and Theodor Adorno.

Said attracted an entire generation of critical thinkers from every continent on planet Earth. Lewis attracted career opportunists who, like him, wanted to be near and dear to power.

In January 2003, just a few months before Said passed away, he and I were invited to Rabat, Morocco, for the conference Dialogue of Civilization. He could not go. He called me from Spain insisting I go.

I went to Rabat, only to learn upon my arrival that Lewis was there too. For the entire duration of the conference, while I was sitting with the late Egyptian philosopher Nasr Hamid Abu Zayd and literary theorist Ferial Ghazoul discussing hermeneutics, Lewis was chaperoned by the young Noah Feldman, the legal adviser to Paul Bremer, who was the "provisional coalition administrator" of Iraq after the US invasion.

In one shot you could see how Lewis was passing the baton of service to empire to the next generation.

"THE EVIL THAT MEN DO LIVES AFTER THEM"

The current state of opinion about Bernard Lewis, now appearing in various postmortem reflections and obituaries, has him hated by the global left, adored by the right-wing Zionists, and in between, you have these Goody-Two-shoes who try to sound wise and impartial and speak "in nuances." Yes, he was a great scholar early in his career, they now say, but later his scholarship diminished, and he became too political. Such branding of Lewis, loved by some and hated by others, deeply distorts a much more serious issue.

Beyond the political and moral abhorrence for Lewis is the legacy of his mode of thinking and writing, his colonially and racially infested manner of knowledge production that was as much subservient to powers that read and enriched him as it was profoundly at odds with the critical turning point in postcolonial knowledge production.

Lewis was no scholar objectively committed to historical truth. Quite the contrary: he has left behind not a single book in which he was not cherry-picking facts and figures to demonize Muslims, dismiss and denigrate their civilization, and subjugate them normatively, morally, and imaginatively to the colonial domination of those who he served.

His most famous recent book, *What Went Wrong? The Clash Between Islam and Modernity in the Middle East* is not a work of scholarship.[1] It is a manual of style, an indoctrination pamphlet, for teaching security, military, and intelligence officers in the United States and Europe why they must seek to control the Muslim world.

Lewis was always on the wrong side of history, driven by his hatred, animated by the most racist clichés in the trade. His reaction to the rise of Arab revolutions in 2011 is the perfect example of who Bernard Lewis was and how he thought.

"Another thing is the sexual aspect of it," he opined at the commencement of Arab revolutions:

> One has to remember that in the Muslim world, casual sex, Western-style, doesn't exist. If a young man wants sex, there are only

two possibilities—marriage and the brothel. You have these vast numbers of young men growing up without the money, either for the brothel or the bride price, with raging sexual desire. On the one hand, it can lead to the suicide bomber, who is attracted by the virgins of paradise—the only ones available to him. On the other hand, sheer frustration.[2]

This is obscenity in black and white—moral, political, and intellectual bankruptcy on full throttle.

His book *The Assassins: A Radical Sect in Islam*, which serious scholars like Farhad Daftary later dismissed as nonsensical gibberish, was definitive to the manner in which he wanted to portray Muslims—as congenital murderers.[3]

His forte was in manufacturing a cosmic divide between "Islam and the West," between Muslims and the modern world, a subject that was the staple of his writing, most condescendingly in his two books: *The Muslim Discovery of Europe* and *Islam and the West*.[4]

Bernard Lewis was no scholar of Islam. He was a British colonial officer writing intelligence for his fellow officers on how to rule the Muslim world better. *A Handbook of Diplomatic and Political Arabic*—one of his earliest volumes—foretold his career as a colonial scribe at the service of the British and later American empires.[5]

Today, when we think of Bernard Lewis's legacy, we think of the Islamophobic industry that has US President Donald Trump and his gang of billionaires crowned at the White House.

Today, when we think of Bernard Lewis, we think of his political progenies—John Bolton, the national security adviser of the United States, the most degenerate sabre-rattler sitting right behind the US president. Today, when we think of Bernard Lewis, we think of US Secretary of State Mike Pompeo, a notorious bigot with a pathological hatred of Muslims. Today, when we think of Bernard Lewis, we think of Gina Haspel, the newly appointed director of the US Central Intelligence Agency, a woman who ordered the torture of Muslims.

No one was more instrumental in manufacturing the illusion of a fundamental and irreconcilable difference between "Islam and the West" than Lewis—his singular achievement that later Samuel Huntington picked up to produce *The Clash of Civilizations.*

This needs no further evidence and proof than looking at who is praising him after his death. "Bernard Lewis was one of the great scholars of Islam and the Middle East in our time. We will be forever grateful for his robust defence of Israel," said Israeli Prime Minister Benjamin Netanyahu, himself, of course, another world-class authority on Islam and the Middle East![6]

"As a true scholar and a great man," chimed in newly minted US Secretary of State Mike Pompeo, another top-notch scholar in the field of Islamic studies, "I owe a great deal of my understanding of the Middle East to his work... He was also a man who believed, as I do, that Americans must be more confident in the greatness of our country, not less. Thank you, Mr. Lewis, for your life of service."

"You simply cannot find a greater authority on Middle Eastern history," this according to Dick Cheney, the former vice president who brought us waterboarding and Abu Ghraib torture chambers and who, of course, is also a stellar authority on Islamic history and doctrine himself.

You put Netanyahu, Pompeo, and Cheney together, with their vast love and admiration for Lewis, and you can gather the company he kept, the hatred he flamed, the death and destruction he sought visited upon the people he "studied" to death.

DEAD BEFORE HIS DEATH

Bernard Lewis died long before he met his creator. The rich and diversified world of critical thinking—in Asia, Africa, Latin America, as well as in Europe and the United States—to which Said was integral and definitive left Lewis and his books a very long time ago in the dustbin of Orientalist history.

"Lewis's verbosity," as Said put it succinctly some thirty-six years before Lewis died, "scarcely conceals both the ideological underpinnings of his position and his extraordinary capacity for getting everything wrong."

Lewis is often compared with Said as if the two were equal. They were not. They were the polar opposites in every sense. Said was a towering critical thinker who revolutionized the field of literary and postcolonial studies.

Lewis was an ideological functionary, an intelligence officer, on par with Francis Fukuyama and Samuel Huntington, competing for the ears of powerful people to tell them how to hate Muslims more persuasively.

Said enabled the moral authority of a generation of critical thinkers. Lewis taught military strategists how and why to rule Arabs and Muslims more effectively.

The mode of ideological knowledge Orientalists like Lewis produced was not in the interest of truth and understanding. It was meant to be used in humiliating and denigrating human beings and dominating their worlds and cultures, killing their sense of self-respect, telling them the only worthy thing to be was a white European settler colonialist.

This critique is not solely based on Said's magisterial book *Orientalism*. What Lewis produced, French philosopher Michel Foucault, long before Said, called *le savoir-pouvoir* or power-knowledge: the knowledge that serves power. And it was works like Lewis's that Argentinian philosopher Enrique Dussel referred to when he wrote in his book *Philosophy of Liberation*: "That ontology did not come from nowhere. It arose from a previous experience of domination over other persons, of cultural oppression over other worlds. Before the ego cogito, there is an ego conquiro; 'I conquer' is the practical foundation of 'I think.'"[7]

Both Said and Lewis are now gone. But Lewis left behind a racist legacy of raising a fictitious "West" at the expense of "the Rest," while Said summoned the best and most noble in each for a better future for all.

Acknowledgments

I put the final touches on this book while in quarantine with my family in our apartment in New York during the Covid-19 Pandemic. Soon the Black Lives Matter uprising had engulfed the country, and the oscillation between the daily anodyne chores and the exhilarating prospects of hope was hovering in the air as I relived my memories of Edward Said. I am grateful to Anthony Arnove and his colleagues at Haymarket for their extraordinary care and competence to get this volume ready for publication. I could not think of a better home for my book on Edward Said. My longtime research assistant Laila Hisham Fouad has been, as always, diligent and resourceful in locating and preparing Word versions of my various pieces on or about Edward Said scattered all over various publications. I thank Ida Audeh, the exceptionally gifted copyeditor who gave the book its final look. I am grateful to my young colleague Thaer AlSheikh Theeb for reading the entire book one last time for typographical mistakes. I thank my dear friend and colleague Joseph Massad for having read an earlier version of this book and alerted me to some necessary emendations for the final publication. I thank the Chair of my Department at Columbia Gil Hochberg for her exceptional care to make our research, writing, and teaching life easy for us while running a tight ship through some turbulent seas.

Hamid Dabashi
New York, June 2020

Notes

Introduction

1 Hamid Dabashi, *Persophilia: Persian Culture on the Global Scene* (Cambridge, MA: Harvard University Press, 2015); *Europe and its Shadows: Coloniality after Empire* (London: Pluto Press, 2019); *Brown Skin, White Masks* (London: Pluto Press, 2011). Edward W. Said, *Orientalism* (New York: Vintage, 1978); *Culture and Imperialism* (New York: Alfred A. Knopf, 1993); *Representations of the Intellectual: The 1993 Reith Lectures* (New York: Pantheon Books, 1994).

Prologue

1 Edward Said, *Orientalism* (New York: Vintage, 1978).

2 Jacques Barzun, *From Dawn to Decadence: 1500 to the Present: 500 Years of Western Cultural Life* (New York: Harper Collins, 2000).

3 Barzun, *From Dawn to Decadence*, 176.

4 Barzun, *From Dawn to Decadence*, 422.

5 Samuel Huntington, *The Clash of Civilizations and the Remaking of World Order* (New York: Simon & Schuster, 1996); Allan Bloom, *The Closing of the American Mind* (New York: Simon & Schuster, 1987); Francis Fukuyama, *The End of History and the Last Man* (New York: Free Press, 1992).

6 Northrop Frye, "'The Decline of the West' by Oswald Spengler," *Daedalus: Twentieth Century Classics Revisited* 103, no. 1 (Winter 1974): 1–13.

7 Daryush Shayegan, *Cultural Schizophrenia: Islamic Societies Confronting the West* (Syracuse, NY: Syracuse University Press, 1997).

The Moment of Myth

1   Edward W. Said, *Orientalism* (New York: Vintage, 1978).
2   Edward W. Said, *Out of Place: A Memoir* (New York: Alfred A. Knopf, 1999).
3   Said, *Out of Place*, 295.

Dreams of a Nation

1   Edward Said, *Representations of the Intellectual: The 1993 Reith Lectures* (New York: Pantheon Press, 1994).
2   Alexis de Tocqueville, *Democracy in America* (Garden City, NY: Doubleday, 1969), 3.
3   Tocqueville, *Democracy in America*, 4.
4   Philip Rieff, *On Intellectuals* (Garden City, NY: Doubleday, 1969).
5   Paul Johnson, *Intellectuals: From Marx and Tolstoy to Sartre and Chomsky* (New York: Harper Perennial, 2007).
6   Russell Jacoby, *The Last Intellectuals: American Culture in the Age of Academe* (New York: Basic Books, 1987).
7   Bruce Robbins, *Intellectuals: Aesthetics, Politics, Academics* (Minneapolis: Minnesota University Press, 1990).
8   For a study of this group of intellectuals and the impact they had on American social and political ideas, see Claus-Dieter Krohn, *Intellectuals in Exile* (Amherst: University of Massachusetts Press, 1993).
9   Said, *Representations of the Intellectual*, 52–53.
10   Max Weber, *The Protestant Ethic and the Spirit of Capitalism* (New York: Charles Scribner's Sons, 1958), 182.
11   Edward Said, *Orientalism* (New York: Vintage, 1978).
12   For further details, see James Tully, ed., *Meaning and Context: Quentin Skinner and His Critics* (Princeton, NJ: Princeton University Press, 1988).
13   See Dominick Lacapra, *Rethinking Intellectual History: Texts, Contexts, Language* (Ithaca, NY: Cornell University Press, 1983).
14   Allan Bloom, *The Closing of the American Mind* (New York: Simon & Schuster, 1987).
15   Said, *Representations of the Intellectual*, 56.
16   Said, *Representations of the Intellectual*, 57.
17   Said, *Representations of the Intellectual*, 59.
18   Said, *Representations of the Intellectual*, 72.

19 Said, *Representations of the Intellectual*, 61.
20 Said, *Representations of the Intellectual*, 62.
21 Antonio Gramsci, *Selections from the Prison Notebooks*, Quintin Hoare and G. N. Smith, eds. (New York: International Publishers, 1971), 20.
22 Richard Rorty, "Self-Creation and Affiliation: Proust, Nietzsche, and Heidegger," in *Contingency, Irony and Solidarity* (New York: Cambridge University Press, 1989), 96.
23 Rorty, "Self-Creation and Affiliation," 96.
24 Rorty, "Self-Creation and Affiliation," 97.
25 Rorty, "Self-Creation and Affiliation," 97.

ON COMPRADOR INTELLETCTUALS

1   See Russell Jacoby, *The Last Intellectuals: American Culture in the Age of Academe* (New York: Basic Books, 1987).
2   See Edward W. Said, *Representations of the Intellectual* (New York: Pantheon Books, 1994), 52–53.
3   See Kwame Anthony Appiah, *My Father's House: Africa in Philosophy of Culture* (London: Methuen, 1992), 149.
4   See http://www.famous-speeches-and-speech-topics.info/famous -speeches/malcolm-x-speech-message-to-the-grassroots.htm.
5   Albert Memmi, *The Colonizer and the Colonized* (Boston: Beacon Press, 1991), 15–16.
6   See http://www.famous-speeches-and-speech-topics.info/famous -speeches/malcolm-x-speech-message-to-the-grassroots.htm.
7   Joseph Massad, "Political Realists or Comprador Intelligentsia: Palestinian Intellectuals and the National Struggle," *Critique* (Fall 1997): 23.
8   Massad, "Political Realists or Comprador Intelligentsia," 32.
9   See Adam Shatz, "The Native Informant," *The Nation*, April 10, 2003.
10 See Ibn Warraq, *Why I Am Not a Muslim* (Amherst, NY: Prometheus Books, 1995).
11 See "Azar Nafisi: Author of Reading Lolita in Tehran Converses with Robert Birnbaum," http://www.identitytheory.com/azar-nafisi/.
12 Mark Lilla, *The Reckless Mind: Intellectuals in Politics* (New York: New York Review of Books, 2001). Lilla is today the picture-perfect example of what the great American historian Richard Hofstadter (1916–70) detected and thoroughly analyzed more than half a century ago in his classic *Anti-Intellectualism in American Life* (New York: Vintage, 1966).

The detection of this anti-intellectual streak in American culture goes back at least to Alexis de Tocqueville early in the nineteenth century.

13 See Lilla, *The Reckless Mind*, xi.

14 Lilla, *The Reckless Mind*, 196.

15 Lilla, *The Reckless Mind*, 197.

16 Lilla, *The Reckless Mind*, 198.

17 Lilla, *The Reckless Mind*, 203–4.

18 See Lewis H. Lapham, "Notebook: Dar al-Harb," *Harper's*, March 2004, 9.

19 Lapham, "Notebook," 8.

20 Lapham, "Notebook," 7.

21 As reported by BBC News, "Blame Widens for Abu Ghraib Abuse," August 26, 2004, and the *New York Times*, August 27, 2004.

22 See Alan Dershowitz, "Is There a Torturous Road to Justice," *Los Angeles Times*, November 8, 2001.

23 See Alan Dershowitz, "When All Else Fails, Why Not Torture?" *American Legion Magazine*, July 2002.

24 See David Kohn, "Legal Torture?" www.cbsnews.com/stories/2002/01 /17/60minutes/main324751.shtml.

25 "Dershowitz: Torture Could Be Justified," CNN.com, March 3, 2003, http://www.cnn.com/2003/LAW/03/03/cnna.Dershowitz/.

26 See Alan M. Dershowitz, *Why Terrorism Works* (New Haven, CT: Yale University Press, 2002).

27 See Michael Ignatieff, *The Lesser Evil: Political Ethics in an Age of Terror* (Princeton, NJ: Princeton University Press, 2004), 140.

28 Ignatieff, *The Lesser Evil*, 143.

29 Ignatieff, *The Lesser Evil*, 136.

30 Ignatieff, *The Lesser Evil*, 138.

31 Ignatieff, *The Lesser Evil*, 138.

32 Ignatieff, *The Lesser Evil*, 137.

33 Ignatieff, *The Lesser Evil*, 137.

34 Ignatieff, *The Lesser Evil*, 139.

35 Ignatieff, *The Lesser Evil*, 140.

36 Ignatieff, *The Lesser Evil*, 140.

37 Ignatieff, *The Lesser Evil*, 140.

38 Ignatieff, *The Lesser Evil*, 142.

39 Ignatieff, *The Lesser Evil*, 141.

40 Ignatieff, *The Lesser Evil*, 141.

41 Ignatieff, *The Lesser Evil*, 142.

42 Ignatieff, *The Lesser Evil*, 142.
43 Ignatieff, *The Lesser Evil*, 142.
44 Ignatieff, *The Lesser Evil*, 142.
45 Ignatieff, *The Lesser Evil*, 143.
46 Ignatieff, *The Lesser Evil*, 144.
47 See Georg Simmel, *Conflict and the Web of Group Affiliations* (New York: The Free Press, 1964).
48 See William Kornhauser, *The Politics of Mass Society* (New York: The Free Press, 1959), 184–85.
49 Kornhauser, *The Politics of Mass Society*, 185.
50 Kornhauser, *The Politics of Mass Society*, 187.
51 See Theodor Geiger, *Aufgaben und Stellung der Intelligentz in der Gesellschaft* (Stuttgart: Ferdinand Enke Verlag, 1949), as quoted in Kornhauser, *The Politics of Mass Society*, 187, footnote 8.
52 For more details on this, see the chart Students and Scholars (2001 estimates) in Lewis H. Lapham's "Tentacles of Rage: The Republican Propaganda Mill, A Brief History," *Harper's*, September 2004, 39.
53 See Ali al-Nezami al-Aruzi al-Samarqandi, Kuliyyat Chahar Maqaleh, edited with an introduction by Muhammad Abd al-Wahab Qazvini (Leiden: Brill, 1909), 26–53.

The Discrete Charm of European Intellectuals

1 Slavoj Žižek, "Berlusconi in Tehran," *London Review of Books* 31, no. 14, July 23, 2009; http://www.lrb.co.uk/v31/n14/slavoj-zizek/berlusconi-in-tehran.
2 Slavoj Žižek, "Iran on the Brink," *In These Times*, July 13, 2009, http://inthesetimes.com/article/4559/iran_on_the_brink.

Orientalism Today

1 Talal Asad, ed., *Anthropology and the Colonial Encounter* (Ithaca, NY: Ithaca Press, 1973).
2 Hamid Dabashi, *Post-Orientalism: Knowledge and Power in Time of Terror* (New York: Transaction, 2009).

230   On Edward Said

Edward Said's *Orientalism*

1   Edward Said, *Orientalism* (New York: Vintage, 1978). Here is the link to the video: https://www.youtube.com/watch?v=JncXpQQoZAo.

2   Here is the link to that interview, the content of which is now chapter 11 of this book: https://www.youtube.com/watch?v=heyuHiGqmu0.

3   Hamid Dabashi, *Post-Orientalism: Knowledge and Power in Time of Terror* (New York: Transaction, 2009).

4   Ranajit Guha, *History at the Limit of World-History* (New York: Columbia University Press, 2002).

5   Gayatri Chakravorty Spivak, "Can the Subaltern Speak?" http://abahlali .org/files/Can_the_subaltern_speak.pdf.

6   Hamid Dabashi, *Persophilia: Persian Culture on the Global Scene* (Cambridge, MA: Harvard University Press, 2015).

Rosa Luxemburg

1   Rosa Luxemburg, *The Accumulation of Capital,* trans. Agnes Schwarzschild (New York: Routledge, 2003).

2   Vladimir Lenin, *Imperialism: The Highest Stage of Capitalism* (New York: International Publishers, 1939).

3   Kevin Anderson, *Marx at the Margins: On Nationalism, Ethnicity, and Non-Western Societies* (Chicago: University of Chicago Press, 2010).

Alas, Poor Bernard Lewis

1   Bernard Lewis, *What Went Wrong? The Clash Between Islam and Modernity in the Middle East* (New York: Oxford University Press, 2002).

2   David Horovitz, "A Mass Expression of Outrage against Injustice," *Jerusalem Post*, February 25, 2011, https://www.jpost.com/opinion/columnists /a-mass-expression-of-outrage-against-injustice.

3   Bernard Lewis, *The Assassins: A Radical Sect in Islam* (London: Weidenfeld & Nicolson, 1967).

4   Bernard Lewis, *The Muslim Discovery of Europe* (New York: W. W. Norton, 1982); Bernard Lewis, *Islam and the West* (New York: Oxford University Press, 1993).

5   Bernard Lewis, *A Handbook of Diplomatic and Political Arabic* (London: Luzac, 1956).

6   "From Netanyahu to Leftists, Praise and Scorn for Late Middle East Schol-
     ar Bernard Lewis," *Haaretz*, May 21, 2018, https://www.haaretz.com
     /middle-east-news/praise-and-scorn-for-late-middle-east-scholar-bernard
     -lewis-1.6104535.
7   Enrique Dussel, *Philosophy of Liberation* (Maryknoll, NY: Orbis Books,
     1985).

INDEX

ABOUT THE AUTHOR

© Sorin Furcoi

Hamid Dabashi is the Hagop Kevorkian Professor of Iranian Studies and Comparative Literature at Columbia University in New York, an internationally renowned cultural critic, and award-winning author, with over twenty-five books to his name. He also offers commentary as a current affairs essayist, and his articles have appeared on major international print, digital, and broadcast media. He is regularly featured on CNN, BBC, CBC, Al Jazeera, and other global, national, and local venues. His essays have regularly appeared in *al-Ahram Weekly* in Egypt, *Bir Gun* in Turkey, and CNN in the United States. He currently writes a regular column for *Al Jazeera*.

About Haymarket Books

Haymarket Books is a radical, independent, nonprofit book publisher based in Chicago. Our mission is to publish books that contribute to struggles for social and economic justice. We strive to make our books a vibrant and organic part of social movements and the education and development of a critical, engaged, international left.

We take inspiration and courage from our namesakes, the Haymarket martyrs, who gave their lives fighting for a better world. Their 1886 struggle for the eight-hour day—which gave us May Day, the international workers' holiday—reminds workers around the world that ordinary people can organize and struggle for their own liberation. These struggles continue today across the globe—struggles against oppression, exploitation, poverty, and war.

Since our founding in 2001, Haymarket Books has published more than five hundred titles. Radically independent, we seek to drive a wedge into the risk-averse world of corporate book publishing. Our authors include Noam Chomsky, Arundhati Roy, Rebecca Solnit, Angela Y. Davis, Howard Zinn, Amy Goodman, Wallace Shawn, Mike Davis, Winona LaDuke, Ilan Pappé, Richard Wolff, Dave Zirin, Keeanga-Yamahtta Taylor, Nick Turse, Dahr Jamail, David Barsamian, Elizabeth Laird, Amira Hass, Mark Steel, Avi Lewis, Naomi Klein, and Neil Davidson. We are also the trade publishers of the acclaimed Historical Materialism Book Series and of Dispatch Books.

Also Available from Haymarket Books

Apartheid Israel: The Politics of an Analogy
Edited by Sean Jacobs and Jon Soske, foreword by Achille Mbembe

Azadi: Freedom. Fascism. Fiction.
Arundhati Roy

Confronting Empire
Eqbal Ahmad and David Barsamian
Foreword by Pervez Hoodbhoy and Edward W. Said

Culture and Resistance: Conversations with Edward W. Said
David Barsamian

The Impossible Revolution: Making Sense of the Syrian Tragedy
Yassin al-Haj Saleh

Lineages of Revolt:
Issues of Contemporary Capitalism in the Middle East
Adam Hanieh

On Palestine
Noam Chomsky and Ilan Pappé, edited by Frank Barat

The Pen and the Sword: Conversations with Edward Said
David Barsamian, introduction by Eqbal Ahmad,
preface by Nubar Hovsepian

Syria After the Uprisings: The Political Economy of State Resilience
Joseph Daher